MYTHS AMERICA LIVES BY

Myths
America
Lives By

RICHARD T. HUGHES

Foreword by Robert N. Bellah

UNIVERSITY OF ILLINOIS PRESS

URBANA AND CHICAGO

First paperback edition, 2004
© 2003 by the Board of Trustees
of the University of Illinois
All rights reserved
Manufactured in the United States of America
5 4 3 2 1 C P 7 6 5

∞ This book is printed on acid-free paper.
The Library of Congress cataloged the cloth edition
as follows:
Hughes, Richard T. (Richard Thomas), 1943–
Myths America lives by / Richard T. Hughes ;
foreword by Robert N. Bellah.
p.   cm.
Includes bibliographical references and index.
ISBN 0-252-02860-0 (cloth : acid-free paper)
1. United States—History—Philosophy. 2. United States—
Foreign relations—Philosophy. 3. United States—
History—Religious aspects—Christianity. 4. National
characteristics, American. 5. Nationalism—United States.
6. Myth—Political aspects—United States. I. Title.
E175.9.H84   2003
973—dc21   2002156582

Paperback ISBN 0-252-07220-0 / ISBN 978-0-252-07220-8

For Samuel S. Hill Jr.

Faithful friend, esteemed colleague,

encourager, hospitable Christian gentleman,

distinguished scholar

Contents

ROBERT N. BELLAH

Foreword

I have spent a good deal of my life thinking about the United States of America, its history, its role in the world, and above all its self-understanding in the light of religious belief. Since I have found it increasingly difficult to make sense of the changes that have occurred even in my own lifetime, I am happy to see that Richard Hughes is contributing so thoughtfully to a task that I have come to feel is almost beyond me.

If we look at the history of our country in the last 250 years, we cannot but be truly amazed. In 1750 we were a set of thirteen small, sparsely settled, colonial dependencies at the fringe of what was fast becoming the greatest empire of the age. Our Declaration of Independence of 1776 was a presumptuous one in view of the enormous disparity in power between the American colonies and the home country. That we did indeed become independent in 1781 was due in no small part to the rivalry between Britain and the second-greatest colonial power of the day, France. We like to think that we gained our independence because of our own bravery alone, but it was an unlikely outcome had it not been for French assistance. Even after gaining our independence, we were a small country of no consequence in the larger world, and we very nearly lost our independence again during the War of 1812, the last time we suffered an attack on the continental United States before September 11, 2001.

During the nineteenth century, when we pushed our frontier across the continent and then, as a result of the Spanish-American War of 1898, gained a couple of overseas colonies (Puerto Rico and the Philippines), we still heeded the words of George Washington in his Farewell Address about avoiding "foreign entanglements." The Monroe doctrine, which attempted to declare the whole Western Hemisphere "off limits," so to speak, in the increasingly intense competition of the European powers for world empire, we saw as fending off foreign incursion more than creating an empire of our own. Though most Americans wanted to stay out of World War I, once we were drawn in we committed ourselves to it ferociously. But no sooner was it over than we withdrew once again into our cocoon. We even refused to join the League of Nations, the brainchild of our own President Woodrow Wilson, and isolationism was a powerful influence on American policy right up until Pearl Harbor.

Already by 1900 it had become evident that we were a world power, and our intervention in World War I was decisive. But for many Americans we were still that small agricultural nation of 1776, cut off, thank God, by two mighty oceans, from the corruption and fratricide of the Old World. World War II was in this regard a turning point. Although an undertone of isolationism exists in America even to the present day, from that time on most Americans knew we had to exercise leadership in the world, even if only for our own security. Soon after defeating world fascism, we took on the threat of world communism. The cold war for forty years brought us or our agents into every corner of the world outside the boundaries of the communist nations themselves. We called the noncommunist world the "Free World," overlooking the dictatorial nature of many of the regimes we sponsored, and we saw ourselves as the leader of this Free World, a far cry indeed from the role that Washington's Farewell Address had envisioned for us.

In 1989 the door on which we had been pushing for forty years suddenly and unexpectedly collapsed: There was no longer a communist world; the evil empire had vanished. It is true that there were a few remnant communist states around, but we could either quarantine them as in the case of North Korea and Cuba or befriend them as in the case of China and Vietnam. Things looked so rosy that some proclaimed "the end of history" and others resurrected the longstanding American hope that we could quietly withdraw from the world and tend to our own affairs. During the 1990s the minuscule amount of foreign aid, 0.2 percent of GDP, the lowest among the rich nations, was cut in half to 0.1 percent of GDP. It might be amusing, if it were not so sad, that Americans when polled believed that we were spending 10 to 15 percent of our federal budget on foreign aid, and that we were doing too much.

It is not that the decade of the 1990s was entirely quiet. The Gulf War at the beginning of the decade (leading the first President Bush to declare a "new world order," much to the dismay of many Americans), and later in the decade several terrorist attacks on American facilities abroad, and even one at home—the 1993 bombing of the World Trade Center—reminded us that the world was still restless. But it was the terrifying attacks of September 11, 2001, that will probably prove to be another historical turning point, warning us unmistakably that we are part of the world and that we can ignore the rest of the world only at our gravest peril.

The question of what it means to be part of the world, however, remains unresolved. At the moment it is defined largely by the War on Terrorism and the exercise of American military power, explicitly or implicitly, everywhere in the world. But what other responsibilities do we have? Should we be concerned that the gap between the developed nations and the undeveloped nations grows greater every year, that half the world's population subsists on less than two dollars a day and one-sixth of the world's population (one billion people) subsists on less than one dollar a day? Should we be concerned with the fact that several so-called nations are at or near complete internal collapse? Our president has said that he doesn't believe in nation building, but can it be that there is no relation between collapsing nations and terrorism?

I have spoken so far as though our involvement with the world is primarily political and military, but that is far from the case. Economic globalization has been underway for a long time, but it has sped up enormously in recent decades and we are at the center of it. Our economy is the most dynamic in the world and the engine of world growth. Mirroring our economic influence is our cultural influence. American films, television, popular music, and the World Wide Web pervade the globe, and American English is the new international language. America is the center of a new kind of empire, but it is the only empire there is. Americans are, like it or not, citizens of that empire and responsible for the whole world.

Our reaction to September 11 suggests we are far from ready for that responsibility. After so devastating and brutal an attack, it is natural that we see ourselves as victims and respond with flag-waving patriotism, more concerned with homeland security than with global responsibility. Not since Pearl Harbor has America suffered such an attack, and not since the War of 1812, as I have said, have we suffered an attack on this continent. So it is natural now that we look within rather than contemplate the staggering job of leading the whole world.

It is precisely at this moment that Richard Hughes's book is so appropriate. In this hour of danger and anxiety he invites us indeed to look within, to examine the myths we have lived by, and to consider which of them we need to reaffirm and which to revise or even discard. But the inward gaze to which Hughes invites us is not merely so that we can better understand ourselves. It is also so that we can assess our cultural resources for taking on the role of world empire that has been thrust upon us. America's world power has no precedent; we could even say that everyone in the world today has two nationalities—the one they were born with and American. How are we going to cope with that?

Hughes has wisely argued that the myths that we have spun about ourselves, though containing much truth, can also be disabling unless critically reappropriated. John Winthrop saw us as a city on a hill, a light to the nations. We are, more than ever, a city on a hill. The eyes of all people are truly on us. But do we bring light or darkness, a blessing or a curse to the rest of the world? Hughes argues that all the myths he describes still have much to teach us, however critically we must now rethink them, except one: the myth of innocence. That we must discard. Neither our military nor our economic intervention in the rest of the world has been innocent. No empire with any duration has ever believed in its own innocence. Humility about who we are and what we can do is essential if we are to avoid the many disasters that await us.

Chosen it seems we are, if not by God then by geopolitics. But the historical example of that original Chosen People should warn us against turning our chosenness into triumphalism. Chosenness today is our burden, and we must think long and hard about how to bear it. I could make a similar case about the other myths that Hughes describes, but that is unnecessary, since the book itself is designed to do that.

I may add only one more comment. Hughes has included in his discussion of every American myth the perspective of African Americans, a perspective often sharply different from that of the majority population, a perspective of those who have many times taken the brunt of our history and seldom fully shared in its successes. I believe that in a moment when we are no longer just *a* nation, but in many respects *the* nation, those African American voices can be heard as speaking for the rest of the world, over which we exercise such power, but which often lacks even the simplest ingredients of our way of life.

Richard Hughes writes as a Christian and so do I. His book is a thoughtful contribution to a decision that all of us who are Christians must make: To what extent can we help America become a responsible empire and to what extent must we stand against empire altogether?

Acknowledgments

In this book, I stand on the shoulders of scores of other scholars who have taught me much about the mythic history of the United
States.

I stand indebted, first, to my major professor at the University of Iowa,
James C. Spalding, who first taught me about William Tyndale's understanding of a national covenant and how that notion was subsequently
mediated to an entire generation of Puritans, both in England and in
America.

Two other scholars have profoundly shaped the way I think about the
United States. One was Sidney E. Mead, who taught me at the University of Iowa also and who has mentored me through his published works
and through extensive personal correspondence and conversation for three
decades. Mead taught me much about the "religion of the Republic" and
its relation both to American Christianity and to the myth of a Christian America. I have not been able to consult Mead directly about this
text, since he passed away on June 9, 1999, but I continue to consult his
books, especially *The Lively Experiment* and *The Nation with the Soul
of a Church.*

The other scholar who has helped shape the way I think about the
United States is Robert N. Bellah, Elliott Professor of Sociology Emeritus at the University of California, Berkeley, who taught me in 1975 in
the summer seminar, "Civil Religion in America," sponsored by the
National Endowment for the Humanities. Like Mead, Bellah has continued to teach me for all these years, mainly through his published works

on American civic faith and the meaning of community in the United States. His book *The Broken Covenant: American Civil Religion in Time of Trial* helped me to conceive both the content and the structure of this text. I am especially grateful to Bellah, both for his critical reading of the manuscript of this book and for contributing the Foreword to this volume.

I also owe a special debt of gratitude to Professor Martin E. Marty, Fairfax M. Cone Distinguished Service Professor Emeritus of the History of Modern Christianity, University of Chicago, who, since the late 1980s, has taken a particular interest in my work and has offered me support, advice, and encouragement in countless ways. I have never studied with Marty in a classroom setting, though I have been a student of his books and articles on American religious history for many years. Most recently, Marty read this text in manuscript form and offered numerous suggestions, many of which turned out to be enormously beneficial.

I also stand indebted to Professor Conrad Cherry, Distinguished Professor Emeritus in the Department of Religious Studies at Indiana University/Purdue University at Indianapolis, especially for his work on the mythic dimensions of the United States as reflected in his book *God's New Israel: Religious Interpretations of American Destiny.*

In addition to Martin Marty and Robert Bellah, a number of other scholars read the manuscript for this text and offered extraordinarily helpful suggestions. From my own institution, Pepperdine University, those readers were professors David Holmes, Ira Jolivet, and Stephen Monsma and Tabatha Jones, associate dean of student life, and several of my current and former students, including Raymond Carr, Marco Prouty, and my son, Christopher Andrew Hughes. Scholars from other institutions who provided substantial help with this project were Molefe Kete Asante, professor of African American studies at Temple University; Dan G. Danner, professor emeritus at the University of Portland; Douglas Jacobsen, Distinguished Professor of Religion at Messiah College; Larry James, director of Central Dallas Ministries; and Rodney Sawatsky, president of Messiah College. In addition, I thank Joshua Fleer, one of my graduate students, for his help with the copyedited manuscript, and Geof Garvey, the copy editor assigned to this project by the University of Illinois Press, whose work was nothing less than magnificent.

I also wish to thank Pepperdine University for two sabbaticals, one in the winter term of 1995 and the other in the fall term of 2001, both of which I devoted to this project.

I should acknowledge that I am a Christian who has learned to see the world, at least in part, through the eyes of such Christian thinkers as Martin Luther, sixteenth-century Anabaptists like Menno Simons and

Conrad Grebel, and Reinhold Niebuhr, all of whom have helped me to frame a critique of the various American myths that I hope readers of this book will find meaningful.

Still and all, this book is mine and I must take final responsibility for its deficiencies.

As always, I wish to thank my wife, Jan, not only for her support for my work but also for the fact that she routinely interacts with me about ideas that matter and, in that way, continues to challenge my thinking. She has helped in this way with reference to this book, just as she has with reference to everything I have sought to accomplish over the course of a long career and an even longer marriage. To her, I renew my ultimate devotion and offer my deepest thanks.

MYTHS AMERICA LIVES BY

Introduction

There is perhaps no more compelling task for Americans to accomplish in the twenty-first century than to learn to see the world through someone else's eyes. Those of us who view America as a good and compassionate nation are almost always people who have benefited from its policies. We are not victims of oppression and persecution. To the contrary, we are comfortable and, by and large, content. We have food to eat and houses in which to sleep. We have sources of income and, while there are occasional insecurities, on the whole, we do well.

There is, however, another side to this story. It comes from those whose voices are seldom heard—from the poor and the dispossessed, not only in this country but also throughout the world.

This book is meant to help us hear those voices more clearly. How do these people understand the United States? What connection do they see between American wealth and power, on the one hand, and their own poverty and deprivation, on the other? At the height of the Vietnam War in 1967, Martin Luther King Jr. even argued that Americans should hear the voices of our enemies: "Here is the true meaning and value of compassion and nonviolence when it helps us to see the enemy's point of view, to hear his questions, to know his assessment of ourselves. For from his view, we may indeed see the basic weaknesses of our own condition, and if we are mature, we may learn and grow and profit from the wisdom of the brothers who are called the opposition."[1]

The fact that we hear these voices does not necessarily mean that we will agree. But hear we must. A world as dangerous as ours will not deal kindly with those who close their ears to the voices of discontent, who

I

avert their eyes from the realities of injustice, and who refuse to entertain the question, "Are there ways in which I might be responsible?" In order to achieve its objectives, this book will focus on two extremely powerful realities in American life: the American Creed and a variety of American myths.

The American Creed

The Declaration of Independence captures the American Creed in these immortal words: "We hold these Truths to be self-evident, that all Men are created equal, that they are endowed by their Creator with certain unalienable Rights, that among these are Life, Liberty, and the Pursuit of Happiness."

What do I mean by the phrase *American myths*? Contrary to colloquial usage, a myth is not a story that is patently untrue. Rather, a myth is a story that speaks of meaning and purpose, and for that reason it speaks truth to those who take it seriously.

The English word *myth* derives from the Greek word *mythos*, which literally means "story." Our national myths, then, are national stories—stories that serve the nation in important and crucial ways. An American myth, therefore, is a story that conveys commonly shared convictions on the purposes and the meaning of the nation.

John H. Westerhoff III helps us understand this issue at greater depth when he recalls Peter Shaffer's play *Equus*, in which a psychiatrist tells his patient, "We need a story to see in the dark." Reflecting on that pregnant line, Westerhoff comments, "We all need such a story. Stories are the means by which we see reality. Without a story it would appear as if we lived in an unreal world. Without a story we cannot live. Without a story we cannot have community. . . . Without a story life makes no sense. The story that is foundational to our life provides us with the basis for our perceptions and for our faith. Faith is manifested in story; story communicates faith. . . . Stories are the imaginative way of ordering our experience."[2]

Our national myths, then, are the stories that explain why we love our country and why we have faith in the nation's purposes. Put another way, our national myths are the means by which we affirm the meaning of the United States.

From this perspective, the American Creed is itself a myth, for in that creed we find the primal meaning of the nation. According to the story embedded in the creed, God made all men equal, and for that reason, all men are endowed with "certain unalienable rights." When Jefferson used the phrase "all men," he meant all white men of property. Over the course of American history, however, we have enlarged the meaning of that story to include not only men but also women, and not only people of light complexion but also people of every race on the face of the earth. Here we find the primal myth that inspires faith in the nation and that binds us together as one, united American people, regardless of race, creed, or national origin.

In spite of the power of the American Creed, we can respond to that creed in ways that are fundamentally damaging to the Republic. There are two ways in which this might happen. On the one hand, we can respond to the American Creed with such depths of cynicism that we rob the nation of any meaning at all. On the other hand, we can absolutize the righteousness of the United States, confuse the ideals of the creed with the realities of the present moment, and eliminate dissent.

THE CYNICAL RESPONSE

If we wish to understand the first form of abuse, we might ask, "What would happen to the United States if we entered a period when no one could agree on the meaning of America, when a large number of Americans were cynical about the American Creed, and when—in short—the spiritual glue that had bound the nation together in previous years had simply collapsed?"

In *The Broken Covenant*, Robert N. Bellah argued that America has experienced three such periods. The time of the founding was one of those periods, since it was by no means clear that the American people could actualize the American Creed. Then, during both the Civil War and the 1960s, many Americans grew cynical about the creed.

Before and during the Civil War, many Americans asked the obvious question "How can we claim a commitment to the proposition that 'all men are created equal' when millions of Americans are kept in bondage simply because of the color of their skin?" One of the leading abolitionists of that time, William Lloyd Garrison, called the Constitution "a pact with the devil" that ought to be abolished, since the founders had failed to outlaw slavery when they had the opportunity to do so. Garrison's opinion on the meaning and purpose of America typified the feelings of many abolitionists of that period.

Then, during the 1960s, many Americans raised similar concerns. "How can we take seriously the nation's commitment to the American Creed," they asked, "since for a hundred years after the Civil War, white

Americans still treat black Americans as second-class citizens with no significant rights whatsoever? And how can we take seriously the nation's commitment to the American Creed in the face of America's military venture in Vietnam?" Many believed that venture to be an unjust war, fought mainly to protect American investments abroad.

Bellah describes these three periods as times "of testing so severe that not only the form but even the existence of our nation has been called in question."[3] Bellah, of course, was right, for if Americans fought over the fundamental meaning of the nation—a meaning that had ceased to be clear—then it is obvious that the glue that held the nation together was rapidly deteriorating, and America stood in peril of disintegration.

The problem sometimes ran even deeper than this, for some Americans, both during the 1860s and the 1960s, essentially stripped the nation of any meaningful myths at all. The myths, they said, were nothing but lies, meant only to deceive the public and maintain the power and privileges of an established class. If Westerhoff was right when he claimed "Without a story we cannot live" and "Without a story life makes no sense," then it is obvious that those who stripped the nation of its myths also stripped the nation of its capacity to survive.

Here we find the enduring problem that the fundamentalists of the left, who can find no good in America whatsoever, have posed. If Americans in significant numbers finally conclude that the American story is both false and bankrupt, precisely at that point the nation is in danger of disintegration.

THE ABSOLUTIST RESPONSE

The absolutist response has also emerged at a variety of critical periods in American history. For example, some responded to the tumult of the 1960s with uncritical affirmations of the nation's righteousness and offered this pointed advice to the nation's dissidents: "America: love it or leave it." A similar dynamic emerged in the aftermath of the terrorist attacks on the Pentagon and the World Trade Center of September 11, 2001. Few at that time wished to hear what was wrong with America, and few could bear to engage in national self-examination.

Thus, for example, the American Council of Trustees and Alumni, founded by Lynne Cheney and committed, in part, to the "free exchange of ideas on campus," nonetheless issued a report that roundly condemned university professors who called for a more thoughtful approach to that crisis than dividing the world neatly between the forces of good and the forces of evil.[4] Some of the comments the report found unacceptable were these:

[We should] build bridges and relationships, not simply bombs and walls.
—speaker at Harvard Law School

[O]ur security can only come by using our national wealth, not for guns, planes, and bombs, but for the health and welfare of our people, and for people suffering in other countries.
—professor emeritus, Boston University

If we perpetuate a cycle of hate and revenge, this conflict will escalate into a war that our great-grandchildren will be fighting.
—professor of anthropology, Brown University

[W]e need to hear more than one perspective on how we can make the world a safer place. We need to understand the reasons behind the terrifying hatred directed against the United States and find ways to act that will not foment more hatred for generations to come.
—professor emerita of women's studies, University of Oregon[5]

The irony of the absolutist response is the fact that, while it seeks to affirm the American Creed, it simultaneously undermines one of the most precious of all American rights—the right to dissent.

The Other American Myths

I have explored in some detail the meaning of the American Creed. But what about those other myths I mentioned earlier in this chapter? How do they function in our national life? There are five of these secondary myths. Each is rooted in a religious understanding of reality, and each has emerged in a particular period of American history. If we understand these myths, we will understand much about the historic periods that produced them. At the same time, all these myths flourish to varying degrees today, often in combination with one another.

Most of these myths hold great potential for good. Yet Americans have often absolutized these myths in ways that undermine the virtues that otherwise stood at their respective cores. This is the irony that lies at the heart of American history, as Reinhold Niebuhr pointed out many years ago. In his classic text *The Irony of American History,* Niebuhr spoke of "the ironic tendency of virtues to turn into vices when too complacently relied upon."[6] Moreover, it is precisely when powerful people absolutize their virtues that the interests of the poor and marginalized are most at risk. That is the fundamental premise of this book.

While each major chapter in this book examines one of these myths in substantial detail, readers may find it helpful if I provide at this point a brief synopsis of each myth along with an assessment of its assets and liabilities.

The first myth—the myth of the Chosen People—emerged among the Puritans in the colonial period of American history. In its best and highest form, this myth summoned the Puritans to "love brotherly without dissimulation" and to "beare one anothers burthens," as John Winthrop, the first governor of Massachusetts Bay Colony, reminded the settlers in 1630. In its original form *chosenness* meant "chosen for the good of the neighbor."

In time, however, Americans would absolutize this myth and claim that God chose the American people for special blessings and privileges in the world. At the very least, many still believe today that, in some mysterious way, God chose the American people for a special, redeeming role on the stage of world history. The origins and development of this myth are the subject of chapter 1.

The second myth—the myth of Nature's Nation—was a construct of the Enlightenment and emerged in the Revolutionary Era. In its highest and noblest form, this myth essentially affirmed the promise of the American Creed, for it grounded the rights of all humankind in "nature," that is, in the way things were meant to be.[7]

In order to justify the oppressive dimensions of American culture in the nineteenth century, some Americans would absolutize this myth as well. Many would argue, for example, that "nature" had "decreed" the removal of Native Americans and the enslavement of blacks. In addition, the myth of Nature's Nation contributed significantly to American myopia. To this day, our particular versions of democracy and capitalism seem so "natural" that many Americans cannot imagine that there might be any viable alternatives. From this perspective, other traditions and other folkways often seem perverse. I will explore in chapter 2 how the myth of Nature's Nation began, the role it has played in American history, and how it sometimes undermines the promise of the American Creed.

The third myth—the myth of the Christian Nation—was a byproduct of the Second Great Awakening and emerged in the early national period. At its best, it summoned Americans to embrace behavior in keeping with the teachings of Jesus. Ironically, however, this myth married itself rather quickly to the myth of the Chosen People and the myth of Nature's Nation. In this way, Americans absolutized this myth and the notion of a Christian Nation became a badge of cultural superiority, not an incentive to extend compassion to the poor and the oppressed. In due time, therefore, many came to believe that God had chosen America for special privilege in the world, precisely because America was thought to be a Christian Nation. The myth of the Christian Nation is the subject of chapter 3.

The fourth myth—the myth of the Millennial Nation—also emerged in the early national period. Struck with the wonders of the American system of government, and especially with the newness of American freedoms, many believed that the United States would usher in a millennial age of freedom that would eventually bless all the peoples of the earth. Americans have often absolutized this myth as well. Accordingly, Americans have sometimes been willing to *force* others to be free, as was the case with the Philippines in the Spanish-American War. More often, Americans imagined they would liberate the world through the sheer force of their example. Thus, when communism collapsed in Eastern Europe, President George Bush attributed that collapse to the compelling power of the American presence in the world. Here was another step on the road to the millennial dawn. I will consider this myth in chapter 4.

The absolutized versions of these myths—Chosenness, Nature's Nation, Christian Nation, and Millennial Nation—came together in the nineteenth century to define the doctrine of manifest destiny. Manifest destiny is not one of the myths highlighted in this book. Rather, manifest destiny is an outgrowth of the absolutized versions of earlier myths. As such, manifest destiny was a doctrine that completely undermined the promise of the United States, especially for Native Americans, Mexicans, and African Americans. Along with the myth of the Millennial Nation, therefore, I will also explore the history and dynamics of the doctrine of manifest destiny in chapter 4.

After the Civil War, laissez-faire capitalism flourished in the United States. Like manifest destiny, capitalism is not one of the myths I seek to examine in this book. Rather, capitalism, as it developed in America in the late nineteenth century, was a doctrine grounded in the absolutized form of earlier national myths.

While capitalism promoted hard work and individual effort and therefore held great potential for good, it also had the potential to nurture greed and exploitation of the economically deprived. This is precisely what happened when Americans of the late nineteenth century began to promote capitalism, self-interest, and greed as fundamentally natural, as inherently Christian, as the handmaid to American chosenness, and as the presupposition for the dawn of the final golden age.

These assumptions about American capitalism sustained the Gospel of Wealth at home and economic imperialism abroad in the waning years of the nineteenth century, and they helped to crush the poor in many corners of the world, including our own. Yet, because the mythic dimensions of American capitalism seemed so self-evident, many Americans could never see the ways in which capitalism helped to undermine the American Creed. In chapter 5, therefore, I will consider the mythic dimensions of American capitalism.

The fifth and final myth—the myth of the Innocent Nation—emerged in the twentieth century and draws its strength from all the other myths that have defined American life in previous epochs. The myth of innocence is therefore, in many ways, the most powerful myth of all. Yet this myth alone seems without redemptive value. It tells no meaningful story because it is finally grounded in self-delusion.

The emergence of this myth depended to a great extent on America's participation in two world wars. World War II was especially important in this regard, for it allowed Americans to imagine that because they faced great evil, they themselves were altogether righteous in both intent and behavior and therefore innocent in the world. Even though America's involvement in the Vietnam War made the claim to innocence highly questionable, the forces that wished to maintain the myth of an innocent and righteous America finally prevailed.

In the aftermath of the attacks on the Pentagon and the World Trade Center and in the midst of a war against terrorism, the myth of innocence resurfaced with extraordinary power in 2001. In that context, most Americans could not even begin to hear answers to the question, "Why do they hate us?" Even the president of the United States seemed bewildered when he told reporters, "I'm amazed that there's such misunderstanding of what our country is about that people would hate us. I am—like most Americans, I just can't believe it because I know how good we are. And we've got to do a better job of making our case."[8]

I will examine the myth of the Innocent Nation in chapter 6.

Finally, it should be noted that each of these myths functions at an unconscious level for most Americans. This means that these myths are essentially invisible and must remain invisible unless we name them, bring them to consciousness, and explore the way they have functioned—and continue to function—in American culture. Unless we undertake this task, they may well be the means by which we continue to undermine the promise of the American Creed, especially for the poor, the marginalized, and the dispossessed.

An African American Perspective

Each chapter in this book relies on minority voices—especially the voices of African Americans—to critique the myth presented in that chapter. Why would I adopt that strategy? The reasons are both simple and clear: African Americans have much to teach and much to share, for they have suffered in unique and extraordinary ways, prompting a passion for human freedom and equality. Perhaps this is why W. E. B. Du Bois suggested in 1903 that "there are to-day no truer exponents of the pure human spirit of the Declaration of Independence than the American Negroes."⁹

Second, African Americans did not simply suffer; they suffered at the hands of the rich, the powerful, and the privileged. If we can view the American experience through their eyes, we will learn much about the capacity of the rich and powerful to exploit those less fortunate than themselves. Indeed, we may learn much about ourselves.

And third, because of these facts, African Americans often provide a perspective on the American experience that differs dramatically from the perspective of the historically privileged classes.

The fact that I have structured this book to include minority voices will sometimes make for unpleasant reading. One colleague who read this text in manuscript form raised the question "Why tell a story that is so one-sided? Sure, America has its foibles. But America is also an extraordinarily good country. Why not balance your stories that portray the negative side of our national life with stories that reflect America's incomparable goodness?" The answer to that question lies in the objective that defines this text: to take seriously the voices of those who have been enslaved, segregated, and disenfranchised. That approach virtually foreordains that this book will not always make for pleasant reading.

Nor is it my concern in this book to explore the ways in which America has provided freedom and opportunity for millions of its citizens. That is a fact that everyone already knows. Rather, my concern is to explore the ways in which our American myths have sometimes obscured and subverted the promise of the American Creed, especially for its minority populations. That objective also lends to this book, at least to some degree, a certain melancholy character.

Why would I wish to write such a book? The answer is grounded in my own Christian convictions, for it seems beyond dispute that concern for the poor and the disenfranchised stands at the very heart of the Christian message. But this book is not a simple morality lesson, for it also seeks to highlight the role of irony in American history. Irony, after all, is a theme that also stands at the center of Christian faith. As Reinhold Niebuhr told us many years ago, "The Christian faith tends to make the ironic view of human evil in history the normative one." The Christian faith, he explained, regards "evil in human history [as] the consequence of man's wrong use of his unique capacities. The wrong use is always due to some failure to recognize the limits of his capacities of power, wisdom, and virtue. Man is an ironic creature because he forgets that he is not simply a creator but also a creature."[10]

For all these reasons, this book will take seriously voices of black Americans like Sara G. Stanley, who wrote in 1856 that the American ideal of liberty was, for her and her people, "a phantom, shadowy and indistinct—a disembodied form, impalpable to our sense or touch." She added, "In the broad area of this Republic, there is no spot, however small or isolated, where the colored man can exercise his God-given rights."[11]

Another African American, John Mercer Langston, wrote in 1845, "We have been in the habit of boasting of our Declaration of Independence, of our Federal Constitution, of the Ordinance of 1787, and various enactments in favor of popular Liberty, for so long, that we verily believe that we are a Free people." Yet, he concluded, the American people had been deceived. Because the spirit of slavery dominated the nation, there was no one—black or white—who enjoyed a "full share of Liberty."[12]

Still another black man, Charles Lenox Remond, proclaimed that "it does very well for nine-tenths of the people of the United States to speak of the awe and reverence they feel as they contemplate the Constitution, but there are those who look upon it with a very different feeling, for they are in a very different position. What is it to *them* that it talks about peace—tranquility—domestic enjoyments—civil rights?"[13]

Another black man, William Wells Brown, spoke these words in Great Britain in 1849:

> Wherever the Constitution proclaims a bit of soil to belong to the United States, there it dooms me to be a slave the moment I set my foot upon it; and all the 20,000 or 30,000 of my brethren who have made their escape from the Southern States, and taken refuge in Canada or the Northern States, are in the same condition. . . . I cannot look at the Constitution or laws of America as a protection to me; in fact, I have no Constitution, and no country. I cannot, like the eloquent gentleman who last addressed you say—"I am bound to stand up in favor of America." I would to God that I could; but how can I! America has disfranchised me, driven me off, and declared that I am not a citizen, and never shall be, upon the soil of the United States. Can I, then, gentlemen, stand up for such a country as that?[14]

This was the same William Wells Brown who reported his punishment for having run away from his master when he served as a slave in Missouri: "I was tied up in the smokehouse, and was very severely whipped. After the major had flogged me to his satisfaction, he sent out his son Robert, a young man eighteen or twenty years of age, to see that I was well smoked. He made a fire of tobacco stems, which soon set me to coughing and sneezing. . . . After giving me what they conceived to be a decent smoking, I was untied and again set to work."[15]

The great abolitionist Frederick Douglass—also a black man—concurred with Brown's assessment of the United States when he said in 1847 that "I have no love for America, as such; I have no patriotism; I have no country." And if we were to ask Douglass why he felt as he did, he would tell us what he said then: "I am not thought of, spoken of, except as a piece of property belonging to some *Christian* slaveholder, and all the religious and political institutions of this country, alike pronounce me a slave and a chattel. Now, in such a country as this, I cannot have patriotism."[16]

It may well be that no one in the nineteenth century did more to help Americans see the perspective from the "other side" than did Douglass. In 1852 he pointedly asked the question "What, to the American slave, is your Fourth of July?"

> I answer: a day that reveals to him, more than all other days in the year, the gross injustice and cruelty to which he is the constant victim. To him, your celebration is a sham; your boasted liberty an unholy license; your national greatness swelling vanity; your sounds of rejoicing are empty and heartless; your denunciation of tyrants brass-fronted impudence; your shouts of liberty and equality hollow mockery; your prayers and hymns, your sermons and thanksgivings, with all your religious parade and solemnity, are to Him mere bombast, fraud, deception, impiety and hypocrisy—a thin veil to cover up crimes which would disgrace a nation of savages.

Douglass concluded, "America is false to the past, false to the present, and solemnly binds herself to be false to the future."[17]

Surely the American people in the twenty-first century can hear the words of these nineteenth-century African American prophets and not be threatened. We can hear their words with relative equanimity because today we know their words were true.

Yet most white Americans of the mid-nineteenth century could no more hear these voices of protest than Americans in the twentieth century were able to hear comparable voices of protest in their own time and place. Many, for example, labeled Malcolm X a radical and then refused to take him seriously when he proclaimed in 1964

> I'm not a Democrat, I'm not a Republican, and I don't even consider myself an American. . . . No, I'm not an American. I'm one of the 22 million black people who are the victims of Americanism. One of the 22 million black people who are the victims of democracy, nothing but disguised hypocrisy. So, I'm not standing here speaking to you as an American, or a patriot, or a flag-saluter, or a flag-waver—no, not I. I'm

speaking as a victim of this American system. And I see America through the eyes of the victim. I don't see any American dream; I see an American nightmare.[18]

Today, in the twenty-first century, we understand why Malcolm acted and spoke as he did. We understand today that Malcolm was a victim of a racist, segregated society. White men murdered his father. The welfare system destroyed his family. And even though Malcolm was one of the top students in the seventh grade, when he told his English teacher—a Mr. Ostrowski—that he might want to become a lawyer, Mr. Ostrowski replied, "Malcolm, one of life's first needs is for us to be realistic. Don't misunderstand me, now. We all here like you, you know that. But you've got to be realistic about being a nigger. A lawyer—that's no realistic goal for a nigger. You need to think about something you *can* be. You're good with your hands—making things. Everybody admires your carpentry shop work. Why don't you plan on carpentry?"[19]

In spite of the severity of these voices, it is nonetheless true that a great paradox has always stood at the center of African American life. For while African Americans have routinely expressed bitter disappointment at America's failure to live up to the promise of its creed, they have also expressed great faith in the American Creed's validity and their hope that one day, Americans might implement the creed to the fullest measure. Their voices, therefore, have not been voices of utter despair, but voices of despair mixed with hope and affirmation.

Anna J. Cooper, an educator, college president, activist, and one of the first African American women to earn a Ph.D., used sarcasm to capture this paradox when she delivered a speech entitled "The Ethics of the Negro Question" in 1902. She recalled how "the Negro was transplanted to this continent in order to produce chattels and beasts of burden for a nation 'conceived in liberty and dedicated to the proposition that all men are created equal.'" She described the cause of the American Revolution as "a trifling tax on tea, because they [the whites] were not represented in the body that laid the tax." Nonetheless, as a result of that experience, those same whites "drew up their Declaration of Independence, a Magna Carta of human rights, embodying principles of universal justice and equality." But though they professed "a religion of sublime altruism [and] a political faith in the inalienable rights of man as man, these jugglers with reason and conscience were at the same moment stealing heathen from their far away homes, forcing them with lash and gun to unrequited toil, [and] making it a penal offense to teach them to read the Word of God."[20] In other words, Cooper praised the promise of the American Creed while lamenting the failure of the American people to implement that promise.

Martin Luther King Jr. offered another example of this paradox in his "I Have a Dream" speech, the keynote address at the March on Washington of 1963. He registered his despair and his disappointment in America when he recalled that one hundred years after emancipation "the Negro still is not free; one hundred years later, the life of the Negro is still sadly crippled by the manacles of segregation and the chains of discrimination; one hundred years later, the Negro lives on a lonely island of poverty in the midst of a vast ocean of material prosperity; one hundred years later, the Negro is still languished in the corners of American society and finds himself in exile in his own land. So we've come here today to dramatize a shameful condition."[21] At the same time, King expressed his faith in the American Creed and his hope for realistic change when he said

> In a sense we've come to our nation's capital to cash a check. When the architects of our republic wrote the magnificent words of the Constitution and the Declaration of Independence, they were signing a promissory note to which every American was to fall heir. This note was the promise that all men, yes, black men as well as white men, would be guaranteed the unalienable rights of life, liberty, and the pursuit of happiness.
>
> It is obvious today that America has defaulted on this promissory note in so far as her citizens of color are concerned. Instead of honoring this sacred obligation, America has given the Negro people a bad check; a check which has come back marked "insufficient funds." We refuse to believe that there are insufficient funds in the great vaults of opportunity of this nation. And so we've come to cash this check, a check that will give us upon demand the riches of freedom and the security of justice.[22]

One finds this very same paradox—this mixture of despair and hope—in the thought of Frederick Douglass. In his speech "What, to the Slave, Is the Fourth of July?"—which expressed his conviction that "America is false to the past, false to the present, and solemnly binds herself to be false to the future"—he also said this:

> Allow me to say, in conclusion, notwithstanding the dark picture I have this day presented of the state of the nation, I do not despair of this country. There are forces in operation, which must inevitably work the downfall of slavery. *"The arm of the Lord is not shortened,"* and the doom of slavery is certain. I, therefore, leave off where I began, with *hope*. While drawing encouragement from the Declaration of Independence, the great principles it contains, and the genius of American institutions, my spirit is also cheered by the obvious tendencies of the age.[23]

Although Douglass concluded on a note of hope, the question nags, What happens when people have no hope? When people consider themselves victims of a system they feel powerless to change, it is not surprising that they sometimes resort to violence. They resort to violence not only to free themselves from a system they consider oppressive, but also to get the attention of the politicians and the policymakers who—from the perspective of the oppressed—had previously ignored their grievances and perpetuated their injustices.

In Southampton County, Virginia, in 1831, a slave named Nat Turner led just such an insurrection. Armed with hatchets and a sword, Nat and his band intended to go from house to house, murdering the inhabitants as they slept without regard to age or gender. They began at the home of Nat's master, a Mr. Travis. "Will laid him dead, with a blow of his axe, and Mrs. Travis shared the same fate, as she lay in bed," Turner reported to his interrogators. All in all, Turner and his band murdered some fifty-five whites—men, women, and children—before they encountered "a party of white men, who had pursued our blood-stained track."[24] Once they had apprehended the culprits, the authorities indiscriminately killed some 100 blacks in the immediate aftermath of the uprising and later executed another eighteen, including Turner.

Few, if any, were seriously interested in why Nat and his friends had committed this bloody deed. Rather than asking about the legitimacy of slavery, the entire slaveholding South took steps to intensify the repression of black people whom they now viewed as a threat to the peace and tranquility of the nation.

Because the nation refused to respond to the cries of the oppressed in the early and middle years of the nineteenth century, the American people not only endured a series of violent slave insurrections. They also endured a bloody civil war in the 1860s. Then, a hundred years later in the 1960s, having still not addressed the problem of racial discrimination in any meaningful way, the nation endured a rupture in the fabric of the Republic from which it still has not fully recovered.

Finally, I must acknowledge that there were and are some blacks who did not then—and do not now—fully share the viewpoints this book presents under the banner "an African American perspective." Indeed, even in this book, one discovers African Americans who took very different positions toward problems they shared. The very different perspectives of Malcolm X and Martin Luther King Jr., or the disputes between W. E. B. Du Bois and Booker T. Washington, offer perhaps the most obvious examples of radical ideological diversity in the African American community. Still, I trust that the voices I have presented here are representative of broad swaths of opinion in the historic African American community and are therefore appropriate for inclusion in this text.

Likewise, I must also acknowledge that there have always been white Americans who have dissented from the myths I present in this book. Ralph Waldo Emerson, Henry David Thoreau, Nathaniel Hawthorne, James Fenimore Cooper, and Herman Melville, for example, either rejected the myth of Nature's Nation or held to versions quite different from the one I present here. Likewise, in the Gilded Age and the early twentieth century, Social Gospel prophets like Washington Gladden and Walter Rauschenbusch, not to mention a great many significant literary figures, rejected out of hand the premises of the Gilded Age and the Gospel of Wealth. Even Andrew Carnegie, for all the ways he justified American capitalism, nonetheless emerged as an outspoken critic of the imperialist tendencies of the nation at the time of the Spanish American War.

For the most part, I have not included these and similar voices in this text simply because I have confined my presentation of dissenting voices primarily to minorities, especially African Americans.

Looking Forward

In the pages that follow I will explore the meaning of the American Creed in relation to five American myths that emerged in specific periods of American history. What do I hope to accomplish through such a study?

First, I hope to provide insight into the complexities that have always defined that relationship. Second, this text may further our understanding of American history and of the periods in which each of the myths emerged, for the myths in many ways defined the periods in which they were so dominant. Third, I hope to further the understanding of the power of religion in American life, for in every instance, the myths reflect a powerful religious vision. And fourth, by assessing the myths from an African American perspective, I hope to amplify the voices of the poor, the disenfranchised, and the dispossessed.

It is also my hope that presenting these voices that have emerged from within our own country will amplify the voices of the poor and the dispossessed throughout the world. As Robert Bellah observes in the Foreword to this text, these African American voices might well be heard as speaking on behalf of marginalized people around the globe—people who live today in a world defined in so many ways by American wealth and power.

Notes

1. Martin Luther King Jr., "A Time to Break Silence" (1967), in *A Testament of Hope: The Essential Writings and Speeches of Martin Luther King Jr.*, ed. James Melvin Washington (San Francisco: HarperSanFrancisco, 1986), 237.

2. John H. Westerhoff III, *A Pilgrim People: Learning through the Church Year* (Minneapolis: Seabury Press, 1984), 3–4.

3. Robert N. Bellah, *The Broken Covenant: American Civil Religion in Time of Trial*, 2d ed. (Chicago: University of Chicago Press, 1992), 1.

4. "Defending Civilization: How Our Universities Are Failing America and What Can Be Done about It," a project of the Defense of Civilization Fund (Washington, D.C.: American Council of Trustees and Alumni, 2002), 1. The quotation is from the mission statement at the council's Web site, <http://www.goacta.org/missionframeset.htm>.

5. Ibid., 13–29.

6. Reinhold Niebuhr, *The Irony of American History* (New York: Scribner's, 1962), 133.

7. Perry Miller popularized the label "Nature's Nation" in a book by that same title, published in 1967, though he used that term in a much broader sense than I do here. See Perry Miller, *Nature's Nation* (Cambridge, Mass.: Belknap Press, 1967).

8. "This Is a Different Kind of War," *Los Angeles Times*, Oct. 12, 2001, A16.

9. W. E. B. Du Bois, *The Souls of Black Folk* (1903), in *Three Negro Classics* (New York: Avon Books, 1965), 220.

10. Niebuhr, *Irony of American History*, 155–56.

11. Sara G. Stanley, "What, to the Toiling Millions There, Is This Boasted Liberty?" (1856), in *Lift Every Voice: African American Oratory, 1787–1900*, ed. Philip S. Foner and Robert James Branham (Tuscaloosa: University of Alabama Press, 1998), 286.

12. John Mercer Langston, "There Is No Full Enjoyment of Freedom for Anyone in This Country" (1845), in Foner and Branham, *Lift Every Voice*, 274–75.

13. Charles Lenox Remond, "For the Dissolution of the Union" (1844), in Foner and Branham, *Lift Every Voice*, 206.

14. William Wells Brown, "I Have No Constitution and No Country" (1849), in Foner and Branham, *Lift Every Voice*, 215–16.

15. William Wells Brown, *Narrative of William W. Brown, a Fugitive Slave* (1847), in *African American Voices: The Life Cycle of Slavery*, ed. Steven Mintz (St. James, N.Y.: Brandywine Press, 1999), 136.

16. Frederick Douglass, "Speech on American Anti-Slavery Society" (1847), in Foner and Branham, *Lift Every Voice*, 248.

17. Douglass, "What, to the Slave, Is the Fourth of July?" 1852, in Foner and Branham, *Lift Every Voice*, 258.

18. Malcolm X, "The Ballot or the Bullet" (1964), in *Malcolm X Speaks*, ed. George Breitman (New York: Grove Weidenfeld, 1965). For an extended commentary on this statement from Malcolm, see James H. Cone, *Martin and Malcolm and America: A Dream or a Nightmare* (Maryknoll, N.Y.: Orbis Books, 1991).

19. Malcolm X as told to Alex Haley, *The Autobiography of Malcolm X* (1964; reprint, New York: Ballantine Books, 1992), 36.

20. Anna J. Cooper, "The Ethics of the Negro Question" (1902), in *Can I Get a Witness? Prophetic Religious Voices of African American Women: An Anthology*, ed. Marcia Y. Riggs (Maryknoll, N.Y.: Orbis, 1997), 124.

21. Martin Luther King Jr., "I Have a Dream" (1963), in Washington, *A Testament of Hope*, 217.

22. Ibid.

23. Douglass, "What, to the Slave, Is the Fourth of July?" 267.

24. *The Confessions of Nat Turner, the Leader of the Late Insurrection in Southampton, Va.* (Baltimore: Thomas R. Gray, 1831). The full text is in Henry Irving Tragle, ed., *The Southampton Slave Revolt of 1831: A Compilation of Source Material Including the Full Text of the "Confessions" of Nat Turner* (New York: Vintage, 1973), 311, 314.

1 The Myth of the Chosen Nation

THE COLONIAL PERIOD

Among the most powerful and persistent of all the myths that Americans invoke about themselves is the myth that America is a chosen nation and that its citizens constitute a chosen people. Scholars and statesmen often refer to this myth as the myth of American exceptionalism. The label "American exceptionalism," however, obscures the profoundly religious origins of the chosenness vision. It is one thing to claim that America is exceptional in its own eyes. It is something else to claim that America is exceptional because God chose America and its people for a special mission in the world.

. The myth of the Chosen Nation has its oldest and deepest roots in the Hebrew Bible. According to the author of the Old Testament book Deuteronomy, God spoke to the Jews as follows: "The Lord your God has chosen you out of all the peoples on the face of the earth to be his people, his treasured possession. The Lord did not set his affection on you and choose you because you were more numerous than other peoples, for you were the fewest of all peoples. But it was because the Lord loved you and kept the oath he swore to your forefathers that he brought you out with a mighty hand and redeemed you from the land of slavery, from the power of Pharaoh king of Egypt" (Deut. 7:6–8, NIV).

In time, the American people would appropriate this very myth regarding themselves and the land in which they lived. How that happened is the subject of this chapter.

The English Reformation

In order to understand how the myth of the Chosen Nation migrated from ancient Israel to the United States, it is important to turn the clock back some five hundred years to England during the early sixteenth century. There, a man named William Tyndale popularized the notion that England stood in a covenant relationship with God. If England obeyed God's commands, it would be blessed. If not, it would be cursed. Implied in this notion of a national covenant was the assumption that England, like Israel of old, had been chosen by God for a special mission in the world.

HENRY VIII

Our story begins with Henry VIII, king of England from 1509 to 1547. Dismayed because his queen, Catherine of Aragon, had not given birth to a male heir to the English throne, and enamored of another woman, Anne Boleyn, Henry asked the pope for a divorce. When the pope refused, Henry, in effect, fired the pope, proclaimed himself head of the church in England, and demanded that his archbishop of Canterbury, Thomas Cranmer, ratify the divorce. In taking these actions, Henry divorced not only his wife. He also divorced England from the Roman Catholic Church. In its place, he created the Church of England, often known as the Anglican Church and, in America, as the Episcopal Church.

All this took place in 1534, seventeen years after Martin Luther had drafted the Ninety-five Theses and launched the Protestant Reformation. By breaking with the Roman Catholic Church, Henry opened the door for reformation in England, but Henry had little interest in real reform. He was interested mainly in divorcing Catherine and marrying Anne Boleyn, and if the only way to achieve those objectives was to break with the pope, then so be it. Though Henry had broken with the pope, he was devoutly Catholic in almost every other way and strenuously resisted the Protestant movement. The Church of England in its earliest years, therefore, resembled the Catholic Church, but without the pope.

If there was to be serious reform, therefore, it had to begin in other quarters, far from the courts of the king. As early as 1519, visions of reform stirred in the minds of several Cambridge University scholars who met regularly in a local pub, the White Horse Tavern, to drink beer and discuss the ideas of Martin Luther.[1] For several years, William Tyndale played a prominent role in that group and rapidly developed a deep admiration for Luther and his teachings. He also determined to translate the New Testament into English so that his own people could read it firsthand. When he approached the Bishop of London for permission to undertake this project, the bishop rejected his proposal out of hand. Tyndale therefore left England for Germany, where he took up residence in Wittenberg in 1524. There he learned from Luther himself and worked on his English translation of the New Testament.

That translation appeared in print in 1526. Tyndale wrote an assortment of prefaces and prologues that he included with that text, explaining to the reader how the New Testament should best be understood. Because Tyndale was so devoted to Luther's theology, these prefaces clearly identified the Lutheran notion of "justification by grace through faith" as the central, overarching theme of the New Testament. Since Henry VIII so strongly resisted all things Protestant, that particular Bible never enjoyed much circulation in England.

In 1530 Tyndale published the Pentateuch (five books of Moses) as a pocket book. In translating the Old Testament book of Deuteronomy, Tyndale was especially struck with the theme of covenant. There, he found the story of a God who had made a covenant, or an agreement, with his chosen people. Essentially, that covenant embodied God's promise to bless his people if they remained faithful to him, but to curse them if they disobeyed him and followed other gods. This was not for Tyndale just one more biblical saga. Rather, it was the very essence of the biblical saga and a story terrifying in its implications. The twenty-eighth chapter of Deuteronomy, especially, struck fear into Tyndale's heart. That chapter tells, first, of the blessings that would come upon Israel if the Israelites obeyed all God's commands (verses 3–6). Tyndale translated that material in the following way: "Blessed shalt thou be in the town and blessed in the fields, blessed shall be the fruit of thy body, the fruit of thy ground and the fruit of thy cattle, the fruit of thine oxen, and thy flocks of sheep, blessed shall thine almery be and thy store. Blessed shalt thou be, both when thou goest out, and blessed when thou comest in." On the other hand, that chapter also tells (verses 22–29) that God would send the most devastating curses upon Israel if it violated its covenant with God:

> And the Lord shall smite thee with swelling, with fevers, heat, burning, weathering, with smiting and blasting. And they shall follow thee, until thou perish.
>
> And the heaven that is over thy head shall be brass, and the earth that is under thee, iron. And the Lord shall turn the rain of the land unto powder and dust: even from heaven they shall come down upon thee, until thou be brought to nought. And the Lord shall plague thee before thine enemies. Thou shalt come out one way against them, and flee seven

ways before them, and shalt be scattered among all the kingdoms of the earth. And thy carcase shall be meat unto all manner fowls of the air and unto the beasts of the earth, and no man shall fray them away.

And the Lord shall smite thee with the botches of Egypt and the emerods, scall and manginess, that thou shalt not be healed thereof. And the Lord shall smite thee with madness, blindness and dazing of the heart. And thou shalt grope at noonday as the blind gropeth in darkness, and shalt not come to the right way.[2]

Upon reading these words, Tyndale exclaimed, "A christian man's heart might well bleed for sorrow at the reading of it, for fear of the wrath that is like to come upon us according unto all the curses which thou there readest. For according unto these curses hath God dealt with all nations, after they were fallen into the abominations of blindness."[3]

In 1534 Tyndale issued a second edition of the New Testament. Because the Old Testament notion of national covenant had now shaped his thinking so profoundly, Tyndale substantially rewrote for his 1534 New Testament the prologues and prefaces he had composed for the 1526 edition. While still maintaining a strong belief in justification by grace through faith, Tyndale now argued that the central theme of scripture is the covenant God has made with his people. When Tyndale's Bible came from the press, Henry was preoccupied with Catherine, Anne, and the pope. As a result, it did not face the restrictions the 1526 edition had encountered. It therefore achieved a significant circulation among literate English people.

It is difficult to overestimate the importance of that 1534 New Testament, for it helped define and popularize in England the concept of the national covenant. Tyndale did not restrict the covenant to ancient Israel but envisioned the possibility that God had extended his covenant to England as well. "The general covenant wherein all other are comprehended and included is this," he wrote. "If we meek ourselves to God, to keep all his laws, after the example of Christ: then God hath bound himself unto us to keep and make good all the mercies promised in Christ, throughout all the scripture."[4]

He made this point especially clear in his preface to the book of Jonah, published separately probably in 1531. He argued there that in years past, God had sent prophets to England, but England had refused to repent. "Gildas preached repentance unto the old Britains that inhabited England," Tyndale wrote. "[T]hey repented not, and therefore God sent in their enemies upon them . . . and destroyed them. . . . Wicliffe preached repentance unto our fathers not long since: they repented not for their hearts were indurate." Then Tyndale made the crucial point: "And now

Christ to preach repentance, is risen yet once again out of his sepulcher in which the pope had buried him and kept him down with his pillars and poleaxes and all disguisings of hypocrisy. . . . And as I doubt not of the examples that are past, so am I sure that great wrath will follow, except repentance turn it back again, and cease it."[5]

Tyndale never claimed that England was God's chosen people, but the theme of the national covenant implied as much. After all, God had struck a covenant with ancient Israel precisely because he had chosen Israel from all the nations of the earth. Tyndale's vision of covenant, therefore, was the soil in which the notion of chosenness would slowly germinate until, finally, it would spring full-blown in the United States.

One can hardly overestimate the importance of the various biblical materials that Tyndale translated and made available to his compatriots. Never having seen or read the Bible in their own language, a whole generation of English people eagerly devoured both his translations and his commentaries. And through his prologues and prefaces, Tyndale became a preacher to the nation. By the time Henry VIII died and Edward VI took the throne (1547), the notion that England was in some sense a chosen people, standing in covenant relation with God, had become a working assumption for many English people.

EDWARD VI AND "BLOODY" MARY

Edward VI (1547–53) was only nine years old when he became king of England, a fact that allowed the king's privy council extraordinary powers. Because some on the council favored the Protestant cause, the king and his council suppressed Catholicism and implemented Protestant reforms with astonishing rapidity. Quick to compare their nation with ancient Israel, many in England saw in Edward a reflection of Josiah, the eight-year-old king of Israel who reestablished the laws of God and, on the basis of those laws, initiated far-reaching reforms (2 Kings, chapters 22 and 23). Clearly, the myth of the Chosen People was working its way into the English imagination.

Still, Edward VI was not altogether certain what it might mean for England to keep covenant with God. He therefore instructed Thomas Cranmer, his archbishop of Canterbury, to consult Heinrich Bullinger, the successor to Ulrich Zwingli, the great Protestant reformer in Zurich, Switzerland. In effect, Bullinger replied, "You must restore the primitive church." Others sustained that advice. Martin Bucer, a leading Christian humanist and Reformed theologian from Strasbourg, for example, wrote a treatise, *De Regno Christi* ("The Kingdom of Christ"), which he dedicated to King Edward. There, Bucer argued that by emulating the ancient Christian faith, England could become the kingdom of Christ.

Many during Edward's reign linked Tyndale's covenant theology to the Reformed emphasis on primitive Christianity. England could keep the covenant, they argued, but only if England abolished human traditions in religion and restored the ancient Christian faith. In this way, Reformed Protestantism first began to shape British religious thought.

When Edward died in 1553, Mary Tudor (1553–58), daughter of Henry VIII and Catherine of Aragon, became queen. Deeply resentful of both her father and the Protestant faith, Mary determined to turn England back to the Church of Rome. She thought she could achieve that objective through the sheer force of persecution. She therefore executed hundreds of Protestants, earning for herself the sobriquet "Bloody Mary."

Many Protestants, fearing for their lives, fled England, hoping to live in peace abroad as long as Mary was on the throne. These Marian Exiles, numbering some 800 in all, took up residence in several cities on the continent, among them Strasbourg, Basel, Frankfurt, and Geneva. While abroad, they pondered Tyndale's claim that God would curse England if the nation wandered from his will. Since they could regard the deaths of so many godly Protestants only as a curse, the pressing question emerged, "What did we do, or fail to do, that we should deserve such devastation from the hand of God?"

The answer seemed clear. They had not restored the ancient Christian faith as Bullinger and others had advised. Instead, they had settled for mere reform. Many exiles therefore determined that when Mary died, they would return to England and devote themselves to a thoroughgoing restoration of the ancient Christian faith. Only by taking such a course might England be saved from divine wrath to come.

This was a radical goal, for those who took this position hoped to replace the Anglican establishment with a church that conformed at every significant point to an ancient model revealed, they thought, in the biblical text. When one realizes that the Anglican Church was now the legally established church in England and that it functioned as a civic faith for the English people, one then sees what a radical—and risky—objective these visionaries undertook.

The radicals who took this position were England's earliest Puritans. Prior to the exile, there had been no Puritans in England at all. There had been Catholics on the one hand and Protestants on the other, and Protestants had been uniformly Anglican. Now, however, there emerged from the very bosom of the Anglican establishment a Puritan party that would rival the Church of England for religious control of the realm. While some of these Puritans would eventually break from the Church of England, others—still wearing the label "Anglican"—sought to subvert that church from within.

There are two other aspects of Puritanism that deserve mention here. First, Puritans always defined themselves over against Roman Catholic tradition. To them, Catholics had defiled and corrupted the ancient church. They viewed the pope as antichrist and Catholic clerics as vermin from the bottomless pit. To restore the ancient faith therefore meant to abandon every vestige of Catholic practice, and to return to biblical norms that predated the rise of the papacy. Puritans quarreled with the Church of England mainly because that church retained so many beliefs and practices rooted in Catholic tradition. Second, the Reformed tradition, especially the Zwinglian side of that tradition, had begun to influence English Protestantism during the reign of Edward VI. Now, during the exile, many Puritans found themselves in Geneva where they experienced firsthand contact with John Calvin, the undisputed leader of the Reformed wing of the Protestant Reformation.

Calvin influenced the exiles in at least two ways. First, the exiles learned from Calvin the notion that God alone was sovereign, and that he had chosen certain people for salvation and others for damnation, from the foundation of the earth. The exiles also saw in Calvin's Geneva a presbyterian model of church government that they found compelling. The presbyterian model called for individual congregations or churches to select delegates to a presbytery, a governing body higher than the local church. Because the congregations selected delegates and could recall those delegates at will, the congregations ultimately maintained control.

Calvin never argued that the presbyterian model was the only biblical model, but these early Puritans did. The truth is, the presbyterian model suited their political objectives remarkably well, for it took power out of the hands of a ruling bishop and placed it in the hands of the people. A populist model like this was necessary for the kind of revolution the Puritans would soon seek to launch. For this reason, the earliest Puritans were presbyterian and formed the vanguard of what eventually would be known as the Presbyterian Church.

Finally, a caveat is in order. Many historians speak of Puritans as English Calvinists. This is true only in a limited sense. They did learn from Calvin the heart of Reformed thought—the sovereignty of God over all the earth. They did embrace Calvin's doctrine of predestination. And most took from Geneva a presbyterian model of church government. These were all defining characteristics of Puritanism. But other defining characteristics came not from Calvin but from Tyndale, who taught them about the covenant England had with God, and from Zwingli, Bullinger, and other Reformed thinkers who insisted that covenant keeping required the restoration of the ancient church.

ELIZABETH I, JAMES I, AND CHARLES I

Mary died in 1558 and Elizabeth I, the daughter of Henry VIII and Anne Boleyn, succeeded her. Elizabeth would rule over England for forty-five years—from 1558 to 1603. How ironic it was that Henry divorced Catherine because she had given birth to no male heirs to the British throne, and then married Anne who bore Elizabeth, destined to rule for almost half a century as one of the greatest monarchs in British history.

Upon Elizabeth's accession to the throne, the Puritans returned home and launched what amounted to a virtual revolution. It was not a revolution with guns, but one of words and propaganda, fought on three separate fronts. First, they secured for themselves strategic teaching positions in the English universities, especially Cambridge, where they could shape the thinking of the next generation of clerics. Second, they sought appointments to some of England's most influential pulpits, where they could shape the thinking of the general population. And third, they wrote. They wrote books, pamphlets, and broadsides. Propaganda poured from their pens as they sought to explain why England must abolish a church built on tradition and restore a church built on God's word.

The Puritans did not at that time separate from the Church of England. Instead, they worked inside the established order, seeking to bring change from within. So while their hopes and objectives made them Puritans, their actual membership made them Anglicans.

Elizabeth, then, inherited a volatile situation. She had Puritans on her left and Catholics on her right, both agitating for special privilege. Elizabeth, however, resolutely cast her lot with the Anglican establishment, what historians call the *via media* or middle way. From time to time, she made minor concessions to the Puritans designed to pacify them. But for the most part, she ignored their demands and thwarted their agenda.

By the 1580s and 1590s, long before Elizabeth's reign was complete, the Puritans found themselves thoroughly discouraged. Some began to argue that they had pursued the wrong strategy from the beginning. It would never work, they said, to seek reform from *within* the Church of England. Instead, they must *separate* from the Church of England and establish a true church, one that conformed to the word of God at every point. The Puritans who took this position soon became known as the Separatists.

The Separatists' decision was momentous, for they thereby abandoned all hope of controlling the national church and purging that church of Catholic tradition. In the meantime, however, many other Puritans continued their efforts to transform the Anglican establishment from within.

After a long and fruitful reign, Elizabeth died in 1603, and James I succeeded her until 1625. Since 1567, James had ruled Scotland as James VI. There he developed an intense dislike of all things Puritan, having known all too well the Scottish version of the Puritan party. He therefore determined, as he once put it, to "harry them out of the land." James harassed the Puritans and made their lives extraordinarily difficult. He blocked publication of their books. He deprived Puritan ministers of their livings. He even encouraged Anglican clerics to burn two "heretics" at the stake.

Perhaps the most notable symbol of his policy toward Puritans was his *Book of Sports,* published in 1618. James knew full well that the Puritan revolution depended on propaganda, and that a staple in their arsenal of propaganda was the Sabbath sermon. Normally, a sermon lasted for several hours, and Puritans encouraged the people to spend their Sunday afternoons in meditation and discussion, reflecting on the meaning of the message they had heard. To undermine the Puritan Sabbath, James's *Book of Sports* designated Sunday as sports day and granted people permission to spend Sunday afternoon racing, gaming, and engaging in other sports as they saw fit.

It is little wonder that a colony of Puritans left England for Leyden in the Netherlands in 1608 and then settled Plymouth Colony, Massachusetts, in 1620. This was the earliest Puritan settlement in America.

James I died in 1625, and his son, Charles I, assumed the throne. Charles ruled until 1649. From the beginning, Charles made himself enormously unpopular with the Puritans. In the first place, Charles adopted an openly pro-Catholic, anti-Puritan policy. He married a Catholic princess, Henrietta Maria, and built for her a Catholic chapel in the heart of London. From the Puritan perspective, such actions by the king could only bring upon England the wrath of God. In addition, Charles appointed as his archbishop of Canterbury a man resolutely opposed to the Puritan movement, William Laud.

If his father had harassed the Puritans, Charles persecuted them, sometimes viciously. In 1637, for example, Laud arrested three Puritan extremists, Henry Burton, John Bastwick, and William Prynne, whose chief crimes were their frequent complaints about Catholics in high places. The court convicted all three on trumped-up charges and then issued the sentence: All three would have their ears severed from their heads and their noses split, and all three would go into perpetual exile on separate islands off the British coast.

It is easy to see, therefore, why another wave of Puritans fled England in 1630 to establish a second settlement in America: the Massachusetts Bay Colony. These Puritans were neither Presbyterians nor Separatists but Congregationalists, that is, members of the Church of England who sought to reform that church according to a congregational model of church polity.

The Covenant People in America

Americans have shrouded in myth the reasons for the Puritan migration to the New World. Every schoolchild learns that the Puritans settled America for the sake of freedom. To a degree, that is true. The freedom the Puritans envisioned, however, was a far cry from the freedom Americans prize today. The Puritans sought freedom for themselves but for no one else.

To acknowledge that Puritans came to the New World in order to secure freedom for themselves still misses the principal motivation for their migration. Puritans never sought liberty for its own sake as Americans do today. They rather sought freedom to place themselves under the absolute control of the law of God, revealed in scripture.

But why? Why was that concern so important, and why could they not pursue that objective in England? The answer to those questions points us once again to William Tyndale's covenant theology. As far as the Puritans could see, the English crown had little interest in keeping covenant with God. Since 1558, when Elizabeth took the throne, the Puritans had done everything in their power to bring England to repentance, and to hold forth clearly the way of the ancient church. More than sixty years had elapsed since then, and little had changed. A host of events made this clear—the refusal of the crown to cooperate with the Puritan agenda, the repression of Puritan literature, the harassment of Puritan ministers, the infamous *Book of Sports,* Charles's flirtations with the Catholic faith and his marriage to a Catholic princess. All these things convinced them that God's wrath hung heavy over England's future.

The Puritans had one more card to play. They could flee into the American wilderness, erect there a church that conformed to biblical norms, and hold that example forth for the English to see and perhaps even to emulate. This would be a last-ditch attempt to rescue England from the wrath of God.

Within a very few years, however, New England Puritans generally despaired of any hope of meaningful change in Old England. A clear example of this sentiment appears in a sermon that Thomas Hooker, founder of Connecticut, preached to friends and acquaintances who gathered at the dock to bid him farewell as he departed England for the New World in 1633. Hooker claimed that God would soon turn his back on England, apparently to accompany the Puritans to a land where people took his law with greater seriousness. "God is going," he told his friends and well-wishers, "his glory is departing, England hath seen her best days, and now evil days are befalling us. God is packing up his gospel because nobody will buy his wares nor come to his price."[6]

Even in New England, Puritans built their experiment squarely on the concept of covenant. No one made this point more clearly than did John Winthrop, first governor of Massachusetts Bay Colony, who assembled the Puritans on the deck of the ship *Arbella* and preached them a sermon before they set foot on dry land. "Thus stands the cause between God and us," he told them. "We are entered into a Covenant with him for this work. . . . Now if the Lord shall please to hear us, and bring us in peace to the place we desire, then hath he ratified this Covenant and sealed our Commission."[7]

As Winthrop understood the notion of covenant, however, it had little to do with special privilege and everything to do with responsibilities for one another. In fact, he explained that *covenant* meant that "we must be knit together in this work as one man, we must entertain each other in brotherly affection, . . . we must delight in each other, make others' conditions our own, rejoice together, mourn together, labor and suffer together, always having before our eyes our Commission and Community in the work." If the Puritans would fulfil the covenant in these ways, he said, "we shall find that the God of Israel is among us."

THE CHOSEN PEOPLE IN THE PROMISED LAND

In the colonies, however, the metaphor of the covenant pointed more and more to the notion of chosenness. After all, the myth of the Chosen Nation had lingered in the shadows of covenantal thought ever since the days of Tyndale. Now, in the American colonies, it stepped forward into the full light of day.

There were several reasons for this. First, New England Puritans believed that other Protestants had accomplished mere reform, while they alone had successfully restored the ancient church. John Robinson, pastor of the Leyden pilgrims, affirmed, for example, that the Puritan way was "cast in the apostolical and primitive mould, and not one day nor hour younger, in the nature and form of it, than the first church of the New Testament." And John Cotton, a leading minister in the Massachusetts Bay Colony, smugly claimed that the New England churches were as close as could be to what "the Lord Jesus [would erect] were he here himself in person." Little wonder that Cotton Mather, a third-generation Puritan minister, could proclaim to old England, "Let us humbly speak it, it shall be profitable for you to consider the light which from the midst of this outer darkness is now to be darted over unto the other side of the Atlantic Ocean."[8]

Second, New England Puritans now found themselves isolated both geographically and spiritually. While initially hopeful that their holy experiment might prompt England to serious reform, that hope soon turned to despair. Separated from their homeland by perilous waters and thousands of miles, Puritans in New England grew increasingly certain that the English monarch and the majority of the English people would not support their cause. From the Puritan perspective, the English church remained entrenched in Catholic tradition and practice and refused to conform itself to the ancient Christian faith. New Englanders therefore found themselves isolated spiritually and felt they stood alone against the world. Because they stood alone in covenant with God, they found it easy to think of themselves as a chosen people.

Third, since the days of Tyndale, English Protestants had drawn a parallel between England and ancient Israel. Now, in their migration to New England, Puritans found that parallel even more compelling. Centuries earlier, for example, God had led the Jews out of Egypt, through the Red Sea, and into the Promised Land. Now God led the Puritans out of England, across the Atlantic Ocean, and into another promised land. The Puritans made the most of this comparison. In the Puritan imagination, England became Egypt, the Atlantic Ocean became the Red Sea, the American wilderness became their own land of Canaan, and the Puritans themselves became the new Israel.

THE "CHOSEN PEOPLE" AND NATIVE AMERICANS

If one imagines one's tribe or clan or nation a chosen people, then it is also clear that others are not. That is the simple long and short of this understanding. The Puritans' identification of themselves as a chosen people took on particular significance in this regard with respect to Native American peoples in New England. If ancient Israel had encountered "heathen tribes" in the land of Canaan, the Puritans thought of native peoples in the same terms. William Bradford, the governor of Plymouth Colony, for example, described the land and its inhabitants like this: "What could they [Puritans] see [upon landing] but a hideous and desolate wilderness, full of wild beasts and wild men—and what multitudes there might be of them they knew not."

This description suggests that the Puritans attributed to the land and its native occupants two very different meanings. On the one hand, New England was a promised land, now to be inhabited by God's new Israel. At the same time, Puritans believed that Satan ruled the wilderness areas of the world and its inhabitants. Only when the gospel penetrated these regions would the tyranny of Satan recede. Puritans therefore believed that God had called them to dispel the influence of Satan in this new, promised land.

The well-known Puritan poet Michael Wigglesworth gave clear expression to this conviction in his verse of 1662, "God's Controversy with New England."

> Beyond the great Atlantick flood
> > There is a region vast,
> A country where no English foot
> > In former ages past:
> A waste and howling wilderness,
> > Where none inhabited
> But hellish fiends and brutish men
> > That devils worshiped.
>
> This region was in darkness plac't
> > Far off from heavens light,
> Amidst the shadows of grim death
> > And of eternal night.
> For there the Sun of righteousness
> > Had never made to shine
> The light of his sweet countenance,
> > And grace which is divine:
>
> Until the time drew nigh wherein
> > The glorious Lord of hostes
> Was pleasd to lead his armies forth
> > Into those forrein coastes.
> At whose approach the darkness sad
> > Soon vanished away,
> And all the shaddows of the night
> > Were turned to lightsome day.
>
> The dark and dismal western woods
> > (The Devils den whilere)

Beheld such glorious gospel-shine,
    As none beheld more cleare.
Where sathan had his scepter sway'd
    For many generations,
The King of Kings set up his throne
    To rule among the nations.[9]

Even though Puritans viewed Native Americans as agents of Satan, they also believed that God could use Native Americans as agents of mercy and hospitality to his chosen people. Puritans, therefore, seldom viewed native hospitality as marks of their inherent goodness, but as evidence of the power of God in an otherwise depraved people. For these reasons, Puritans seldom took Native Americans very seriously. They sometimes spoke of the land that Native Americans had occupied for many generations as "vacant." John Cotton, for example, defended Puritan occupation of Native American lands in the following terms: "Where there is a vacant place, there is liberty for the son of Adam or Noah to come and inhabit, though they neither buy it, nor ask their leaves. . . . In a vacant soil, he that taketh possession of it, and bestoweth culture and husbandry upon it, his right it is. And the ground of this is from the Grand Charter given to Adam and his posterity in Paradise, Genesis 1:28. Multiply and replenish the earth, and subdue it."[10] The truth is, New England Puritans seldom had to buy native lands or wrest them from Native Americans by military might. Instead, smallpox epidemics so greatly reduced and subdued native populations that Puritans encountered little resistance to their settlements in the early years.

While most in New England took for granted the claim that God had singled out the American Puritans as his chosen people, there was one man in Puritan New England who completely rejected that premise. His name was Roger Williams. Many Americans know Williams as the father of the Baptists in America and as a person instrumental in the creation of the colony of Rhode Island. The truth is, Williams was a seeker, searching for the restoration of the primitive church. For a very brief period of time, he embraced the Baptist Church as the embodiment of the ancient Christian faith, but he soon grew disillusioned and moved even further to the left. Williams completely rejected the Puritans' claim that they were a chosen people. God chose only one people, Williams thundered, and those were the Jews. There has never been another. As he put it, "The State of the Land of Israel, the Kings and people thereof in Peace & War, is proved figurative and ceremonial, and no pattern nor precedent for any Kingdom or civil state in the world to follow."[11] For that reason, the white population of New England was a people like any other people—the Germans, the French, or the Spaniards, for example—but certainly not a chosen people.

On the basis of that premise, Williams vigorously criticized the Puritan appropriation of Native American land. In effect, he argued, Puritans had stolen the land and should buy it or return it.

It is hardly surprising that the magistrates banished Williams from Massachusetts Bay Colony four years later. They intended to ship Williams back to England, but it was winter when they made that decision, and so they allowed Williams to remain in his house until spring. In the meantime, Williams slipped out of the colony and made his way to Rhode Island, a region the Bay Colony Puritans routinely described as the "cesspool of New England" since it harbored so many dissenters. There, Williams learned Native American languages and, in 1644, won from the English Parliament a charter for the new colony of Rhode Island.

The Legacy of the Myth of the Chosen Nation

In spite of Williams's objections, the notion that the people of New England were chosen by God for a special mission in the world intensified over the years and eventually became central to the larger American imagination. This happened for one fundamental reason: the Puritans told a focused, compelling, and convincing story that no other immigrant group could match. Nevertheless, it was a story with which many immigrant groups could identify. In numerous books, treatises, and sermons, the Puritans told how God had led them from oppression into a promised land. Immigrants from all over Europe—and from many parts of the world—found this story immensely compelling and adopted it as if it were their very own. In this way, the myth of the Chosen Nation became a permanent part of the American consciousness.

Two examples will suffice. Rabbi Isaac Mayer Wise immigrated to America from Bohemia in 1846. Here he became the paramount spokesperson for Reform Judaism, a form of Judaism that sought to adapt the Jewish heritage to modern culture. Ironically, this Jewish leader could speak of the wars that whites waged against the Native American population as "the wars of 'the Israelites against the Philistines,' of 'God's chosen people against the Indian Gentiles.'" Further, Wise argued that "George Washington and his heroic compatriots were the chosen instruments in the hands of Providence, to turn the wheel of events in favor of liberty forever."[12] In this speech, Wise articulated a myth that he, like millions of immigrants to these shores, ultimately learned from the Puritans of New England.

Another example: several years ago, when a colleague and I taught a course in world religions at Pepperdine University, we took a group of students to a Buddhist temple in Los Angeles. I was excited, for I knew that the priest would explain the Buddhist faith to my students in ways that I could not. My anticipation grew as we entered the temple. Fragrances unfamiliar to me filled the building. Around the walls, pictures told the story of the Buddha's life.

Soon, the priest emerged. He was a first-generation Japanese immigrant. I could hardly wait to hear what this man would say. He instructed our students to sit in the first several rows of chairs. And then he began. "Students," he said, "I have one message for you today: If the United States does not turn back to God, we are in serious trouble."

I hope my amazement didn't register on my face too visibly. This wasn't Buddhism. It was the message of William Tyndale, proclaimed in a Buddhist temple by a first-generation immigrant to the United States in the closing years of the twentieth century. I was struck once again by the power with which the twin myths of covenant and Chosen People have captivated generation after generation of people who have immigrated to the United States from the far corners of the world.

THE MYTH OF THE CHOSEN PEOPLE IN THE REVOLUTIONARY PERIOD

Since the Puritans told their story so often and so well, one should not be surprised to find the myth of the Chosen Nation central even to the thinking of the American founders. In fact, when Congress appointed a committee of Franklin, Jefferson, and Adams to design a seal for the United States, Franklin suggested a seal that would portray "Moses lifting his hand and the Red Sea dividing, with Pharaoh in his chariot being overwhelmed by the waters, and with a motto in great popular favor at the time, 'Rebellion to tyrants is obedience to god.'" No less concerned than Franklin to link the United States to the image of ancient Israel, Jefferson suggested "a representation of the children of Israel in the wilderness, led by a cloud by day and a pillar of fire by night."[13]

Images of the children of Israel and of America as a chosen people likewise informed the rhetoric of the Revolution. In a sermon with the significant title "God Arising and Pleading His People's Cause," for example, Abraham Keteltas, a preacher in Newburyport, Massachusetts, told his congregation in 1777, "Our cause is not only righteous but, most important, it is God's own cause. It is the grand cause of the whole human race. . . . If the principles [adopted] . . . by the American colonies . . . were universally adopted and practiced upon by mankind, they would turn a vale of tears into a paradise of God." Keteltas had by no means finished with that rhetorical flourish. He went on. The cause of the American Revolution, he proclaimed, "is the cause of truth against error and falsehood, the cause of righteousness against iniquity, the cause . . . of benevolence against barbarity, of virtue against vice. . . . In short, it is the cause of heaven against hell. . . . It is the cause for which heroes have fought, patriots bled, prophets, apostles, martyrs, confessors, and righteous men have died. Nay, it is a cause for which the Son of God came down from his celestial throne and expired on a cross."[14]

Keteltas was not unique in his presentation of these themes. Nicholas Street, for example, preached a sermon in East Haven, Connecticut, in 1777, in which he claimed that God had sent the Revolutionary War to scourge the colonies for their sins. He entitled that sermon, appropriately enough, "The American States Acting over the Part of the Children of Israel in the Wilderness and Thereby Impeding Their Entrance into Canaan's Rest." While Street clearly lamented the colonists' sins, he shared with Keteltas the fundamental assumption that the American colonies constituted a latter-day chosen people.

Then, in 1796, twenty years after the revolution, another patriot named John Cushing spoke at a Fourth of July celebration at Ashburnham, Massachusetts. He told the crowd that in all of history "God dealt with no people as with Israel. But in the history of the United States, particularly New England, there is as great similarity perhaps in the conduct of Providence to that of the Israelites as is to be found in the history of any people."[15] And Jefferson, in his second inaugural address, once again appealed to the image of ancient Israel as an appropriate model for the United States. "I shall need," he proclaimed, "the favor of that Being in whose hands we are, who led our fathers, as Israel of old, from their native land and planted them in a country flowing with all the necessaries and comforts of life."[16]

THE MYTH OF THE CHOSEN PEOPLE AFTER THE REVOLUTION

Intellectuals and literary elites, no less than politicians, have resorted to the myth of the Chosen People to describe the United States. Herman Melville in his novel *White Jacket* (1850) depicted America as "the peculiar, chosen people—the Israel of our time." "Escaped from the house of bondage," he wrote, "We Americans are the peculiar, chosen people— the Israel of our time; we bear the ark of the liberties of the world. . . . God has predestinated, mankind expects, great things from our race. . . . Long enough have we been skeptics with regard to ourselves, and doubted whether, indeed, the political Messiah had come. But he has come in *us*, if we would but give utterance to his promptings."[17]

By the time Americans fought the Civil War, the myth of the Chosen Nation continued to hold an extraordinary power over the American imagination—so powerful, in fact, that both northerners and southerners appealed to the motif to legitimate their cause. Numerous examples could be given, but two will suffice.

Henry Ward Beecher, son of the famed Lyman Beecher, brother of Harriet Beecher Stowe (author of *Uncle Tom's Cabin*), and one of America's most popular pulpit preachers in the mid-nineteenth century, has been described as "that magnificent weathervane of respectable opinion."[18] In a sermon he preached at Plymouth Church of Brooklyn in 1861, he explicitly drew the comparison between the northern states and ancient Israel. He reflected on the fact that God had "brought the Egyptians behind the children of Israel" as Israel prepared to cross the Red Sea. Then he made his point. "And now our turn has come. Right before us lies the Red Sea of war. It is red indeed. There is blood in it. We have come to the very edge of it, and the Word of God to us to-day is, 'Speak unto this people that they go forward.'"[19]

Benjamin Palmer served as the first moderator of the General Assembly of the Presbyterian Church in the Confederate States of America. In a sermon he delivered in 1861, Palmer also appealed to the myth of the Chosen Nation, in this case on behalf of the South: "Eleven tribes sought to go forth in peace from the house of political bondage: but the heart of our modern Pharaoh is hardened, that he will not let Israel go. In their distress, with the untried sea before and the chariots of Egypt behind, ten millions of people stretch forth their hands before Jehovah's throne, imploring him to 'stir up his strength before Ephraim and Benjamin and Manasseth, and come and save them.'"[20]

At the end of the nineteenth century, patriots in the Spanish-American War once again appealed to the myth of the Chosen Nation to justify American intervention in Cuba and the Philippines. Senator Orville Platt of Connecticut, for example, expressed on the floor of the U.S. Senate his conviction that "the same force was behind our army at Santiago and our ships in Manila Bay that was behind the landing of the Pilgrims on Plymouth Rock," adding that "we have been chosen to carry on and to carry forward this great work of uplifting humanity on earth."

Among those who sought to justify American involvement in the Philippines, no one employed the myth of the Chosen Nation with greater force than Albert Beveridge, senator from Indiana from 1899 to 1911. According to Beveridge,

> God has not been preparing the English-speaking and Teutonic peoples for a thousand years for nothing but vain and idle self-contemplation and self-admiration. No. He made us master organizers of the world to establish system where chaos reigned. He has given us the spirit of progress to overwhelm the forces of reaction throughout the earth. He has made us adept in government that we may administer government among savage and senile peoples. Were it not for such a force as this the world would relapse into barbarism and night. And of all our race He has marked the American people as His chosen nation to finally lead in the redemption of the world.[21]

In this passage, several things seem obvious. First, Beveridge defines America strictly in terms of "English-speaking and Teutonic peoples." This conception of America has no room for people of color. This point is fundamental to the thesis of this book, for in making the claim that "English-speaking and Teutonic peoples" were God's "chosen nation to finally lead in the redemption of the world," Beveridge implicitly defined people of color as "the other"—those people who were not chosen and who needed to be redeemed.

Second, in the rhetoric of Beveridge, the earlier definition of covenant that for so many years had accompanied the myth of the Chosen Nation now disappeared. John Winthrop, for example, argued in the seventeenth century that "we are entered into a Covenant with him [God] for this work" and defined "this work" as love for the neighbor. By the late nineteenth century, Beveridge argued that America was God's "chosen nation to finally lead in the redemption of the world."

One finds here little if any sense of responsibility to the neighbor, and certainly nothing comparable to Winthrop's assertion that "we must be knit together in this work as one man, we must entertain each other in brotherly affection, . . . we must delight in each other, make others' conditions our own, rejoice together, mourn together, labor and suffer together, always having before our eyes our Commission and Community in the work."

Instead, we find in Beveridge only the claim that the Teutonic peoples of America were the "master organizers of the world" who would "administer government among savage and senile peoples." Here one finds only an appeal to power, domination, and control. No wonder that H. Richard Niebuhr could write in 1937 that "the old idea of American Christians as a chosen people who had been called to a special task was turned into the notion of a chosen nation especially favored. . . . As the nineteenth century went on, the note of divine favoritism was increasingly sounded."[22] In this sense, the American people absolutized the myth of the Chosen Nation.

It is precisely that understanding of chosenness as divine favoritism that would continue to dominate the thinking of many Americans through the twentieth century and into the twenty-first. However, the explicit language of chosenness seldom emerged as blatantly in the twentieth century as it had in the nineteenth, and it often appeared in the guise of one of the other myths that I shall consider in this book.

African Americans and the Myth of the Chosen People

Because white Americans increasingly embraced the myth of the Chosen Nation as a sign that the Almighty had favored them with power, dominion, and control, minority peoples often had to devise alternate but comparable myths in order to survive in a hostile and alien culture. The African American slave population was a case in point, and their creation of alternate Chosen People myths provided a telling critique of the dominant white understandings.

Like the whites, black slaves also identified with the saga of ancient Israel. If whites, however, imagined themselves a new Israel in a promised land, slaves identified with Israel in Egyptian bondage, longing for deliverance to the Promised Land. In this way, the white South became Egypt, the land of oppression, and the North became the Land of Canaan, flowing with milk and honey.

If whites celebrated John Winthrop and other Puritan leaders as "Moses" who had led them into the Promised Land, slaves eagerly looked for just such a Moses who would lead them out of the house of bondage. From time to time, such a "Moses" emerged. Nat Turner, Denmark Vesey, and a slave known only as Gabriel announced themselves as messianic liberators who would overpower the white population and lead the slaves to freedom. During the days of the Underground Railroad, "conductors" smuggled slaves out of the South to freedom in the northern states. One of the most famous of those conductors, a black woman named Harriet Tubman, soon acquired the designation "Black Moses."

Sometimes blacks identified not just the South, but also the entire American nation as the "house of bondage," symbolized by Egypt or, alternatively, Babylon. For example, Maria W. Stewart, a pamphleteer and activist, suggested in an 1833 lecture at the African Masonic Hall in Boston that "America has become like the great city of Babylon, for she has boasted in her heart, 'I sit as a queen, and am no widow, and shall see no sorrow.' She is indeed a seller of slaves and the souls of men; she has made the Africans drunk with the wine of her fornication; she has put them completely beneath her feet, and she means to keep them there." God, Stewart claimed, would soon deliver the slaves from the house of bondage. "The oppression of injured Africa has come up before the Majesty of Heaven; and when our cries shall have reached the ears of the Most High, it will be a tremendous day for the people of this land; for strong is the arm of the Lord God Almighty."[23]

Often slaves celebrated the theme of liberation from the house of bondage in their hymnody. To sing these songs was risky business, however, since white overseers often punished them severely if they spoke of escape. To fool the overseers, therefore, slaves routinely employed the metaphors of heaven and the afterlife when they spoke of liberation. They were interested in heaven, to be sure, but they also longed for freedom in this life. And so they sang songs like this one.

> I got shoes, you got shoes,
>   All God's children got shoes.
> When I get to heaven, gonna put on my shoes,
>   Gonna dance all over God's heaven.

Sometimes they described the Underground Railroad as a chariot and sang songs like these.

> Good news, chariot's comin',
>   Good news, chariot's comin',
> Good news, chariot's comin',
>   And it's coming for to carry me home.

Or again,

> Swing low, sweet chariot,
>   Comin' for to carry me home,
> Swing low, sweet chariot,
>   Comin' for to carry me home.
>
> If you get there before I do,
>   Comin' for to carry me home.
> Tell all my friends I'm comin' too.
>   Comin' for to carry me home.

By the late twentieth century, many African Americans still identified themselves as a chosen people bound for the Promised Land. On the evening before he was assassinated in 1968, Martin Luther King Jr.

identified himself with Moses and his black audience as a latter-day children of Israel. He told a crowd of striking sanitation workers and their supporters that "He's allowed me to go up to the mountain. And I've looked over. And I've seen the promised land. I may not get there with you. But I want you to know tonight, that we, as a people will get to the promised land."[24]

At the same time, some black Americans found it necessary to devise alternate Chosen People myths in order to cope in the United States. One such story is "Yacub's History," which appears in *The Autobiography of Malcolm X*. According to this narrative from the Black Muslim religious tradition, the first human beings on earth were black. Then, some 6,600 years ago, an angry and bitter scientist named Mr. Yacub decided to seek revenge on his peers. He therefore created through selective breeding and genetic manipulation "a devil race—a bleached-out, white race of people." The people that resulted from this effort were "pale-skinned, cold-blue-eyed devils—savages, nude and shameless; hairy, like animals, they walked on all fours and they lived in trees." The devil race wreaked so much havoc that blacks finally rounded them up, marched them to Europe, and placed them in caves. Once they left the caves, they grew strong, ruled the earth, and exploited other peoples around the world.[25]

The meaning of this myth is clear. Blacks are good and, since they came from the hand of God, they were the world's first human beings. Whites, on the other hand, are evil, and since they came from the hand of a mad scientist, they constitute an aberration on the natural order of things.

If one imagines that this story is nothing more than a fanciful tale, one should hear Malcolm explain its significance to the black community, especially to black prisoners:

> Among all Negroes the black convict is the most perfectly preconditioned to hear the words, "the white man is the devil."
>
> You tell that to any Negro. Except for those relatively few "integration"-mad so-called "intellectuals," and those black men who are otherwise fat, happy, and deaf, dumb, and blinded, with their crumbs from the white man's rich table, you have struck a nerve center in the American black man. He may take a day to react, a month, a year; he may never respond, openly; but of one thing you can be sure—when he thinks about his own life, he is going to see where, to him, personally, the white man sure has acted like a devil. . . .
>
> You let this caged-up black man start thinking, the same way I did when I first heard Elijah Muhammed's teachings: let him start thinking how, with better breaks when he was young and ambitious he might have been a lawyer, a doctor, a scientist, anything. You let this caged-up black man start realizing, as I did, how from the first landing of the first slave

ship, the millions of black men in America have been like sheep in a den of wolves. That's why black prisoners become Muslims so fast when Elijah Muhammed's teachings filter into their cages by way of other Muslim convicts. "The white man is the devil" is a perfect echo of that black convict's lifelong experience.[26]

Conclusions

It is clear that the myth of the Chosen Nation has been a powerful theme in American life. It is also clear that this myth can serve good and constructive purposes, especially when yoked to the notion of national covenant, for "covenant" implies responsibilities to other human beings. Thus, William Tyndale argued that God would bless England, but only "if we meek ourselves to God, to keep all his laws, after the example of Christ." And for John Winthrop, first governor of colonial Massachusetts, covenant meant that "we must be knit together in this work as one man, we must entertain each other in brotherly affection, . . . we must delight in each other, make others' conditions our own, rejoice together, mourn together, labor and suffer together, always having before our eyes the Commission and Community in the work." But when shorn of the notion of covenant and mutual responsibility, the myth of the Chosen Nation easily becomes a badge of privilege and power, justifying oppression and exploitation of those not included in the circle of the chosen.

Further, it is possible to take seriously the notion of covenant in the context of one's immediate peers and fail to extend that covenant understanding to a larger circle of humanity. In this case, the myth of the Chosen Nation can justify oppression of those outside the bounds of the covenant, as surely as if there were no conception of covenant whatsoever. This is precisely the posture that the New England Puritans took toward Native Americans.

The myth of the Chosen Nation, defined in terms of power and privilege and cut loose from the chastening effects of covenant duties, therefore, cripples our ability to implement the American Creed and its promise that *all human beings* "are created equal, that they are endowed by their Creator with certain unalienable rights, that among these are Life, Liberty, and the pursuit of Happiness."

Perhaps this is why Senator J. William Fulbright so roundly criticized this myth. "We are not God's chosen saviour of mankind," Fulbright wrote, "but only one of mankind's more successful and fortunate branches, endowed by our Creator with about the same capacity for good and evil, no more or less, than the rest of humanity."[27]

While Fulbright could roundly critique the myth of America as a chosen nation in the context of international affairs, he found it far more difficult to critique that same myth in the context of race relations. His voting record on civil rights legislation in the U.S. Senate was nothing short of dismal.

In spite of its potential shortcomings, the myth of the Chosen Nation is in many ways a fixture on the American ideological landscape. Recognizing this fact, national leaders at various times in America's past have sought to reconstruct this myth in terms of covenant duties and responsibilities. In all of American history, there is no more notable example of this attempt than Abraham Lincoln's second inaugural address.

There, Lincoln made it clear that to claim divine favoritism for one's own nation or cause is presumptuous in the extreme and ignores the fact that God stands in judgment on all human pretensions, even on claims to be a chosen people. Speaking of both the North and the South in the midst of the Civil War, Lincoln affirmed, "Both [sides] read the same Bible and pray to the same God, and each invokes His aid against the other. It may seem strange that any men should dare to ask a just God's assistance in wringing their bread from the sweat of other men's faces, but let us judge not, that we be not judged. The prayers of both could not be answered. That of neither has been answered fully. The Almighty has His own purposes."

The notion that God has his own purposes was crucial to Lincoln's understanding of covenant. This is precisely why he could fervently but contingently pray "that this mighty scourge of war may speedily pass away." Nonetheless, he said, "if God wills that it continue until all the wealth piled by the bondsman's two hundred and fifty years of unrequited toil shall be sunk, and until every drop of blood drawn with the lash shall be paid by another drawn with the sword, as was said three thousand years ago, so still it must be said 'the judgments of the Lord are true and righteous altogether.'"

Within this context, Lincoln understood the war as a judgment from a righteous God on a sinful people on both sides of the Mason-Dixon Line: "If we shall suppose that American slavery is one of those offenses which, in the providence of God, must needs come, but which, having continued through His appointed time, He now wills to remove, and that He gives to both North and South this terrible war as the woe due to those by whom the offense came, shall we discern therein any departure from those divine attributes which the believers in a living God always ascribe to Him?"[28]

In spite of Lincoln's warnings, many Americans over the years have failed to see the liabilities inherent in the Chosen Nation mythology. Indeed, the notion that God chose America for power and privilege has often seemed altogether obvious and beyond dispute. How and why that myth could appear virtually self-evident to so many Americans for so many years are questions I will seek to answer in the next chapter.

Notes

1. For a discussion of these men and their contributions, see William A. Clebsch, *England's Earliest Protestants, 1520–1535* (New Haven, Conn.: Yale University Press, 1964), esp. 42 and 139.

2. William Tyndale, trans., *Tyndale's Old Testament*, ed. David Daniell (New Haven, Conn.: Yale University Press, 1992), 292–93.

3. William Tyndale, "A Prologue into the Fifth Book of Moses Called Deuteronomy," in Tyndale, *Tyndale's Old Testament*, 256.

4. William Tyndale, "W. T. unto the Reader," in Tyndale, *Tyndale's New Testament*, ed. David Daniell (New Haven, Conn.: Yale University Press, 1989), 4.

5. William Tyndale, "The Prologue to the Prophet Jonas," in Tyndale, *Tyndale's Old Testament*, 634–35. Tyndale published *Jonas* as a separate work in 1531. (See Tyndale, *Tyndale's Old Testament*, xi.) In the Yale University Press edition, the editor combines Tyndale's *Pentateuch* of 1530, his *Joshua* through 2 *Chronicles* of 1537, and *Jonas*. On Tyndale and his translations, see James C. Spalding, "Restitution As a Normative Factor for Puritan Dissent," *Journal of the American Academy of Religion* 44 (Mar. 1976): 47–63.

6. Thomas Hooker, *The Danger of Desertion, a Farewell Sermon Preached Immediately before His Departure* [1633] *Out of Old England*, in *Nationalism and Religion in America*, ed. Winthrop Hudson (London, 1641; reprint, New York: Harper and Row, 1970), 25.

7. John Winthrop, *A Modell of Christian Charity*, in *God's New Israel: Religious Interpretations of American Destiny*, ed. Conrad Cherry, rev. ed. (Chapel Hill: University of North Carolina Press, 1998), 40.

8. Robert Ashton, ed., *The Works of John Robinson, Pastor of the Pilgrim Fathers* (Boston: Jonathon Cape, 1851), 2:43; Cotton Mather, *Magnalia Christi Americana; or, The Ecclesiastical History of New England* (London: Thomas Parkhurst, 1702), 1:26–27.

9. Michael Wigglesworth, *God's Controversy with New England*, in Cherry, *God's New Israel*, 42–43.

10. John Cotton, "God's Promise to His Plantations" (1630), *Old South Leaflets*, no. 53 (Boston: Directors of the Old South Work, 1896), 6, cited in Charles M. Segal and David C. Stineback, *Puritans, Indians, and Manifest Destiny* (New York: G. P. Putnam's Sons, 1977), 31–32.

11. Roger Williams, *The Bloudy Tenent of Persecution for the Cause of Conscience*, in *American Christianity: An Historical Interpretation with Representative Documents*, vol. 1, *1607–1820*, ed. H. Shelton Smith, Robert T. Handy, and Lefferts A. Loetscher (New York: Scribner's, 1960), 153.

12. Isaac Mayer Wise, *Our Country's Place in History*, in Cherry, *God's New Israel*, 230.

13. Irving L. Thompson, "Great Seal of the United States," *Encyclopedia Americana* (1967), 13:362.

14. Abraham Keteltas, "God Arising and Pleading His People's Cause," in Hudson, *Nationalism and Religion in America*, 49, 52.

15. John Cushing, "A Discourse Delivered at Ashburnham, July 4, 1796," in Hudson, *Nationalism and Religion in America*, 18.

16. Thomas Jefferson, "Second Inaugural Address," in *The Writings of Thomas Jefferson*, vol. 10, ed. A. E. Bergh (Washington, D.C.: Thomas Jefferson Memorial Association, 1907), 217.

17. Herman Melville, *White Jacket; or, The World in a Man-of-War* (Boston: St. Botolph Society, 1892), 144.

18. Sidney E. Mead, *The Lively Experiment: The Shaping of Christianity in America* (New York: Harper and Row, 1963), 143.

19. Henry Ward Beecher, "The Battle Set in Array," in Cherry, *God's New Israel*, 171–72.

20. Benjamin Palmer, "National Responsibility before God," in Cherry, *God's New Israel*, 184. For Palmer's use of the Israel motif, see Richard T. Hughes, "A Civic Theology for the South: The Case of Benjamin M. Palmer," in *Illusions of Innocence: Protestant Primitivism in America, 1639–1875* by Richard T. Hughes and C. Leonard Allen (Chicago: University of Chicago Press, 1988), 194–95. See also Stephen R. Haynes, *Noah's Curse: The Biblical Justification of American Slavery* (Oxford, Eng.: Oxford University Press, 2002), 125–60.

21. *Congressional Record* 33 (Washington, D.C.: Government Printing Office, 1900), 711.

22. H. Richard Niebuhr, *The Kingdom of God in America* (1937; reprint, New York: Harper and Row, 1959), 179.

23. Maria W. Stewart, "An Address Delivered at the African Mason Hall, Boston, February 27, 1833," in "Productions," a pamphlet published in 1835, in *Pamphlets of Protest: An Anthology of Early African American Protest Literature, 1790–1860*, ed. Richard Newman, Patrick Rael, and Phillip Lapsansky (New York: Routledge, 2001), 127.

24. Martin Luther King Jr., "I See the Promised Land" (April 3, 1968), in *A Testament of Hope: The Essential Writings and Speeches of Martin Luther King Jr.*, ed. James Melvin Washington (San Francisco: HarperSanFrancisco, 1986), p. 286.

25. Malcolm X as told to Alex Haley, *The Autobiography of Malcolm X* (1964; reprint, New York: Ballantine Books, 1992), 164–67.

26. Ibid., 183.

27. J. William Fulbright, "The Arrogance of Power," in Cherry, *God's New Israel*, 340.

28. Abraham Lincoln, "Second Inaugural Address," in Cherry, *God's New Israel*, 202.

2 The Myth of Nature's Nation

THE REVOLUTIONARY PERIOD

Studying the myths that have shaped the American people quickly leads one to realize that from one important perspective, at least, the revolutionary and early national periods (between 1776 and 1825) stand at the center of American self-understanding, for several reasons. First, the myths that emerged in those years seemed so self-evident, especially to Americans of European descent, that it was difficult to contest them at all. The American experiment simply reflected the way things were meant to be.

Repressed minorities like African Americans and Native Americans, however, could see the holes in these myths. So, for example, could many women, many impoverished whites, and radicals and dissenters of various stripes. Their protests, however, were seldom heard in the larger culture. As a result, these myths stood virtually unchallenged from the Revolution to the 1960s, when, under the assaults of a massive countercultural and multicultural revolution, they finally began to unravel.

Second, the myths that emerged in this period had about them a certain timeless quality. According to these myths, America virtually transcended the particularities of time and place. These myths implicitly denied, for example, that the nation had particular historical roots. At one level, of course, everyone knew that Europe, especially Britain and France, had profoundly shaped the political structures of the United States. At another level, however, many believed that the American founders simply exploited a design they found in nature itself, a design as old as creation, rooted in the mind of God.

Because in the popular imagination the nation embodied timeless truths, many assumed that America eventually would enlighten the rest of the world and usher in a final golden age of peace, justice, and democratic self-government. In this way, Americans rooted their identity in a golden age of the past and a golden age yet to come. They stood, as it were, with one foot in the dawn of time and the other in the world's evening shadows. Defined by the beginning of the world, they would define its end. Like a bridge that spanned a mighty river, they spanned in their imaginations the particularities of time and place that had molded all cultures and civilizations except themselves. They therefore thought themselves untouched in any significant way by the power of human history.

Because these myths were so thoroughly ahistorical and seemed so completely self-evident, they had the capacity to absorb and reshape other American myths that were more obviously rooted in a particular past. The myth of the Chosen Nation, for example, had its roots in the particularities of Israel's past and the English Protestant experience. In the context of the early national period, however, chosenness became a self-evident truth that helped to undergird the doctrine of manifest destiny. Or again, by the late nineteenth century, the doctrine of free enterprise capitalism emerged not as one economic system among others, but as a fundamentally natural system, rooted in the way things were meant to be. For all these reasons, myths born of the revolutionary and early national periods have defined American culture in far-reaching ways and, by any measure, stand at the center of American life.

What were these myths? There were two. One emerged especially in the revolutionary period. The other emerged especially in the early years of the nineteenth century. One looked to the beginning of time. The other looked to its end. I will explore the first of these myths in this chapter and the other in chapter 4.

Nature's Nation

We shall call the myth that emerged in the revolutionary period the myth of Nature's Nation.[1] It had its deepest roots in the European Enlightenment, especially in Britain. The early seventeenth century provides the backdrop for understanding this development.

ENLIGHTENMENT BACKGROUNDS TO THE MYTH OF NATURE'S NATION

If the sixteenth century had been a period of religious reformation, the seventeenth century was a period marked by religious warfare. Before the Reformation, religious wars were virtually unthinkable, since one monolithic faith—the Roman Catholic Church—dominated Western Europe. This dominance dated from the fourth century when, in 313 A.D., the emperor Constantine's Edict of Milan legalized Christianity and when, in 380 A.D., the emperor Theodosius made the Christian faith the official religion of the Roman Empire. For the next 1,100 years and more, therefore, the monolithic power of a single religious faith virtually guaranteed that if war marred the face of Western Europe, it would not be religious in nature.

Then, in the sixteenth century, Christianity in Western Europe fragmented into competing faiths. Two embryonic Christian movements—Lutheran and Reformed—soon rivaled the Catholic Church for dominance in Western Europe. This situation was complicated by the fact that most Europeans—with the notable exception of the Anabaptists—still believed that a single state church was crucial to the welfare of the social and political order. The question quickly arose, therefore, of which church would serve as the legally established religion of a given state.

By the early seventeenth century, Europeans sought to resolve this question on the field of battle. The first religious war erupted in France in the late sixteenth century and pitted Catholics against Calvinists. Then, from 1618 to 1648, the Thirty Years' War virtually devastated the entire European Continent as Catholics and Protestants vied for power and control. In England, the Puritan Revolution erupted in 1640 and raged for the rest of the decade. This seventeenth-century background is crucial to understanding the Enlightenment of the eighteenth century.

In 1624 an Englishman named Edward Lord Herbert of Cherbury sought to find a way to resolve the religious crisis in Europe apart from bloodshed. In his book, *De Veritate*, he argued that the Bible stood at the heart of the problem. Before the sixteenth century, he observed, there had been only one version of the Bible, the Latin Vulgate, for which the church provided the single, official interpretation. With one version of the Bible and a single, unified interpretation, there was no theological basis for schism or for war.

Then, in the course of the Reformation, Herbert explained, religious leaders like Martin Luther and William Tyndale translated the Bible into the languages of the people. With that development, the Bible became an open book, subject to a variety of interpretations. The diverse interpretations legitimated the religious schisms that ultimately led to war. Under these circumstances, Herbert warned, religious warfare was inescapable.

Yet, Herbert noted, God had authored two books, not just one. If the first book was complex, the second was simple. If the first was susceptible to a variety of interpretations, the second was crystal clear to everyone who read it. In fact, the truths taught by this second book were self-evident. If the first book was the Bible, the second was the world of nature.

Herbert believed that nature taught the fundamental truths that stood at the heart of all religious faiths. Nature taught, for example, that God exists. Who could possibly observe the finely tuned symmetry of the natural world and conclude there was no God? Or again, nature taught the existence of a moral order that defined right and wrong. No one needed to read the Bible or any other religious text to learn that he or she should lead a virtuous life, or to discover that he or she should not kill or steal or abuse another human being, Herbert argued. One needed only to heed the laws God had written on the human heart. Nature also taught, Herbert believed, that human beings should repent of wrongdoings, and that God would reward the righteous and punish the wicked after death.

Then Herbert asked what to him was the pivotal question: "Who could possibly quarrel with these propositions?" Would Catholics disagree with these truths? Would Protestants? The answer obviously was "no," since these themes, Herbert thought, stood at the center of all religious faiths. Further, in Herbert's view, these notions were self-evident to the rational mind. Herbert therefore suggested that Christians of all persuasions place the book of nature at center stage and relegate the Bible to the wings. In this way, Christians could rob religious warfare of its theological basis and help put an end to the wars of religion.

Herbert's objectives were fundamentally pragmatic and not theological at all. Herbert's question was simply this: How can we put an end to the killing? His answer was to reduce religion to a set of self-evident essentials upon which all reasonable human beings could agree. By arguing for a religion grounded in nature and knowable through the powers of reason, Herbert helped give birth both to the English Enlightenment and to English Deism.

These two phenomena—the Enlightenment and Deism—were related but were not the same. The term *Enlightenment* refers to a broad philosophical outlook that especially valued the powers of human reason and flourished in the eighteenth century. It manifested itself in many parts of Europe and even in the American colonies. In the context of the Enlightenment worldview, natural science as we know it today took root and flowered.

On the other hand, the term *Deism* refers to a particular religious perspective that reflected the Enlightenment worldview. Deism focused exclusively on the deity, that is, on God. In Herbert's zeal to seek religious truth in nature alone, for example, he scuttled all those doctrines that could be known only from the biblical text. In Deism, therefore, theologies about Jesus Christ as the Son of God went out the window. So did any teachings about the Holy Spirit. All that was left was God—a God who could be known through human reason, attentive to the natural order. This was the meaning of Deism.

In America, Deism institutionalized itself in the Unitarian Church. The word *Unitarian* says it all, for Unitarians affirmed the unity of God and rejected the trinitarian notion of God the Father, God the Son, and God the Holy Spirit. Put another way, they focused their faith on God alone.

When Herbert's *De Veritate* appeared in 1624, few in England took it seriously. After all, while the continent was embroiled in the Thirty Years' War, England was still at peace and would remain so for another sixteen years. Few in England, therefore, saw the urgency of the issues Herbert raised.

By the 1640s, however, when the streets of London ran red with the blood of young soldiers, giving their lives for religious zealotry, Herbert's arguments suddenly made a great deal of sense. Others now took up Herbert's banner and argued that authentic Christianity had little to do with the mysteries found in scripture but everything to do with the simple, rational, self-evident truths taught in nature.

John Toland, for example, wrote an influential book in 1696 that he called *Christianity Not Mysterious*. He argued that authentic Christianity could be discerned in nature by the rational mind. He therefore rejected any so-called religious truths that originate in revelation, outside the sphere of human reason.

The English Deistic tradition reached its pinnacle in a work by Mathew Tindal, published in 1730: *Christianity As Old As the Creation; or, The Gospel a Republication of the Religion of Nature*. If the gospel was a republication of nature's truths, Tindal asked, why bother with the gospel at all? Why not focus instead on God's second book, the book of nature?

THE RELIGIOUS VIEWS OF AMERICA'S FOUNDERS

At this point, one might ask, how is any of this pertinent to the American myths that emerged in the founding years of the United States? The relevance becomes apparent when one takes note of the fact that the United States, born as it was in 1776, is a child of the eighteenth-century Enlightenment. Even more to the point, most of the American founders embraced some form of Deism, not historically orthodox Christianity.

On this particular point, I must be especially clear. To suggest that most of the American founders embraced some form of Deism is not to suggest that they did not *think of themselves* as Christians, for most certainly did. Jefferson, in fact, argued that his own Deist sentiments represented the heart of Jesus' teachings and the purest form of Christianity. In addition, Michael Novak has demonstrated how the biblical tradition informed in significant ways the political ideas of the founders.[2] Still, it is difficult to describe the founders as "orthodox Christians" when many rejected classic Christian doctrines like the divinity of Jesus. That is why it is fair to say that most of the American founders embraced some form of Deism, not orthodox Christianity.

Thomas Jefferson is a notable case in point. Though technically not a founder, Jefferson was part of the founding generation, was the principal author of the Declaration of Independence, and was held in the highest esteem by his peers. His religious views, therefore, are worth noting.

One finds Jefferson's religious perspectives mainly in his private correspondence. In a letter to Benjamin Waterhouse, dated June 26, 1822, for example, Jefferson wrote,

> The doctrines of Jesus are simple, and tend all to the happiness of man.
>
> 1. That there is one only God, and he all perfect.
> 2. That there is a future state of rewards and punishments.
> 3. That to love God with all thy heart and thy neighbor as thyself is the sum of religion. . . .
>
> But compare with these the demoralizing dogmas of Calvin.
>
> 1. That there are three Gods.
> 2. That good works, or the love of our neighbor, are nothing.
> 3. That faith is everything, and the more incomprehensible the proposition, the more merit in its faith.
> 4. That reason in religion is of unlawful use.
> 5. That God, from the beginning, elected certain individuals to be saved, and certain others to be damned; and that no crimes of the former can damn them; no virtues of the latter save.[3]

In a letter to Jared Sparks, dated November 4, 1820, Jefferson described the teachings of traditional Christian orthodoxy as "metaphysical insanities . . . , mere relapses into polytheism, differing from paganism only by being more unintelligible." On the other hand, he argued in that same letter that "the religion of Jesus is founded in the unity of God. . . . Thinking men of all nations rallied readily to the doctrine of one only God, and embraced it with the pure morals which Jesus inculcated."[4] Put another way, Jefferson believed that Jesus taught religious truths that harmonized beautifully with the truths proclaimed by God's second book, the book of nature.

On the other hand, Jefferson claimed, Christian orthodoxy emerged centuries after Jesus when Christian leaders embellished his simple teachings for the sake of profit and power. Accordingly, Jefferson wrote to Mrs. Harrison Smith on August 6, 1816, "There would never have been an infidel, if there had never been a priest. The artificial structures they have built on the purest of all moral systems, for the purpose of deriving from it pence and power, revolts those who think for themselves."[5]

Unmistakably, one finds in Jefferson the perspectives of a classic Deist.

Because he believed so strongly in the moral teachings of Jesus, Jefferson in 1803 extracted from the New Testament those teachings of Jesus that he thought reflected the essence of Christian faith. This book has been called "The Jefferson Bible."

As a Deist, Jefferson strongly advocated religious toleration. In a letter to Miles King, dated September 26, 1814, he wrote

> I must ever believe that religion substantially good which produces an honest life, and we have been authorized by one whom you and I equally respect, to judge of the tree by its fruit. Our particular principles of religion are a subject of accountability to our God alone. I inquire after no man's, and trouble none with mine. . . . Nay, we have heard it said that there is not a Quaker, or a Baptist, or a Presbyterian or an Episcopalian, a Catholic or a Protestant in heaven; that on entering that gate, we leave those badges behind, and find ourselves united in those principles only in which God has united us all.[6]

One finds in Benjamin Franklin very similar perspectives. A single passage will suffice. To Ezra Stiles, the president of Yale University, Franklin wrote, "Here is my creed. I believe in one God, Creator of the Universe. That He governs it by His providence. That he ought to be worshipped. That the most acceptable service we render Him is doing good to His other children. That the soul of man is immortal, and will be treated with justice in another life respecting its conduct in this. These I take to be the principal principles of sound religion." Here, Franklin claimed for himself the central themes of classic Deism. But he went on.

> As to Jesus of Nazareth . . . , I think the system of morals and his religion, as he left them to us, the best the world ever saw or is likely to see; but I apprehend it has received various corrupt changes, and I have, with most of the present dissenters in England, some doubts as to his divinity; though it is a question I do not dogmatize upon, having never studied it, and think it needless to busy myself with it now, when I expect soon an opportunity of knowing the truth with less trouble. I see no harm, however, in its being believed, if that belief has the good consequence, as probably it has, of making his doctrines more respected and better observed; especially as I do not perceive that the Supreme [Being] takes it amiss, by distinguishing the unbelievers in His government of the world with any peculiar marks of His displeasure.[7]

What difference did it make that those in the founding generation embraced Deism to the extent that they did? The answer to that question lies in the potential that religion held for the new nation. On the one hand, religion was a potential asset. As Franklin noted in the passage just cited, religious beliefs helped to sustain moral behavior, and that could only be good for the state.

Religion also presented serious liabilities, since so many competing Christian traditions existed in the colonies on the eve of the Revolution. Puritans, Presbyterians, Baptists, Quakers, Anglicans, Catholics, Lutherans, Methodists, Dutch Reformed people, and more—all these traditions, imported from Europe, had taken root in the American colonies. This diversity stood in marked contrast to the religious situation in Europe, where for one state only one established church existed.

In addition, many of the churches in the colonies had held legally established status back in Europe, or at least had sought that status for themselves. This was true of Catholics, Anglicans, Puritans, Lutherans, and various churches descended from the Reformed tradition. Now, with the birth of the new nation, each of these churches nurtured the hope that it might become the established church of the United States. Precisely those kinds of ambitions and hopes had fueled the wars of religion back in Europe in the seventeenth century. It was hardly inconceivable that religious wars, or at least serious religious conflicts, might erupt in the new nation. What could anyone do to prevent them?

The founders had several options. Obviously, they could have made one church the legally established church of the United States. That course of action, however, would have undermined their vision of what

America should become—a land where its citizens were free to believe what they chose to believe. On the other hand, they could have provided for complete freedom of religion. That provision, however, would have opened the door once again to the potential for religious conflict. Then what could be done?

Here, the Deism that characterized the founding generation served the nation remarkably well. Like Herbert of Cherbury, the founders asked the pragmatic question, "How can we prevent religious conflict, even religious bloodshed?" To answer that question, they turned directly to their Deist faith and, like Herbert, sought to reduce religion to a set of self-evident essentials upon which all reasonable people could agree.

Nowhere was this strategy more apparent than in Thomas Jefferson's Declaration of Independence. In fact, in that document Jefferson borrowed a page from Herbert of Cherbury and other Deistic thinkers and grounded America's religious faith squarely in a Deistic perspective. For example, he clearly affirmed in that document the existence of God. "All Men," he wrote, "*are created* equal [and] . . . are endowed by their *Creator*" (italics mine) with certain rights. He even identified this God as "Nature's God," that is, the God all human beings can know through nature.

Second, Jefferson affirmed the existence of a self-evident moral order. "We hold these Truths to be self-evident," he wrote, "that all Men are created equal, that they are endowed by their Creator with certain unalienable Rights, that among these are Life, Liberty, and the Pursuit of Happiness." In this context, he grounded the right of the colonies to break their political bonds with Britain as a right to which they were entitled by "the Laws of Nature and of Nature's God."

What Jefferson did not say is as important as what he said. He said nothing in the Declaration about Jesus, or the Trinity, or the church, or the Virgin Mary, or Moses, or Buddha, or Mohammed. He did not appeal to the New Testament, the Old Testament, the Koran, or to any other body of sacred scripture. Instead, he rooted the American Revolution in the existence of a God, apparent to all human beings in nature, and in a moral order that he proclaimed as self-evident.

While the American Creed, therefore, is grounded in certain ways in biblical metaphysics, as Michael Novak has pointed out, it has little to do with historic Christian orthodoxy. This point is worth noting in light of the frequently heard claim that America is a Christian nation. The truth is, the American Creed is rooted squarely in a Deistic worldview that was common to the eighteenth century.

By appealing to this perspective, Jefferson sought to place on the nation's center stage a minimal religious vision that virtually all Americans in his day could affirm. At the same time, he sought to banish to the wings of the national stage those religious themes that were important to certain denominations or faiths but not to the American people at large. In this way, he believed, Americans could embrace a religious faith that could unite them, not divide them.

How successful was this strategy? Immensely so. From Jefferson's day to this, many Americans have commonly claimed that it makes very little difference what particular religious faith one embraces, just so long as one believes in God and lives a good moral life. These are not the values of any particular religious faith such as Christianity, Judaism, or Islam, much less the values of any particular Christian denomination such as Baptist, Methodist, or Catholic. Instead, these are the values of eighteenth-century Deism, made incarnate in the Declaration of Independence.

If anything, therefore, the Declaration made Deism America's national faith. In part, this was Jefferson's intent. This should not be surprising in light of Jefferson's prediction, confided to James Smith in letter dated December 8, 1822, "I confidently expect that the present generation will see Unitarianism become the general religion of the United States."[8] Jefferson could make that prediction only because Unitarianism was the institutional embodiment of the Deist faith, a religion broad enough, he thought, to embrace all Americans willing to take "Nature and Nature's God" as the standard for their lives. And he imagined that all reasonable Americans would embrace just that option.

In 1791 the Bill of Rights, the first ten amendments to the Constitution of the United States, became effective. First among those amendments was Article 1, which contained this affirmation: "Congress shall make no law respecting an establishment of religion, or prohibiting the free exercise thereof."

While Article 1 of the Bill of Rights did not ground its provisions in an explicitly Deistic frame of reference as had the Declaration, it did put legal teeth into one of the Declaration's main concerns. It disallowed any possibility that the federal government could ever make one single faith the established religion of the nation. Further, it applied to the realm of religion one of the truths that the Declaration had proclaimed as "self-evident"—the right to liberty. In other words, it denied to the federal government the right to "prohibit the free exercise" of religion on the part of any citizen. Finally, if the Declaration had *implicitly* pushed denominational religion to the wings of the national stage, the First Amendment to the Constitution made that point explicit: as far as the government was concerned, religion was simply off limits.

The First Amendment thereby provided the classic American doctrine of separation of church and state. It is a gross mistake nonetheless to imagine that separation of church and state also meant the separation of religion from culture. To make that mistake is to ignore the power both of the American Creed and of the various American myths. It is to ignore as well the many ways in which religious assumptions, often unspoken, have shaped the common life of the United States.

If one sought to illustrate the role religion has played in American culture, one could find no better example than the case of the First Amendment itself. It may appear ironic that the secularizing provisions of the First Amendment grew from deep religious convictions, but that is nonetheless the case.

First, James Madison, author of the Bill of Rights, clearly embraced the sentiments of Deism. In 1785 Madison wrote his famous "Memorial and Remonstrance," protesting a proposal that Virginia assess upon all citizens a tax that would support the Christian religion. In that document we can clearly discern Madison's religious commitments that would later undergird the First Amendment. Madison started with the assumption that "before any man can be considered as a member of Civil Society, he must be considered as a subject of the Governor of the Universe." He therefore argued that freedom of religion "is in its nature an unalienable right. It is unalienable," he said, because "it is the duty of every man to render to the Creator such homage, and such only, as he believes to be acceptable to him." This, Madison believed, was one of those truths taught by "Nature and Nature's God."[9]

Partly on that ground, Madison rejected the Virginia proposal that government has the right to raise a religious tax. On that same ground, he argued in the First Amendment that "Congress shall make no law respecting an establishment of religion, or prohibiting the free exercise thereof."

There is another sense in which the secularizing provisions of the First Amendment grew from deep religious convictions. For example, in colonies with established churches, Baptists and Methodists suffered severe disabilities because they refused to support the legally established faith. Because they sought religious freedom for themselves, dissenters like Baptists and Methodists made common cause with Deists in their effort to abolish religious establishments wherever they were found. It is doubtful, in fact, that people like Jefferson and Madison could have won religious freedom to the extent that they did without the support of those dissenting Christians.

Once religious freedom became a reality, however, many of those same dissenting Christians grew fearful that a nation without explicitly Christian supports might lack the moral character necessary to survive. They therefore snuggled up to those Christians of established churches who had treated them so badly for so long. Together, those two groups now launched an attack on the Deist perspective in which religious freedom was grounded. I will explore that development more fully in the following chapter.[10]

ELABORATING THE MYTH OF NATURE'S NATION

Because the American founders grounded the American experiment in their vision of "Nature and Nature's God," it was easy to imagine that the United States simply reflected the way God himself intended things to be from the beginning of the world. In other words, the American system was not spun out of someone's imagination or contrived by human wit. Instead, it was based on a natural order, built into the world by God himself.

Jefferson said as much when he spoke of "self-evident truths." John Adams concurred when he affirmed that "the United States of America have exhibited, perhaps, the first example of governments erected on the simple principles of nature." The fullest expression of this conviction came from Jefferson's friend and confidant, Thomas Paine, who announced that "the case and circumstance of America present themselves as in the beginning of the world." Indeed, Paine wrote, "We are brought at once to the point of seeing government begin, as if we had lived in the beginning of time. The real volume, not of history, but of facts, is directly before us, unmutilated by contrivance, or the errors of tradition."[11] Here one finds the myth of Nature's Nation full blown.

At its core, this myth encouraged Americans to ignore the power of history and tradition as forces that shaped the nation. Paine's words epitomize this perspective: when we live in the United States, it is "as if we had lived in the beginning of time." Here was a nation untouched by the hand of human tradition, a nation that had escaped the molding power of history and culture, a nation that had sprung, as it were, directly from the hand of God. At the most fundamental level, therefore, American identity derived not from British history and culture, not even from ancient Greece and Rome, but from nature, formed directly by the Creator.

If one would like a graphic example of how this myth has found expression in American popular culture, a film that appeared in the late 1980s, *Rocky IV,* is particularly instructive. In this film, Rocky, an American boxer, goes to the Soviet Union to fight the Russian giant, Drago. A marvelous sequence depicts the two fighters training for the bout. Rocky trains in the Siberian wilderness. He lifts logs, drags heavy boulders, and runs on mountaintops. Clearly he is the natural man. On the other hand, Drago trains in a high-tech gym, full of the latest scientifically produced equipment. If Rocky is natural, Drago is contrived, a creature of human design and ingenuity.

Finally, the fight begins before a huge crowd of Muscovites. The fight is hardly underway before Drago begins to pummel Rocky unmercifully. It appears as though Rocky has more than met his match and will surely fall before the great Russian giant. But then, suddenly, Rocky gets a second wind. Boom! Boom! He lands a right, then a left, then another right. Drago stumbles, and finally falls. Suddenly, we see an American flag unfurl and we hear a chant go up from this crowd of Russian spectators. "Rocky! Rocky! Rocky!" It is clear what has happened. The Russians have witnessed the irresistible power of the American, the Natural Man.

Precisely because the myth of Nature's Nation downplayed the power of history and tradition, it found a ready and receptive audience among many American Christians. The Reformed tradition, as I have noted, revered the founding period of the Christian faith, and many in that tradition rejected Christian history and tradition as carrying any significant authoritative weight. While Reformed Christians did appeal to Calvin and other leaders in the sixteenth-century Reformation, those leaders carried weight only to the extent that they pointed beyond themselves to Scripture and the first Christian age. Significantly, Christians from the Reformed tradition enjoyed extraordinary strength in the early national period throughout the United States. Puritans in New England, Presbyterians and Dutch Reformed Christians in the Middle Colonies, and Baptists in the South were all bona fide representatives of the Reformed tradition.

In addition, a variety of new Christian movements emerged in the United States in the early national period, and almost all of them claimed to have restored the ancient Christian faith in all its purity. Quite apart from the Enlightenment, therefore, fascination with pure beginnings abounded among American Christians in the early nineteenth century. These Christians shared with Deists a bias that favored the authority of the founding age, however that age might be defined. No wonder that the myth of Nature's Nation captured the American imagination in the early nineteenth century.

Critiquing the Myth of Nature's Nation

In so many ways the myth of Nature's Nation failed to deliver on its promise of liberty and justice for all. The reason for this failure is easy enough to grasp: Those who embraced this myth all too often found in nature their own cultural traditions and then defended those traditions as fundamentally natural.

A PHILOSOPHICAL CRITIQUE

Carl Becker made this point many years ago when he wrote that "in the eighteenth-century climate of opinion, whatever question you seek to answer, nature is the test, the standard: the ideas, the customs, the institutions of men, if ever they are to attain perfection, must obviously be in accord with those laws which 'nature reveals at all times, to all men.'" Becker went on to note that the problem lay in the fact that those Enlightenment philosophers who embraced nature as the standard for civilization "do not know that the 'man in general' they are looking for is just their own image, that the principles they are bound to find are the very ones they start out with. That is the trick they play on the dead."[12]

Examples of Becker's point abound. Becker himself offers one striking example when he notes that the natural-rights philosophy "had been, and could again be . . . effectively used as a justification of revolutionary movements." But revolution was precisely what nineteenth-century Americans did not want. They had fought one revolution and that was enough. Now their greatest concern was "to preserve the independence they had won, the institutions they had established, the 'more perfect Union' they had created."[13]

Of course, the political and cultural traditions they had created were deeply rooted in a white, male, European, and Protestant frame of reference. Regardless, those who embraced these traditions and institutions now defended them in the language of natural rights and ideals. In this way, they absolutized their very particular cultural traditions and then heralded those traditions as both natural and universal, and therefore as the standard for all human beings in all places in all times. Not only did they absolutize their cultural traditions; they absolutized the myth as well. The myth of Nature's Nation at its best affirms that *all men* are created equal. In its absolutized form, however, this myth suggests that certain civilizations are grounded in the laws of nature, while others are simply contrived.

One finds another poignant example of Becker's point in the stance of Indiana senator Albert Beveridge. Eager to legitimate America's colonizing ventures at the end of the nineteenth century, Beveridge grounded those ventures in the self-evident laws of nature. In this vein, he spoke in glowing terms of "this self-evident and contemporaneous truth: *Every progressive nation of Europe to-day is seeking lands to colonize and governments to administer.* . . . France declined only when she abandoned that natural law of national power and progress." Accordingly, he spoke of "that universal law of civilization which requires of every people who have reached our high estate to become colonizers of new lands."[14]

It must be clear by now why and how the myth of Nature's Nation was a two-edged sword, cutting in two very different directions. On the one hand, it promised "life, liberty, and the pursuit of happiness" as "unalienable rights" for "all men" and grounded those rights squarely in "Nature and Nature's God." On the other hand, it defined nature in Eurocentric terms that especially served the interests of a white male population descended from European stock.

AN AFRICAN AMERICAN CRITIQUE

No one understood this point better than David Walker, a black man born in Wilmington, North Carolina, in 1785. His father was a slave, but since his mother was free, he also was free in the eyes of the law. Nonetheless, Walker fled the slaveholding South and took up residence in Boston, where, in 1827, he opened a store selling old clothes. In 1829 he published the first thoroughgoing critique of slavery written by a black man. He called his book *Walker's Appeal . . . to the Coloured Citizens of the World.*

Walker's book is notable for many reasons, but especially because he opposed Thomas Jefferson head-on and thereby exposed the ambiguities in the myth of Nature's Nation. He pointed his readers, on the one hand, to the Declaration of Independence that declared that all men were created equal. Then he quoted extensively from another document, *Notes on the State of Virginia,* where Jefferson argued that blacks were *by nature* inferior to whites.

Jefferson resolutely opposed the institution of slavery, which, in his judgment, degraded slaves and masters alike. He therefore claimed there was no more urgent business than the eradication of this barbaric practice. Despite his opposition to slavery, he compromised his conviction for a variety of reasons and consented to the extension of slavery into the territories of the United States. Finally, he died with scores of slaves working his property at Monticello. Paradoxically, he was never able to free himself of the institution he so much despised.[15]

Though he hoped for the abolition of slavery in his lifetime, he thought very poorly of those human beings who served as slaves. In his *Notes on the State of Virginia*, he explored the makeup of African Americans in considerable detail, speaking first of their physical characteristics.

> Are not the fine mixtures of red and white, the expressions of every passion by greater or less suffusions of colour in the one, preferable to that eternal monotony, which reigns in the countenances, that immoveable veil of black which covers all the emotions of the other race? Add to these, flowing hair, a more elegant symmetry of form, their own judgment in favour of the whites, declared by their preference of them, as uniformly as is the preference of the Oran-ootan for the black women over those of his own species. The circumstance of superior beauty, is thought worthy attention in the propagation of our horses, dogs, and other domestic animals; why not in that of man?

When Jefferson turned to the emotional makeup of blacks, he said this:

> A black, after hard labour through the day, will be induced by the slightest amusements to sit up till midnight, or later, though knowing he must be out with the first dawn of the morning. . . . They are more ardent after their female [than whites]: but love seems with them to be more an eager desire, than a tender delicate mixture of sentiment and sensation. Their griefs are transient. Those numberless afflictions, which render it doubtful whether heaven has given life to us in mercy or in wrath, are less felt, and sooner forgotten with them. In general, their existence appears to participate more of sensation than of reflection.

Regarding the mental characteristics of blacks, Jefferson wrote, "Comparing them by their faculties of memory, reason, and imagination, it appears to me, that in memory they are equal to the whites; in reason much inferior, as I think one could scarcely be found capable of tracing and comprehending the investigations of Euclid; and that in imagination they are dull, tasteless, and anomalous." He concluded by advancing the theory that blacks are fundamentally inferior to whites, and that the differences between the two races are rooted *in nature*. "I advance it therefore as a suspicion only," he wrote, "that the blacks, whether originally a distinct race, or made distinct by time and circumstances, are inferior to the whites in the endowments both of body and mind." Further, "it is not their condition, then, but nature, which has produced the distinction."[16]

Recognizing Jefferson's standing among American whites, David Walker understood the importance of these words. Jefferson's efforts to root the inferiority of blacks *in nature*, Walker wrote, "has in truth injured us more, and has been as great a barrier to our emancipation as any thing that has ever been advanced against us." Indeed, Walker surmised that Jefferson's remarks had "sunk deep into the hearts of millions of the whites, and never will be removed this side of eternity."[17]

Walker, of course, was right. A generation later, Frederick Douglass, the former slave turned abolitionist leader, would complain that

> *slavery has bewitched us.* It has taught us to read history backwards. It has given us evil for good. . . .
> The chief and recognized builders of the Republic, almost without an exception, openly condemned . . . the system of Slavery as a great moral and political evil, alien to the laws of nature. But how different from this is the sentiment of the present, among our public men! What was regarded as a curse at the beginning, is now cherished as a blessing. . . . Those who denounced the accursed thing at the beginning, were deemed wise, humane and patriotic. Those who denounce it now, are called disorganizers, enemies of the Union, "freedom-shriekers," "negro-worshippers," infidels and traitors. The contrast is striking and instructive.[18]

In David Walker's judgment, therefore, "unless we try to refute Mr. Jefferson's arguments respecting us, we will only establish them."[19]

Throughout his book, he sought to do precisely that. To Jefferson's reference to "oran-ootans," Walker responded, "Have they [the whites] not, after having reduced us to the deplorable condition of slaves under their feet, held us up as descending originally from the tribes of *Monkeys* or *Orang-Outangs*? O! my God! I appeal to every man of feeling—is not this insupportable? Is it not heaping the most gross insult upon our miseries, because they have got us under their feet and we cannot help ourselves?"[20] When Walker read Jefferson's affirmation that blacks were inferior to whites, both in mind and body, he was amazed that Jefferson would "speak so of a set of men in chains. I do not know what to compare it to," he wrote, "unless, like putting one wild deer in an iron cage, where it will be secured, and hold another by the side of the same, then let it go, and expect the one in the cage to run as fast as the one at liberty."[21]

It was difficult to argue against sheer prejudice. The best Walker could do, therefore, was to affirm his own humanity, and that of other African American slaves: "Are we MEN!!—I ask you, O my brethren! are we MEN? Did our Creator make us to be slaves to dust and ashes like ourselves? Are they not dying worms as well as we? Have they not to make their appearance before the tribunal of Heaven, to answer for the deeds done in the body, as well as we?"[22]

The proof of who was inferior and who was not, Walker suggested, was to be found in moral behavior, and on that score, he claimed that whites had failed miserably. Whether in Greece, Rome, Gaul, Spain, or Britain, he argued, "the whites have always been an unjust, jealous, unmerciful, avaricious and blood-thirsty set of beings, always seeking after power and authority." In a line that anticipated the twentieth-century Black Muslim affirmation that "the white man is the devil," Walker affirmed that, for the most part, whites have acted "more like devils than accountable men." In terms of moral behavior, Walker wondered "whether they are *as good by nature* as we are or not. Their actions . . . have been the reverse."[23]

Walker turned Jefferson's arguments upside down. The fact that whites found it necessary to keep blacks in chains was the strongest possible argument for the full humanity of African American people:

> Man, in all ages and all nations of the earth, is the same. Man is a peculiar creature—he is the image of his God, though he may be subjected to the most wretched condition upon earth, yet the spirit and feeling which constitute the creature, man, can never be entirely erased from his breast, because God who made him after his own image, planted it in his heart; he cannot get rid of it. The whites knowing this, they do not know what to do; they know that they have done us much injury, they are afraid that we, being men, and not brutes, will retaliate, and woe will be to them.[24]

With an ironic twist on the theme of Nature's Nation, Walker claimed that whites had made themselves the "natural enemies" of blacks through the "outrages" they had committed "upon human nature."[25] Finally, Walker raised before his readers the Declaration of Independence itself.

> See your Declaration Americans!!! Do you understand your own language? Hear your language, proclaimed to the world, July 4th, 1776—"We hold these truths to be self evident—that *ALL* men are created EQUAL!! *that they are endowed by their creator with certain unalienable rights; that among these are life, liberty, and the pursuit of happiness*!!" Compare your own language above, extracted from your Declaration of Independence, with your cruelties and murders inflicted by your cruel and unmerciful fathers on ourselves on our fathers and on us, men who have never given your fathers or you the least provocation!!![26]

Walker's words of protest, as powerful as they were, fell on deaf ears. According to the sketch of his life that accompanies Walker's *Appeal*, "This little book produced more commotion among slave-holders than any volume of its size that was ever issued from an American press. They saw that it was a bold attack upon their idolatry, and that too by a black man who once lived among them." Little wonder, then, that "a company of Georgia men . . . bound themselves by an oath, that they would eat as little as possible until they had killed the youthful author." Walker died in 1830 at the age of 34, apparently a victim of murder.[27]

Conclusions

The myth of Nature's Nation is rooted squarely in the principles of the American Creed. The creed proclaims that among all the truths one might encounter in a lifetime, there are certain truths that are simply "self-evident" and require no formal proof. Among those truths are the propositions "that all Men are created equal, that they are endowed by their Creator with certain unalienable Rights, that among these are Life, Liberty, and the Pursuit of Happiness." Those truths are "self-evident," the creed contends, because they are rooted in "Nature and Nature's God" and therefore reflect the way things are meant to be. To the extent that the American people have lived out the meaning of these principles, the American Creed has brought innumerable blessings both to Americans and to others around the globe.

The paradox lies in the fact that the myth of Nature's Nation, rooted as it is in the American Creed, has sometimes devoured itself and undermined the very creed from which it grows. For the notion of Nature's Nation has often annulled America's debt to history, tradition, and culture and led Americans to believe that the contours of American civilization—the way things actually are—simply reflect "the way things are meant to be." Thomas Paine could therefore argue that when we view American government, "We are brought at once to the point of seeing government begin, as if we had lived in the beginning of time. The real volume, not of history, but of facts, is directly before us, unmutilated by contrivance, or the errors of tradition."[28] In other words, the sort of government America had erected was the very kind of government God had ordained from the foundations of the world, and the kind of government God would create if He were here in person. Here one finds no debt whatsoever to history, culture, or tradition.

David Noble argued that Americans of the revolutionary generation supplemented their covenant with God with a covenant with nature. Accordingly, "Americans, as children of nature, were innocents who did not act in the world of historical conflict. . . . Their responsibility was to keep pure and undefiled this New World Garden of Eden."[29]

In this context, Albert Beveridge could view America's colonizing efforts as reflecting a "self-evident truth," grounded in "natural law." From this perspective, it was completely legitimate to subjugate Filipinos to what Beveridge and his comrades viewed as America's superior way of life. And Thomas Jefferson—the very man who spoke of life, liberty, and the pursuit of happiness as "unalienable rights" grounded in "self-evident" truths—this very same Jefferson could argue that whites *by nature* were superior to blacks. If this was so, then blacks were exempted from that "self-evident" truth that "all men are created equal."

Clearly, Carl Becker was right when he claimed that those Enlightenment philosophers who embraced nature as the standard for civilization "do not know that the 'man in general' they are looking for is just their own image, that the principles they are bound to find are the very ones they start out with." Because the principles they were bound to find were the very ones with which they began, Americans folded into the myth of Nature's Nation virtually all the significant contents of their culture. From this perspective, "white" was natural. So was democracy and representative government. In subsequent chapters, I shall explore how nineteenth-century Americans also folded into the myth of Nature's Nation their religion—Protestant Christianity—and their economic system—laissez-faire capitalism.

Notes

1. Perry Miller popularized the label "Nature's Nation" in a book by that same title, published in 1967, though he used the term in a much broader sense than I do here. See Perry Miller, *Nature's Nation* (Cambridge, Mass.: Belknap Press, 1967).

2. Michael Novak, *On Two Wings: Humble Faith and Common Sense at the American Founding* (San Francisco: Encounter Books, 2002), 5–47.

3. Thomas Jefferson to Benjamin Waterhouse, June 26, 1822, in Norman Cousins, ed., *"In God We Trust": The Religious Beliefs and Ideas of the American Founding Fathers* (New York: Harper, 1958), 160–61.

4. Thomas Jefferson to Jared Sparks, November 4, 1820, in Cousins, *"In God We Trust,"* 156.

5. Thomas Jefferson to Mrs. Harrison Smith, August 6, 1816, in Cousins, *"In God We Trust,"* 147.

6. Thomas Jefferson to Miles King, September 26, 1814, in Cousins, *"In God We Trust,"* 144–45.

7. Benjamin Franklin to Ezra Stiles, March 9, 1790, in Cousins, *"In God We Trust,"* 42.

8. Thomas Jefferson to James Smith, December 8, 1822, in Cousins, *"In God We Trust,"* 159.

9. James Madison, "Memorial and Remonstrance" (1785), in Cousins, *"In God We Trust,"* 309.

10. The interpretations in this section are heavily dependent on Sidney E. Mead's two seminal works, *The Lively Experiment: The Shaping of Christianity in America* (New York: Harper and Row, 1963), and *The Nation with the Soul of a Church* (New York: Harper and Row, 1975).

11. John Adams, *A Defense of the Constitutions of the Government of the United States of America*, abridged in *The Political Writings of John Adams: Representative Selections*, ed. George A. Peek (New York: Liberal Arts Press, 1954), 117; and Thomas Paine, *Rights of Man* (1791–92), in *The Complete Writings of Thomas Paine*, ed. Philip S. Foner (New York: Citadel Press, 1945), 1:376.

12. Carl L. Becker, *The Heavenly City of the Eighteenth-Century Philosophers* (1932; reprint, New Haven, Conn.: Yale University Press, 1964), 52–53, 103–4.

13. Carl L. Becker, *The Declaration of Independence: A Study in the History of Political Ideas* (New York: Vintage Books, 1922), 237–38.

14. Albert Beveridge, "The Star of Empire," in *God's New Israel: Religious Interpretations of American Destiny*, ed. Conrad Cherry (1971; reprint, Chapel Hill: University of North Carolina Press, 1998), 153–54. Beveridge's emphasis.

15. For an assessment of this paradox, see John Chester Miller, *The Wolf by the Ears: Thomas Jefferson and Slavery* (New York: Free Press, 1977).

16. Thomas Jefferson, *Notes on the State of Virginia*, ed. William Peden (Chapel Hill: University of North Carolina Press, 1955), 138–43.

17. David Walker, *Walker's Appeal . . . to the Colored Citizens of the World*, 2d ed. (1830; Nashville: James C. Winston, 1994), 38–39.

18. Frederick Douglass, "Freedom in the West Indies: An Address Delivered in Poughkeepsie, New York, August 2, 1858," in *The Frederick Douglass Papers*, ed. John Blassingame, vol. 3 (New Haven, Conn.: Yale University Press, 1985), 224–26. The italics are in the original.

19. Walker, *Walker's Appeal*, 26.

20. Ibid., 20.

21. Ibid., 20–21.

22. Ibid., 27.

23. Ibid., 27–29.

24. Ibid., 72–73.

25. Ibid., 73.

26. Ibid., 85–86. Walker's emphasis.

27. "A Brief Sketch of the Life and Character of David Walker," in *Walker's Appeal*, vi–vii.

28. Paine, *Rights of Man*, 376.

29. David W. Noble, *Historians against History: The Frontier Thesis and the National Covenant in American Historical Writing since 1830* (Minneapolis: University of Minnesota Press, 1965), 30.

3 *The Myth of the Christian Nation*

THE EARLY NATIONAL PERIOD

William G. McLoughlin tells us that when John Adams was president, the United States "concluded a treaty with the Moslem nation of Tripoli (now Libya) in which one article read in part: 'As the government of the United States of America is not, in any sense, founded on the Christian religion.'" McLoughlin further reports, "That treaty was ratified by more than two thirds of the U.S. Senate and signed by John Adams."[1]

McLoughlin's report is not surprising, since the founders of the United States never intended America to be an explicitly Christian nation. With the Declaration of Independence as a measure of their sentiments, one must conclude that they sought to ground this country on the Deist assumption that God exists and rules the affairs of humankind, that God can best be discerned in the book of nature, and that God has built into nature certain moral standards that are equally accessible to all human beings. These were the beliefs that would stand at the core of the new Republic, and because the founders viewed these propositions as "self-evident," they imagined that all Americans could affirm them with ease.

At the same time, if Americans wished to belong to specific religious traditions, or wished to affirm other doctrines—the notion of the Trinity, for example, or the doctrine of substitutionary atonement—they were free to do so. But these other doctrines, peculiar to specific sects and denominations, would never occupy the nation's center stage, would never define the nation's legal tradition, and would be irrelevant to the workings of the American government. The founders sought to guarantee religious liberty by allowing for particular doctrines and creeds but by pushing those doctrines and creeds off the center stage of the Republic and into the wings.

The Declaration therefore affirmed a minimalist religious sentiment, that is, the religious convictions that most Americans held in common. But the Constitution went far beyond the Declaration and essentially created a secular state. Nowhere does the Constitution mention God or any other religious symbol. And when, finally, the First Amendment to the Constitution speaks of religion for the very first time, it makes perfectly clear that "Congress shall make no law respecting an establishment of religion, or prohibiting the free exercise thereof."

In other words, while the American people would be free to practice any religion, they would also be free to practice no religion at all. And the government had no business injecting itself into religion or religious issues in any form, shape, or fashion. In this sense, America would be a secular state.

The paradox lies in the fact that in spite of the stipulations of the First Amendment, America nonetheless emerged in several respects as a Christian nation. First, even though the founders resisted the creation of an explicitly Christian nation, the Deism that they espoused is inexplicable apart from biblical faith. Michael Novak has documented this fact extensively and has shown how Jewish and Christian presuppositions informed American political institutions.[2] And second, the myth of America as a Christian Nation took on objective truth especially in the nineteenth century when Protestants succeeded in Christianizing the country through the power of revivalism. From that time to this, America has indeed been a Christian nation of sorts.

The Attempt to Christianize the Republic

Most Americans are familiar with the charge that secular humanists seek to remove God and even religion from serious discussion in American public life. Few realize, however, that charges like this are not new. In the nation's earliest years, the operative phrase was not "secular humanist" but "infidel." Some Americans regarded the founders of the Republic as the nation's archinfidels who sought to destroy Christianity and remove religion from the public square. The people who hurled that charge against the founders generally were Christians still devoted to the European model of the state church or, at the very least, to the ideal of a state with significant Christian underpinnings.

While most Americans in the twenty-first century are comfortable with the notion of a secular government, with the separation of church and state, and with a multiplicity of religious traditions, many in the nation's earliest years were not. Outside of Maryland, Rhode Island, and Pennsylvania, there were virtually no significant models of the separation of church and state when the nation was born, either in Europe or in the United States. Many Americans during that period, therefore, could not imagine a viable nation without a legally established church.

Equally important is the fact that during the Revolutionary period and into the nineteenth century, the majority of Americans who claimed the Christian faith were Calvinists of one stripe or another. Roman Catholics were still a distinct minority. The Anglican Church—or the Church of England—still thrived, especially in the South, but had lost considerable credibility, especially since so many Americans associated that church with Britain, not with America. Methodism—a distinctly non-Calvinist faith—was growing by leaps and bounds and would soon take the American frontier by storm. Yet, all in all, in the early nineteenth century, Calvinists still dominated religious life in the United States.

Calvinism came in many forms. In New England, the Calvinist faith manifested itself especially in Congregationalism, one of the churches that descended directly from New England Puritanism. In the middle colonies, Presbyterians and Dutch Reformed Christians abounded. And Baptists were numerous in the South. Baptists, however, do not play a significant role in this phase of our story since, at that time at least, they did not share with other Reformed Christians the goal of dominating public life.

As people of the Reformed tradition, Congregationalists, Presbyterians, and Dutch Reformed Christians generally looked to John Calvin and the regime he erected in Geneva to understand how religion should inform the public square. Understanding the Christian resistance to America's founders, therefore, requires some understanding of religion and politics in Geneva in the sixteenth century.

Calvin shared with virtually all European Christians of the sixteenth century the conviction that for one state, there could be only one church, and that church should be legally established and binding on all citizens. To understand the genius of Calvin, however, one must realize that he went far beyond that position. Simply put, Calvin sought to transform Geneva into a model kingdom of God. *Transform* and *transformation*—these are the operative words when discussing Calvin, for Calvin wished to transform every dimension of Geneva's culture—its politics, its art, its education—into a regime controlled by a Christian understanding of reality.

Since that time, Calvin's vision of a godly society has become central to the Calvinist heritage and has flourished wherever Calvinists have lived throughout the world. When Reformed Christians settled in America, therefore, they brought with them this very same understanding of how Christian faith should relate to the state, to the culture, and to the public order. On the basis of this commitment, they determined to transform the colonies, and then the nation, into a model kingdom of God, just as Calvin had transformed Geneva many years before.

Since most American Christians at the time of the Revolution had little or no experience with the separation of church and state, and since most of those Christians stood in the Reformed heritage in one way or another, one can readily understand why so many Christians registered such opposition to the founders of the American Republic. As far as these Christians were concerned, the founders who created a secular state with freedom of religion had declared war not only on the ideal of a Christian republic, but also on the Christian religion itself. These Christians, therefore, unequivocally labeled the founders infidels.

We find a marvelous example of the struggle over these issues in the presidential election of 1800. In that year, Thomas Jefferson ran for the presidency of the United States. His candidacy created a firestorm of controversy. Because he was a Deist who rejected any effort to establish or coerce religious faith, his opponents assailed him as an infidel and a godless atheist. And because he disavowed a great deal of traditional Christian theology, some claimed that his administration would encourage the grossest kinds of immoralities and would hasten the Republic's early demise.

One clergyman, the Reverend John M. Mason, discovered that Jefferson had written in his *Notes on Virginia* that "the legitimate powers of government extend to such acts only as are injurious to others. But it does me no injury for my neighbor to say there are twenty Gods, or no God. It neither picks my pocket nor breaks my leg." To Mason, Jefferson had preached both "atheism" and "the morality of devils which would break in an instant every link in the chain of human friendship, and transform the globe into one equal scene of desolation and horror, where fiend would prowl with fiend for plunder and blood."[3]

Another preacher, the Reverend Clement Clarke Moore, also objected to Jefferson's *Notes on Virginia*. He had only recently read them, he wrote, and found himself "surprised that a book which contains so much infidelity, conveyed in so insidious a manner, should have been extensively circulated in a Christian country, for nearly twenty years, without ever having received a formal answer."[4]

Mason and Moore typified the thousands of Christians in the early national period who were still devoted to the ideals of a state church. More to the point, they could not imagine an America that was not fundamentally Christian, even fundamentally Protestant. Jefferson had challenged all that, and for this reason, he emerged as the archinfidel of his generation.

For all that, the Jeffersonians won that war. They won it when the First Amendment prohibited Congress from making any law "respecting an establishment of religion, or prohibiting the free exercise thereof." They won again when the various states passed their own versions of the First Amendment, striking down religious establishments in state after state. As might be expected, Massachusetts—long dominated by Puritan visions of a Christian commonwealth—was the last state to disestablish, doing so in 1833. Slowly, one indisputable fact became clear even to the most resolute defender of Christian orthodoxy and the state church ideal: America would not be a Christian nation, at least in legal terms.

The Second Great Awakening

Shortly after the nation's birth Christians throughout the country launched a massive revival designed, in part, to achieve through persuasion what they could no longer achieve through coercion or force of law. Through that revival, they sought to transform the United States into a Christian nation. We remember that revival as the Second Great Awakening. This awakening was the second such revival in American life. The Great Awakening, which I shall consider in the next chapter, had swept through the colonies some seventy-five years earlier.

The Second Great Awakening was not simply a response to the loss of an established church. At a far deeper level, it was a two-pronged attempt to realize the old Calvinist vision of a social order responsive to the sovereign will of God. First, the Second Great Awakening sought to Protestantize the nation. Second, it sought to transform the republic into the Kingdom of God, whose social order would be thoroughly reformed according to biblical principles. In these ways, the United States would become a distinctly Christian nation.

FACTORS PROMPTING THE SECOND GREAT AWAKENING

Many factors prompted the rise of the Second Great Awakening. First, as I have noted, many Christians of that time were still devoted to the European model of a state church and could not imagine America without the influence of a Christian establishment. Second, many feared that the Constitution, by disallowing any possibility of an established Christian faith, had opened the door to heresy, skepticism, and irreligion. To some degree, developments since the Revolution confirmed those fears. For example, while the founders were moderate-minded Deists, other freethinkers of the period launched scathing attacks on the Bible and the Christian faith, portraying miracle stories as fairy tales and traditional religion as little more than superstition. Through their various publications, Ethan Allen, Elihu Palmer, and Jefferson's friend and ally, Thomas Paine, made themselves especially prominent in this regard.

Third, the French Revolution began in 1789, and the violence it spawned against religion horrified many Americans and especially American Christians. For example, the French king himself lost his head to the guillotine in 1793. In the chaotic months that followed, the new regime executed literally thousands of Frenchmen. In 1794 the Convention designated Reason the Supreme Being that must be worshiped and transformed Roman Catholic churches into Temples of Reason, where citizens now poured libations to statues depicting the goddess of nature.

These events alarmed many American Christians, since the French Revolution was rooted in the same principles that had undergirded the American Revolution: the equal rights of all people, rooted in Nature and Nature's God. In fact, when Jefferson served as ambassador to France, he assisted the marquis de Lafayette in drafting the Declaration of the Rights of Man, a document patterned directly after Jefferson's own Declaration of Independence.

A fourth factor prompting revival was the virtual flood of settlers pouring over the mountains into regions that soon would become the states of Kentucky, Tennessee, Ohio, Indiana, Illinois, Mississippi, and Alabama—a development that had accelerated especially since 1790. Almost as much as Deism and free thought, these western settlements frightened the older, eastern population. From the eastern perspective, settlers in these new western regions lacked civilizing influences altogether. Easterners typically thought that people on the western frontier lacked serious instruction in the Christian faith. As the western population grew, many easterners imagined that the frontier threatened to overwhelm the entire nation with barbarism.

For all these reasons, many felt that a revival of Christian faith and commitment was sorely needed.

MAJOR DEVELOPMENTS IN THE SECOND
GREAT AWAKENING

Although it is difficult to chart the beginnings of the Second Great Awakening, since spontaneous revivals broke out in several locales, even in the late eighteenth century, three developments stand out and demand attention.

The first occurred in Kentucky. James McGready, a powerful Presbyterian preacher, arrived in 1796 in Logan County, Kentucky, and began preaching for three country churches in that vicinity. Because of the lawlessness that had dominated that region, many described Logan County as "Rogue's Harbor."

McGready, however, more than matched the challenges he encountered there. He was tall, rough-hewn, and plainspoken. With a powerful voice, he condemned sin and vice in all their forms and called upon sinners to repent. By 1798, a stirring revival broke out in his congregations. Another occurred in 1800. At this second revival, something occurred that McGready had never witnessed before: people were "slain in the spirit" and fell to the floor, weeping for their sins. McGready publicized these revivals with reports he sent to various magazines, and news of these events swept the country.

In 1801, the action shifted from Logan County to Bourbon County, where another Presbyterian preacher, Barton W. Stone, preached for two small Presbyterian congregations: Concord and Cane Ridge. In May of that year, Stone visited McGready in order to see with his own eyes the revivals about which he had heard so much. There he saw the Spirit of God send sinners crashing to the floor, where they wept openly and uncontrollably.

As one might imagine, Stone was deeply impressed. He returned to his own congregations where he told of the marvelous things he had seen in Logan County. As he related these events, people in his own congregations began to exhibit the same behavior that Stone had witnessed under the preaching of McGready.

By August 1801 a full-scale revival erupted at Cane Ridge. News of this revival quickly spread and attracted people from miles in every direction. Historians estimate that the crowd finally totaled between ten thousand and twenty-five thousand people. People came to stay for as long as the Spirit moved. They brought with them their cooking utensils, a supply of food, the mule, the hen, and everything they would need to sustain them for the duration of the revival.

To accommodate a crowd that large, they cut trees to create a huge clearing. Then, here and there in the clearing, they parked wagons that served as makeshift pulpits from which preachers representing a variety of denominations delivered their messages. The preachers abandoned their distinctive denominational themes and preached instead the one message upon which they all agreed: God's love for sinners.

Then, as the preachers preached, the strangest things began to occur. People standing, listening to the preachers, suddenly began to jerk and twitch. Then, the jerks grew more violent. Barton Stone, in one of the most vivid accounts of these events, explains that he sometimes saw a person "stand in one place, and jerk backward and forward in quick succession, their head nearly touching the floor behind and before." Sometimes the head snapped back with such force that barks were forced from the throat. To control themselves, some grabbed hold of trees, jerking and barking all the while. To some observers, they appeared to be "barking up a tree."

Stone describes other "exercises" as well. Some danced, and when they did, "the smile of heaven shone on the countenance of the subject." Others laughed with "a loud, hearty laughter," though "the subject appeared rapturously solemn." Still others sang, "not from the mouth or nose, but entirely in the breast, the sounds issuing thence. Such music silenced every thing" and surpassed "any thing we had known in nature."[5]

For Stone and many others, these exercises reflected nothing more nor less than the power of the Holy Spirit. As one preacher asked, "Will people who are not wrought upon by power not their own, roll and dash themselves in the mud, and act as though they would kill themselves? I confess I never done so, nor I believe, none will that can avoid it."[6]

One can hardly overestimate the impact of the Cane Ridge Revival. All across the western frontier, it touched off other revivals that revitalized dying congregations and brought thousands of people into the Christian faith.

The second notable manifestation of the Second Great Awakening also began in 1801, but this time revival erupted far from the Kentucky frontier, in New England. There, Timothy Dwight, president of Yale College and a grandson of Jonathan Edwards, discovered that Yale students generally questioned Christian orthodoxy and admired the skepticism that characterized the French Revolution. Dwight determined to change all that by preaching strong sermons to his students, convincing them of the horrors of "infidelity." Dwight painted the widest possible gulf between authentic Christianity and what he called "infidelity" and suggested that if one placed one's foot on the path that led to "infidelity," there was no stopping point. To Dwight, the natural religion of the Enlightenment led inevitably to "mere Unbelief, then Animalism, then Scepticism, then partial, and then total Atheism."

We perhaps should listen even more closely to his rhetoric and place ourselves in the seats of his students. Perhaps then we can understand why his preaching produced such powerful results. "There can be no halting between two opinions," Dwight told his youthful audience.

> What part hath he that believeth with an Infidel? From a connection with them what can you gain? What will you not lose? Their neighbourhood is contagious; their friendship is a blast; their communion is death. Will you imbibe their principles? Will you copy their practices? Will you teach your children, that death is an eternal sleep? that the end sanctifies the means? that moral obligation is a dream? Religion a farce? and your Saviour the spurious offspring of pollution? . . . Will you enthrone a Goddess of Reason before the table of Christ? Will you burn your Bibles? Will you crucify anew your Redeemer? Will you deny your God?[7]

Revival quickly broke out at Yale under Dwight's preaching. To some degree, the Yale revival resulted from other New England revivals, and to some degree, it helped spread the revival fire even further.

Charles G. Finney ushered in the third and most notable phase of the Second Great Awakening, the phase of consolidation. Finney served that awakening much as George Whitefield had served the first one some seventy-five years before: beginning in the 1820s, he traveled from one community to the next and led revivals in towns and cities throughout the United States. By so doing, he helped to consolidate many local revivals into a great national religious awakening.

Finney was the first person in American history to promote his revivals through what amounted to marketing techniques. These "new measures," as Finney called them, stood in marked contrast to the revival styles that had characterized the Great Awakening of the previous century. In particular, Finney's techniques demonstrated that the old Calvinist notion of predestination had fallen on hard times. In the Great Awakening of the 1730s and 1740s, no one thought that conversion was the work of the preacher. Instead, everyone believed that conversion was the work of God. If sinners responded to the gospel message, so much the better. If they did not, well then, perhaps they were not among the elect.

By the early nineteenth century, however, the popular passion for individual liberties snuffed out practically every trace of predestination. To a people convinced that liberty was among their "unalienable rights," it made little sense to claim that God, from the foundations of the world, had preselected those who would be saved and those who would be damned.

THE HUMANITARIAN CRUSADE OF THE SECOND
GREAT AWAKENING

Charles Finney not only consolidated the revivals of the early nineteenth century into a national spiritual awakening. He also funneled hundreds and perhaps thousands of Christians into a great crusade, designed to alleviate the social ills of the United States. In his revivals, Finney insisted that no one could be a Christian by and for one's self. Genuine Christians, he argued, would seek perfection not only for themselves but also for the world around them. In this way, Finney lived out the standard Calvinist concern to transform the surrounding culture into the Kingdom of God.

Finney told new converts that they must throw themselves into the transformation of society in some meaningful way. Many of his converts committed themselves to prison reform. Others took up the banner of temperance. Still others sought to uplift society through education. Most of all, Finney's converts worked for the abolition of slavery.

Harriet Beecher Stowe, an active participant in the Second Great Awakening, provides one of the most striking examples of the Christian zeal to abolish slavery during that period. In her book *Uncle Tom's Cabin,* she sought to portray the horrors of American slavery in ways that might help end that practice. The book won a wide readership and exerted a broad influence, both in the North and in the South.

In addition to their revivals, Protestants also formed national transdenominational organizations to achieve the purposes of the Second Great Awakening. Before Finney became involved in the Awakening, these organizations sought mainly to extend the influence of Protestantism throughout the nation. The American Bible Society and the American Education Society, both organized in 1816, sought to distribute Bibles and to promote Protestant-oriented education, especially on the western frontier. The American Colonization Society, formed in 1817, sought to obtain freedom for slaves and then to colonize those slaves in their African homeland. The American Sunday School Union appeared in 1824 and the American Tract Society in 1825.

The work of the American Colonization Society and the effort to educate and uplift the American frontier were not unrelated. Lyman Beecher, a famous preacher of that period and the father of Harriet Beecher Stowe, explained that relationship. He saw the nation as a pair of scales on which its various populations rested. On one side was the eastern Protestant establishment. On the other were Catholics, western settlers, and blacks. To Beecher, if no effort were made to educate and uplift the western settlements, and if at the same time the slaves were to win their freedom, those two populations, along with the Catholics, would outweigh the Protestant civilization of New England. In that case, Beecher thought, America would be doomed. His solution was to establish schools throughout the western settlements and to return freed slaves to their African homeland. In that way, a balance of power might be retained. Beecher therefore embraced both these issues with characteristically crusading zeal.

Then, with the preaching of Finney, the burden shifted from the promotion of Protestant principles throughout the nation to genuine social reform. The American Temperance Society, for example, emerged in 1826, and the American Peace Society in 1828. Finally, northern abolitionists organized in 1833 the American Antislavery Society, an organization founded on explicitly Christian grounds and devoted to the destruction of American slavery.

All these organizations had roots in one way or another in the Second Great Awakening.

THE LEGACY OF THE SECOND GREAT AWAKENING

The Second Great Awakening succeeded fabulously in Christianizing the American Republic. It ushered in a period of Protestant domination in the United States that lasted for well over a hundred years, most of those years spanning the nineteenth century.[8] In fact, the Second Great Awakening succeeded so well that even the federal government, in various official statements, sometimes referred to the United States as a "Christian nation," even into the twentieth century. The last official statement of this sort came from the Supreme Court of the United States in 1931. Writing for the majority on *United States* v. *Macintosh,* a case of that year, Justice George Sutherland observed in an offhand way that "We are a Christian people."[9]

A Christian Critique of the Myth of the Christian Nation

We have already argued that when measured by the intentions of America's founders, the notion that America was a Christian nation is questionable at best. The notion is questionable in a second sense as well. This second sense will become apparent in the answer to the question "What does it *really* mean to say that America is a Christian nation?"

THE VOICE OF THE SIXTEENTH-CENTURY ANABAPTISTS

So far in this book, I have presented one important voice from the sixteenth-century Reformation—that of the Reformed tradition. The question before us gains perspective with a second voice from the Reformation, that of the Anabaptists.

If people in the Reformed tradition sought to transform culture into a Christian civilization, the Anabaptists completely rejected any such option. From their perspective, a Christianized culture was a contradiction in terms, since nations were inevitably full of people who would never conform themselves to the moral discipline of the Christian faith. One might therefore hope for a Christian *church*—a community of voluntary believers—but one could not realistically hope for a Christian *nation*.

Because they took this position, the Anabaptists of the sixteenth century rejected the state-church ideal and established their own churches, completely separate and apart from the established church that was sanctioned by the state. They thereby became the first people in the western world to advocate a notion that most Americans hold dear: the separation of church and state.

In their own time, however, they suffered grievously for taking that position. Reformed and Lutheran leaders, the Roman Catholic hierarchy, kings, and princes sought their extermination. All over Europe, thousands of Anabaptists were hanged, drowned, burned at the stake, or run through by the sword. The price they paid suggests how incredibly radical was the ideal of the separation of church and state in the sixteenth century.

The separation of church and state, as the Anabaptists understood the notion, is an incredibly radical ideal even in modern America. For the Anabaptists took that position not to protect the welfare of the state but to protect the integrity of the church. The Anabaptists understood that in order to Christianize the nation, the church would have to make itself acceptable to the larger public. It would therefore have to accommodate itself to values and perspectives commonly accepted in the larger culture.

THE TRADE-OFF OF A CHRISTIANIZED CULTURE

Christianizing the culture, therefore, involved a trade-off: The world might absorb bits and pieces of the Christian faith, while the church would absorb bits and pieces of the values common to the larger society. This is precisely what happened when Christians in the early nineteenth century sought to create an informal Christian establishment in the United States.

Of all the values prevalent in America at that time, none was more important than liberty, that is, freedom for the individual to pursue his or her self-interest. Freedom to pursue self-interest stands diametrically opposed to the Christian understanding of freedom, for the Christian understanding of freedom ultimately means freedom *from* self-interest in order to serve the neighbor. Nonetheless, in order to make itself acceptable to the larger culture, the church would have to lend its support, to one degree or another, to the larger cultural understanding.

There is more, for liberty, as Americans understood that term in the early nineteenth century, was grounded in "Nature and Nature's God," not in the Christian faith. Christians had to argue, therefore, that the faith they promoted was fully compatible with "Nature and Nature's God." They had to argue, in effect, that the Christian faith was both reasonable and natural.

This strategy backfired, however, since by understanding their faith as both reasonable and natural, white Christians typically read their own European American experience not only into nature but also into the Christian faith. In this way, they stripped the Christian faith of much of the ability it might otherwise have had to stand in judgment on ethnocentric cultural norms. It therefore became easy to speak of "unalienable rights" for "all men," but to mean by that rhetoric "unalienable rights" for all *white men.*

In this way, white American Christians domesticated the Christian faith and robbed it of the radical demands one encounters in the ethical teachings of Jesus. By the time they finished their work, an unbiased observer might have found it difficult to distinguish American Christianity from cultural values common to most Americans at the time. We know that some American Christians did challenge the ethical norms and standards of the larger culture. One thinks, for example, of the humanitarian crusade that I have already explored in the context of the Second Great Awakening.

If some white Christians worked tirelessly for the abolition of slavery, however, others worked just as zealously to free the blacks and return them to Africa, on the grounds that a free black population would corrupt a white society. And many white Christians, especially in the South, had so completely interpreted the Christian faith in the light of cultural values that they could actually make the case that the Christian religion sanctioned the institution of slavery.

While segments of American Christianity did challenge prevailing cultural norms and standards, therefore, many American Christians invoked divine approval in order to sanctify the cultural status quo. That was the problem that stood at the heart of the African American critique of the myth of the Christian Nation.

An African American Critique of the Myth of the Christian Nation

If whites had a difficult time discerning the contradictions in the myth of the Christian Nation, blacks did not. If America was really a Christian nation, blacks pointed out, how could the institution of slavery possibly survive? At the very least, one would think that the Christian character of the nation would help to make slavery more humane and less brutal. The reality, however—as blacks so often pointed out—was just the reverse. David Walker, mentioned in the previous chapter, for example, was a devout Christian. Nonetheless, he complained that American whites were bad enough without their religion. As Christians, "they are ten times more cruel, avaricious and unmerciful than ever they were."[10]

Walker spoke specifically of the myth of the Christian Nation and ridiculed it. Slavery, he knew, had existed in many other parts of the world. He pointed out that the sufferings of slaves "in ancient and heathen nations, were, in comparison with ours, under this enlightened and Christian nation, no more than a cypher."[11]

Walker recalled a camp meeting he attended in South Carolina. "To my no ordinary astonishment," he wrote, "our Reverend gentleman got up and told us (coloured people) that slaves must be obedient to their masters—must do their duty to their masters or be whipped." Walker stood amazed. "Here I pause for a moment, to give the world time to consider what was my surprise, to hear such preaching from a minister of my Master, whose very gospel is that of peace and not of blood and whips." Even in Boston, Walker noted, "in the very houses erected to the Lord, they have built little places for the reception of coloured people, where they must sit during meeting, or keep away from the house of God."[12]

Walker felt that most white American Christians simply did not take the Christian faith seriously. "Have not the Americans the Bible in their hands?" he asked. "Do they believe it? Surely they do not."[13] Or again, he asked, "in the name of the Lord, of what kind can your religion be? Can it be that which was preached by our Lord Jesus Christ from Heaven? I believe you cannot be so wicked as to tell him that his Gospel was that of [racial] *distinction.*"[14]

In making these points, Walker was only confirming what the Anabaptists had discerned three hundred years before—that attempts to Christianize the culture often result in the acculturation of the Christian faith.

Frederick Douglass, the black man who taught himself to read and then became the country's most powerful voice for the abolition of slavery, concurred with virtually all Walker's points. In a profoundly eloquent passage in his speech "What, to the Slave, Is the Fourth of July?" he mercilessly assailed American Christianity:

> The church of this country is not only indifferent to the wrongs of the slave, it actually takes sides with the oppressors. . . . It is . . . a religion which favors the rich against the poor; which exalts the proud above the humble; which divides mankind into two classes, tyrants and slaves; which says to the man in chains, *stay there,* and to the oppressor, *oppress on;* it is a religion which may be professed and enjoyed by all the robbers and enslavers of mankind; it makes God a respecter of persons, denies his fatherhood of the race, and tramples in the dust the great truth of the brotherhood of man. All this we affirm to be true of the popular church, and the popular worship of our land and nation—a religion, a church, and a worship which, on the authority of inspired wisdom, we pronounce to be an abomination in the sight of God.[15]

In his autobiography, Douglass returned to this theme:

> Revivals of religion and revivals in the slave-trade go hand in hand together. The slave prison and the church stand near each other. The clanking of fetters and the rattling of chains in the prison, and the pious psalm and solemn prayer in the church, may be heard at the same time. The dealers in the bodies and souls of men erect their stand in the presence of the pulpit, and they mutually help each other. The dealer gives his blood-stained gold to support the pulpit, and the pulpit, in return, covers his infernal business with the garb of Christianity.

Then, so no one would think he was speaking of the South alone, Douglass concluded, "Dark and terrible as is this picture, I hold it to be strictly true of the overwhelming mass of professed Christians in America."[16]

Forrest G. Wood has argued that the majority of slaves never became Christians, and that those who accepted Christianity did so not so much from conviction but rather because Christianity offered privileges, most notably a day of rest.[17] That may be true.

At the same time, many nineteenth-century African Americans who criticized American Christianity most severely were extraordinarily devout in their commitment to the Christian faith. In other words, they clearly recognized the difference between the Christianity they read about in the New Testament and the Christianity they saw practiced in the United States.

David Walker and Frederick Douglass provide notable examples of this point. Indeed, in a particularly scathing passage, Douglass wrote,

> Between the Christianity of this land, and the Christianity of Christ, I recognize the widest possible difference—so wide, that to receive the one as good, pure, and holy, is of necessity to reject the other as bad, corrupt, and wicked. . . . I love the pure, peaceable, and impartial Christianity of Christ: I therefore hate the corrupt, slaveholding, women-whipping, cradle-plundering, partial and hypocritical Christianity of this land. Indeed, I can see no reason, but the most deceitful one, for calling the religion of this land Christianity.[18]

In this passage, Douglass makes it clear that white Americans had absolutized the myth of the Christian Nation. In its highest form, that myth would call on Americans to live out the moral principles of Jesus, especially his admonition to love one's neighbor as one's self. In its corrupted and absolutized form, the myth of the Christian Nation became a self-serving badge of cultural superiority.

The African American critique of this version of the Christian faith did not diminish in the years following emancipation. Among the most prominent voices in this regard was that of Anna J. Cooper, an activist, scholar, and educator. In a speech delivered at the Friends General Conference held in Asbury Park, New Jersey, in 1902, Cooper described the Negro as "the passive and silent rebuke to the Nation's Christianity, the great gulf between its professions and its practices." Then she satirized what she viewed as the perverted gospel preached by most American churches: "Come unto me all ye *whites* who are heavy laden. The Poor (*whites*) have the Gospel preached unto them. Suffer the little *white* children to come unto Me! For of such is the kingdom of heaven. Love the Lord thy God with all thy heart, soul, and strength and thy *white* neighbor as thyself!"[19]

Some sixty-five years later, at the height of the struggle for civil rights in the American South, another black woman, Anne Moody, recalled the mood of the white churches in Mississippi after the murder of black activist Medgar Evers. The Sunday after Evers's funeral, Moody reported, young blacks visited numerous white churches in the city of Jackson in an attempt to worship God alongside the whites. Moody reported, "At each one they had prepared for our visit with armed policemen, paddy wagons, and dogs—which would be used in case we refused to leave after 'ushers' had read us the prepared resolutions."

The following Sunday, they tried again.

> We went first to a Church of Christ, where we were greeted by the regular ushers. After reading us the same resolutions we had heard last week, they offered to give us cab fare to the Negro extension of the church. Just as we had refused and were walking away, an old lady stopped us. "We'll sit with you," she said.
>
> We walked back to the ushers with her and her family. "Please let them in, Mr. Calloway. We'll sit with them," the old lady said.
>
> "Mrs. Dixon, the church has decided what is to be done. A resolution has been passed, and we are to abide by it."
>
> "Who are we to decide such a thing? This is a house of God, and God is to make all of the decisions. He is the judge of us all," the lady said.
>
> The ushers got angrier then and threatened to call the police if we didn't leave. We decided to go.[20]

No single African American was more critical of the white Christian establishment in the American South than Martin Luther King Jr. At the beginning of the freedom movement, he recalled, he fully expected to "have the support of the white church." He found himself bitterly disappointed: "In the midst of blatant injustices inflicted upon the Negro, I have watched white churches stand on the sidelines and merely mouth pious irrelevancies and sanctimonious trivialities. In the midst of a mighty struggle to rid our nation of racial and economic injustice, I have heard so many ministers say, 'Those are social issues with which the gospel has no real concern.'" King found himself completely puzzled by this lack of support.

> On sweltering summer days and crisp autumn mornings I have looked at her [the South's] beautiful churches with their lofty spires pointing heavenward. . . . Over and over again I have found myself asking: "What kind of people worship here? Who is their God? Where were their voices when the lips of Governor Barnett dripped with words of interposition and nullification? Where were they when Governor Wallace gave the clarion call for defiance and hatred? Where were their voices of support when tired, bruised and weary Negro men and women decided to rise from the dark dungeons of complacency to the bright hills of creative protest?[21]

In spite of these scathing criticisms, many blacks who criticized the white American church carefully distinguished between the Christian faith and gospel, to which they fully committed their allegiance, and mainstream American Christianity, which they felt had simply lost its way. This careful distinction was already present in the rhetoric of nineteenth-century blacks like David Walker and Frederick Douglass.

We find this same distinction in the rhetoric of Frances Ellen Watkins Harper, an educator and eloquent orator who gave her considerable energies to the abolitionist cause between 1854 and 1863. In 1891, at the age of sixty-six, she continued to speak on behalf of blacks who now suffered under the constraints of a rigid caste system, especially in the American South. In that year, she addressed the National Council of Women in the United States and carefully distinguished between what she called "the Christianity of the Christ of Calvary" and the perversions of this faith.

> I believe in the Christianity of the Christ of Calvary, but I cannot believe in all its saddest and most terrible perversions. They are the shadow that has followed its sunshine and hindered its unfulfilled mission. . . .
>
> What I ask of American Christianity is not to show us more creeds, but more of Christ; not more rites and ceremonies, but more religion glowing with love and replete with life,—religion which will be to all weaker races an uplifting power, and not a degrading influence. Jesus Christ has given us a platform of love and duty from which all oppression and selfishness is necessarily excluded. While politicians may . . . ask in strange bewilderment, "What shall we do with weaker races?" I hold that Jesus Christ answered that question nearly two thousand years since. "Whatsoever ye would that men should do to you, do you even so to them."[22]

While Martin Luther King Jr. could chastise the white Christian establishment, he also distinguished between his disgust at the behavior of many Christians and his love for the Christian faith: "I have wept over the laxity of the church. But be assured that my tears have been tears of love. There can be no deep disappointment where there is not deep love. Yes, I love the church; I love her sacred walls. How could I do otherwise? I am in the rather unique position of being the son, the grandson and the great-grandson of preachers. Yes, I see the church as the body of Christ. But, oh! How we have blemished and scarred that body through social neglect and fear of being nonconformists."[23]

The Enduring Legacy of the Myth of the Christian Nation

In spite of these critiques, the myth of a Christian America persisted with enormous power into the early years of the twentieth century, when the secularity of the United States threatened to overwhelm that vision.

THE FIRST CHALLENGE TO "CHRISTIAN AMERICA"

The founders, of course, intended America to function as a secular state, even though their vision was grounded in a biblical worldview. Then, in the late nineteenth and early twentieth centuries, secularity emerged with a vengeance in several ways.

First, Charles Darwin's theory of evolution suggested to the popular imagination that human beings were not created in the image of God but in the image of a monkey, the result not of creation but of natural selection. This popular perception, of course, badly distorted Darwin's theory. Nonetheless, that perception was widely embraced by a broad spectrum of the American people.

Second, critical theories on the origins of the biblical text suggested that the Bible was not always the result of divine inspiration. Instead, biblical critics seemed to suggest that the Bible was simply a human creation. Implicitly drawing on evolutionary theory, the critics argued that the biblical text had evolved over a period of hundreds of years as a variety of editors had rearranged and adapted portions of that text to make its message relevant to the needs of particular epochs.

To the traditional Christian mind, these two notions were damaging enough, since they cast serious doubt on the divine origin both of human beings and of the biblical text. But those two suggestions were minor indeed when compared with the third manifestation of secularity. Modern psychology in the early twentieth century—especially under the tutelage of Sigmund Freud—argued that the very idea of God was a myth, a figment of our collective human imagination. Our primitive ancestors, Freud claimed, had created "God" as a way to protect themselves from forces over which they had no control.[24]

How would it be possible to build a Christian civilization when powerful forces in modern American culture had launched a devastating assault on notions that were fundamental to the dominant Christian worldview? How would it be possible to build a Christian civilization when more and more Americans seemed to doubt that humankind was a creation of God, that Scripture was inspired of God, and that the notion of God had any basis in reality?

These developments were all the more disconcerting, since efforts to build a Christian America had seemed so successful in the nineteenth century. To many Christians, the future looked incredibly bright as the twentieth century dawned. A thoroughly Christianized America seemed well within their reach.

But now, this.

Little wonder, then, that some Christians determined to fight the forces of the modern world, to resist the encroachments of secularity, and to preserve a Christian America against all odds. They typically identified Darwin's theory of evolution as the chief culprit, and they hammered that doctrine unmercifully. In case they lost this battle, however, they elaborated a theory of the end times according to which Jesus would return, expunge the secularists from the face of the earth, and reign with his saints for a thousand years. In this way, those Christians who resisted the march of the modern world were guaranteed final victory, regardless of the outcome of any particular skirmish. We know these Christians today as fundamentalists.

From 1925 through the 1970s, however, fundamentalism fell silent on political issues and, in effect, went underground. This transition occurred after the fundamentalist movement at large suffered national embarrassment in the Scopes "Monkey Trial" in Dayton, Tennessee, in the summer of 1925. In that infamous trial, the noted lawyer Clarence Darrow defended John Scopes, a schoolteacher accused of violating the Tennessee statute that forbade the teaching of evolution in the public schools. William Jennings Bryan, a noted statesman and the acknowledged champion of the fundamentalist cause, prosecuted Scopes on behalf of the state of Tennessee.

Simply put, Darrow made Bryan look foolish and held his fundamentalist religious convictions up to ridicule. And journalists who covered the trial from around the country—especially New York's H. L. Mencken—made it appear that fundamentalists at large were ignorant country bumpkins. After suffering such humiliation, it was little wonder that fundamentalists retreated to their churches and turned their backs on American public life for the next half-century.

THE SECOND CHALLENGE TO CHRISTIAN AMERICA

In the 1960s and 1970s, the myth of Christian America suffered additional setbacks. During those decades, many American young people turned their backs on the Christian faith, since they viewed Christianity as the religious arm of a corrupt American establishment. As they saw it, Christianity had long been complicit in American imperialism, since so many American denominations, they thought, had sanctioned both racial discrimination and American involvement in the Vietnam War. Further, they often charged that the Christian doctrine of creation had legitimated the destruction of the environment. For these reasons and more, many young people abandoned the Christian faith and embraced a variety of eastern religions that, up to that point, had largely been foreign to most Americans.

In addition, after the Vietnam War, a flood of immigrants representing a wide variety of non-Christian religions came to these shores. In this context, religious pluralism in the United States began to take on a whole new meaning.[25] Up through the 1950s, religious pluralism in America essentially meant a variety of denominations within the Christian tradition. Now, religious pluralism included Hindus, Buddhists, Muslims, and adherents of a great many other religious traditions, any or all of whom might live in Anytown, USA.

Finally, many Christians worried over what they perceived as a widespread attempt to evict God from the public square and a consequent breakdown in public morality. The first concern focused on the Supreme Court ruling of 1962 in *Engel* v. *Vitale,* striking down prayer in America's public schools. The second focused on the *Roe* v. *Wade* decision of 1973, in which the U.S. Supreme Court legalized abortion in America.

The challenges to the ideal of a Christian America that had broken into American life in the early twentieth century were severe enough. But now, some fifty years later, those who sought to preserve that vision had also to contend with American youth who rejected the Christian faith in large numbers. They had to contend with an American nation that, in point of fact, was growing less and less Christian by virtue of a changing population. And they had to contend with what they viewed as a serious erosion of public morality and the eviction of God from America's classrooms.

Finally, it should also be said that, in the aftermath of the Vietnam War, they also had to cope with what they viewed as a serious erosion of American patriotism.

Pat Robertson, an ordained Baptist minister and a highly influential evangelical leader based in Virginia, was among the first to build Christian institutions specifically designed to recover a Christian America. In 1961 Robertson started a single television station in Norfolk, Virginia (WYAH-TV), and then built that station into the Christian Broadcasting Network. In 1966 he launched a Christian talk show, the "700 Club." In 1977 he established Regent University. And in 1989 he created the Christian Coalition, an organization designed to encourage Christian participation in the political process. All these organizations were crucial to Robertson's goal of re-establishing the United States on a Christian foundation.

Robertson stated his vision for a Christianized America, if not for a Christianized world, in his 1991 book, *The New World Order.*

There will never be world peace until God's house and God's people are given their rightful place of leadership at the top of the world. How can there be peace when drunkards, drug dealers, communists, atheists, New Age worshipers of Satan, secular humanists, oppressive dictators, greedy moneychangers, revolutionary assassins, adulterers, and homosexuals are on top? Under their leadership the world will never, I repeat never, experience lasting peace. Peace will only come when its source is flowing from the benign influence of Almighty God, through the people given to His service who comprise "His house." As long as the cynical politicians and equally cynical media continue to deny God's people their rightful place in God's order for the world, they are condemning their world to violence, turmoil, oppression, and war.[26]

Jerry Falwell emerged as another significant leader in the Christian America crusade. A fundamentalist Baptist preacher in Lynchburg, Virginia, Falwell issued a summons to fundamentalists throughout the country to return to political life in order to reclaim America as a Christian nation. Playing on Richard Nixon's contention that there was in the United States a "silent majority" of people who supported his policies, Falwell claimed that there existed in America a "moral majority" who would support, once again, his vision for a Christian America. In 1979, therefore, Falwell created a Christian political organization that he called, appropriately enough, the Moral Majority. The organization supported conservative candidates for political office throughout the 1980s, supported both prayer and the teaching of creationism in the public schools, and opposed the Equal Rights Amendment, gay rights, abortion rights, and the U.S.-Soviet SALT treaties. (In 1989 the Moral Majority was dissolved.)

Proponents of a Christian America often appeal both to the myth of the Christian Nation and the myth of the Chosen Nation as a basis for their work. For example, in the aftermath of the September 11 bombing of the World Trade Center in New York and the Pentagon in Washington, D.C., Jerry Falwell and Pat Robertson invoked both these myths as ways to explain the disaster. As Falwell and Robertson interpreted those events, because America had turned its back on its Christian moorings, it had violated its covenant with God. God had therefore punished America, and the nation had suffered the fate it deserved.

"God almighty is lifting his protection from us," Robertson proclaimed, declaring the September 11 terrorist attacks a "wake-up call from God."[27] For his part, on the very day of the bombings, Falwell argued during an interview on Robertson's "700 Club,"

The ACLU's got to take a lot of blame for this . . . throwing God out successfully with the help of the federal court system, throwing God out of the public square, out of the schools. The abortionists have got to bear some burden for this because God will not be mocked. And when we destroy 40 million little innocent babies, we make God mad. I really believe that the pagans and the abortionists and the feminists and the gays and the lesbians who are actively trying to make that an alternative lifestyle, the ACLU, People for the American Way—all of them who have tried to secularize America—I point the finger in their face and say, "You helped this happen."

Robertson replied, "Jerry, that's my feeling. I think we've just seen the antechamber to terror. We haven't even begun to see what they can do to the major population."[28]

As the twenty-first century dawned, however, Falwell and Robertson were by no means the only prominent religious figures advocating a Christian America. Other high-visibility organizations promoting this ideal were, among others, David Barton's Wallbuilders, James Kennedy's Center for Reclaiming America, and Beverly LaHaye's Concerned Women for America. All these organizations promoted a conservative political agenda that they typically identified with Christian principles.

When one realizes that by the dawn of the twenty-first century, the Christian Right still represented a potent force in American politics, one also begins to see that the notions of America as a Chosen Nation and a Christian Nation had by no means disappeared from the American public square.

Conclusions

America has always been a Christian nation in certain important respects. This concept ultimately is rooted in the hopes and aspirations of the New England Puritans, but, of course, that was long before there was such a nation as the United States of America. In the second place, the founders grounded their program in a worldview defined by the moral principles of Judaism and Christianity. And in the third place, the notion of America as a Christian Nation did become a reality in the nineteenth century, thanks largely to the work of the Second Great Awakening. It is also clear that while that vision weakened over the course of the twentieth century, it never disappeared and remains potent today, at least in certain quarters.

The myth of a Christian America is problematic on several counts. First, it flies in the face of the founders' intentions. In spite of their Christian grounding, they never intended to create an explicitly Christian nation. Second, the notion of Christian America contradicts the plain fact of religious pluralism in the United States. And third, a Christian America often means an acculturated, Americanized Christianity. This is a principle to which the Anabaptists testified in the sixteenth century and to which African Americans have testified throughout the course of American history.

In the next chapter I shall explore the fourth of America's myths—the myth of the Millennial Nation and show how the three myths I have already considered converged and reinforced one another and then made common cause with the fourth to sustain America's doctrine of manifest destiny.

Notes

1. William G. McLoughlin, *Soul Liberty: The Baptists' Struggle in New England, 1630–1833* (Hanover, N.H.: Brown University Press, 1991), 249.

2. Michael Novak, *On Two Wings: Humble Faith and Common Sense at the American Founding* (San Francisco: Encounter Books, 2002), 5–47.

3. John M. Mason, *The Voice of Warning, to Christians, on the Ensuing Election of a President of the United States* (New York, 1800), 20, cited in G. Adolf Kock, *Religion of the American Enlightenment* (New York: Thomas Y. Crowell, 1968), 271.

4. Clement Clarke Moore, *Observations upon Certain Passages in Mr. Jefferson's "Notes on Virginia," Which Appear to Have a Tendency to Subvert Religion, and Establish a False Philosophy* (New York, 1804), 5, cited in Kock, *Religion of the American Enlightenment*, 271–72.

5. Barton W. Stone, *The Biography of Eld. Barton Warren Stone, Written by Himself* (Cincinnati: J. A. and U. P. James, 1847), 39–42. On the Cane Ridge Revival, see Paul K. Conkin, *Cane Ridge: America's Pentecost* (Madison: University of Wisconsin Press, 1990).

6. Joseph Thomas, *The Life of the Pilgrim Joseph Thomas* (Winchester, Va.: J. Foster, 1817), 160.

7. Timothy Dwight, "A Discourse on Some Events of the Last Century," delivered January 7, 1801, in *American Christianity: An Historical Interpretation with Representative Documents*, ed. H. Shelton Smith, Robert T. Handy, and Lefferts A. Loetscher, vol. 1 (New York: Scribner's, 1960), 533, 537–38.

8. Many scholars have explored the notion of Christian America, most notably Martin E. Marty in *Righteous Empire: The Protestant Experience in America* (New York: Dial Press, 1970), and Robert T. Handy in *A Christian America: Protestant Hopes and Historical Realities*, 2d ed. (New York: Oxford University Press, 1984).

9. *United States* v. *Macintosh*, in *Toward Benevolent Neutrality: Church, State, and the Supreme Court*, ed. Robert T. Miller and Ronald B. Flowers (Waco, Tex.: Baylor University Press, 1977), 161.

10. David Walker, *Walker's Appeal . . . to the Colored Citizens of the World*, 2d ed. (1830; Nashville: James C. Winston, 1994), 28.

11. Ibid., 11; see also 17, 19.

12. Ibid., 50–52.

13. Ibid., 49.

14. Ibid., 55.

15. Frederick Douglass, "What, to the Slave, Is the Fourth of July?" (1852), in *Lift Every Voice: African American Oratory, 1787–1900*, ed. Philip S. Foner and Robert James Branham (Tuscaloosa: University of Alabama Press, 1998), 262–63.

16. Frederick Douglass, *Narrative of the Life of Frederick Douglass, an American Slave, Written by Himself* (1845; New York: Signet Books, 1968), 121, 123.

17. Forrest S. Wood, *The Arrogance of Faith* (New York: Knopf, 1990), 155–56.

18. Douglass, *Narrative*, 120.

19. Anna J. Cooper, "The Ethics of the Negro Question" (1902), in *Can I Get a Witness? Prophetic Religious Voices of African American Women: An Anthology*, ed. Marcia Y. Riggs (Maryknoll, N.Y.: Orbis, 1997), 133, 143.

20. Anne Moody, *Coming of Age in Mississippi* (New York: Dell, 1968), 283–84.

21. Martin Luther King Jr., "Letter from Birmingham City Jail" in *A Testament of Hope: The Essential Writings and Speeches of Martin Luther King Jr.*, ed. James Melvin Washington (San Francisco: HarperSanFrancisco, 1986), 299.

22. Frances Ellen Watkins Harper, "Duty to Dependent Races," speech delivered to the National Council of Women of the United States, 1891, reprinted in *With Pen and Voice: A Critical Anthology of Nineteenth-Century African-American Women*, ed. Shirley Wilson Logan (Carbondale: Southern Illinois University Press, 1995), 40, 42.

23. King, "Letter from Birmingham City Jail," 299–300.

24. Freud made this point in three books, originally published in German: *Totem and Taboo* (1912–13), *The Future of an Illusion* (1927), and *Moses and Monotheism* (1938).

25. On this point, see Diana L. Eck, *A New Religious America: How a "Christian Country" Has Become the World's Most Religiously Diverse Nation* (San Francisco: HarperSanFrancisco, 2001).

26. Pat Robertson, *The New World Order* (Dallas: Word Publishing, 1991), 227.

27. "Robertson Says Attacks Are a 'Wake-Up Call,'" *Los Angeles Times*, Oct. 2, 2001, A6.

28. John Balzar, "Brothers, Fundamentally," *Los Angeles Times*, Sept. 17, 2001, and <http://www.actionagenda.com/petitions>. Falwell later apologized for this assertion, calling his remarks "insensitive, uncalled for at the time and unnecessary as part of the commentary on this destruction. I apologize that, during a week when everyone appropriately dropped all labels and no one was seen as liberal or conservative, Democrat or Republican, religious or secular, I singled out for blame single groups of Americans." "Falwell Apologizes for Blaming Liberals," *Christian Century* 118 (Sept. 26–Oct. 3, 2001): 15.

4 *The Myth of the Millennial Nation*

THE EARLY NATIONAL PERIOD

The myth of Nature's Nation dominated the Revolutionary period and quickly became a staple in the American imagination. This myth held up for emulation the virtues and perfections of a golden age that nature embodied and that stood at the beginning of time.

In the early national period, another myth—equally ahistorical—captured the American imagination. This was the myth of the Millennial Nation.[1] These two visions—Nature's Nation and the Millennial Nation—connected with one another in powerful ways, since they effectively placed brackets around human history. One looked back toward the beginning of time. The other looked forward to its end. If the myth of Nature's Nation suggested that the United States embodied themes built into nature from the time of the Creation, the myth of the Millennial Nation pointed in the opposite direction. This second myth suggested that the United States would illumine the globe with truth, justice, goodness, and democratic self-government and would thereby usher in a final golden age for all humankind.

I attempted to describe in chapter 2 the way the American people related to both these myths in the early national period, and it will be helpful to remind ourselves of that relationship here. Americans, I suggested in chapter 2, "stood . . . with one foot in the dawn of time and the other in the world's evening shadows. . . . [T]hey spanned . . . the particularities of time and . . . therefore thought themselves untouched . . . by . . . human history."

In this chapter, I want to accomplish several objectives. First, I want to explore the backgrounds to the myth of the Millennial Nation, both in the ancient world and in the American colonies. Second, I want to explore how this myth worked in the early national period. And third, I want to explore how the myth of the Millennial Nation combined with all the other myths I have considered to this point to produce the doctrine of manifest destiny.

Background

THE ANCIENT WORLD

The notion of a Millennial Nation ultimately derives from Jewish and Christian understandings of the end of time. Ancient Judaism nurtured a vision of a Messiah who would someday appear and usher in a time when peace, justice, and righteousness would prevail. There is perhaps no biblical passage more descriptive of the messiah and the messianic age than Isaiah 11:2–6 (NIV).

> The Spirit of the Lord will rest on him—
>   the Spirit of wisdom and of understanding,
>   the Spirit of counsel and of power,
>   the Spirit of knowledge and of the fear of the Lord—
> and he will delight in the fear of the Lord.
>
> He will not judge by what he sees with his eyes,
>   or decide by what he hears with his ears;
> but with righteousness he will judge the needy,
>   with justice he will give decisions for the poor of the earth.
> He will strike the earth with the rod of his mouth;
>   with the breath of his lips he will slay the wicked.
> Righteousness will be his belt
>   and faithfulness the sash around his waist.
>
> The wolf will live with the lamb,
>   the leopard will lie down with the goat,
> the calf and the lion and the yearling together;
>   and a little child will lead them.

Christians believed that in Jesus Christ, the Messiah had appeared. It was, nevertheless, apparent that the advent of Jesus Christ had not transformed the world in ways that the messianic vision had predicted. Christians therefore began to apply that vision to the earth's final age, when Christ would reign triumphant.

Only one passage in the entire New Testament fleshes out that vision with any detail—Revelation 20:1–3. The book of Revelation falls into the category of apocalyptic literature, that is, literature that deals with the end time. It is filled with visions and images that often make little sense to the modern reader. To ancient Christian believers, however, it made all the sense in the world. It explained how Christian believers, harassed and persecuted by the Roman Empire, would finally reign victorious with God.

Though most of the book of Revelation focused on final victory in an afterlife, many Christians found in one particular passage a prediction that righteousness would someday reign triumphant even on this earth. That passage was Revelation 20:1–3 (NIV): "And I saw an angel coming down out of heaven, having the key to the Abyss and holding in his hand a great chain. He seized the dragon, that ancient serpent, who is the devil, or Satan, and bound him for a thousand years. He threw him into the Abyss, and locked and sealed it over him, to keep him from deceiving the nations anymore until the thousand years were ended. After that, he must be set free for a short time."

The imagery here seems clear. Satan, as the source of all evil, would be bound and locked away for a thousand years. During that period he could tempt no one. Many Christians interpreted that passage to mean that if the devil would someday be bound for a thousand years, they could therefore expect a thousand-year period, sometime in the future, when peace, justice, and righteousness would prevail over all the earth.

This is the basis for the vision of a millennial age, since the word *millennium* literally means "thousand years." Some believed that the millennium would be a period of a literal thousand years. Others understood the thousand years to be symbolic of a golden age of undetermined duration. In any event, the expectation of a final, golden age of peace, justice, and righteousness has been a powerful theme throughout Christian history.

PREMILLENNIALISM AND POSTMILLENNIALISM

Christians have differed over the means by which this golden age would become reality. Many Christians believed that the golden age could appear only at the second coming. People who held to this position believed that human beings were powerless to create a golden age on their own. The advent of the golden age, therefore, depended entirely on God's power and initiative. At the second coming, therefore, Jesus would set up his throne and rule the earth for a thousand years. The term for this vision is *premillennialism*, since it emphasizes the conviction that Jesus' second coming would be *pre-*, or prior to, the dawn of the *millennium*.

This sort of vision was not foreign to Americans of the late twentieth century. In the 1960s fears of nuclear annihilation, racial strife, overpopulation, and air and water pollution prompted some American Christians to embrace premillennial thinking. Bumper stickers appeared with regularity that read "In case of rapture, this car will be driverless." The transition from the second to the third millennium prompted comparable speculation, as the extraordinary popularity of the *Left Behind* series of novels by authors Tim LaHaye and Jerry Jenkins bore witness.[2]

What might we say about the longer history of the premillennial tradition? To the extent that Europeans concerned themselves with any version of millennial speculation before the eighteenth century, they usually embraced premillennial sentiments. After all, for centuries human beings had been subject to plagues, diseases, natural disasters, and short life spans. What could they possibly do to counteract those devastating forces? They could only live—and die—with these disasters. For all those centuries, therefore, no one really thought that human beings could radically transform their world into a paradise of goodness, peace, and tranquility.

The Enlightenment of the eighteenth century, however, completely transformed the way Europeans envisioned their future. Suddenly, science opened up the possibility that human beings might control far more of their destiny than anyone had ever dreamed. Perhaps, to a degree, they could conquer fate. Perhaps they could conquer disease. Perhaps by taking a rational and scientific approach to life, they could even put an end to wars and bring about an era of peace and justice. And if all this were to occur, what would that era be, if not the golden age so long expected by their forebears?

During the eighteenth century, therefore, the prevalent Christian understanding of the millennium shifted from *premillennialism* to *postmillennialism*.[3] Once again, the prefix had reference to the second coming of Christ. In this case, however, Christ's second coming would occur *post-*, or after, the millennium. What means, then, would make the golden age a reality? The answer was human initiative, especially science, rational thought, and education. If Christ wished to return to the earth, that was his business. But He was not needed to launch a golden age. Human beings would do that.

Postmillennial thinking emerged in the American colonies early in the eighteenth century. In the American context, it is interesting that the shift in millennial thinking had more to do with religion than it did with science or education. To understand this development we need to explore two things. First, we must ask how and why the religious vision of the first Puritan settlers began to collapse. Second, we must see how and why Christianity began to revive throughout the American colonies in a phenomenal spiritual movement called the Great Awakening.

DECLINE IN NEW ENGLAND

When the Puritans first came to America, they sought to create a society dominated by the church and by Christian ideals. They assumed that every citizen would be a faithful member of a Puritan congregation. By and large, the first generation successfully implemented that vision. In the second and third generations, however, that vision slowly dimmed.

By the 1660s, a variety of developments revealed that the spiritual vision that drove the founders had fallen on hard times. Many Puritans now grew discouraged, suspecting that New England was rapidly violating the covenant they had struck with God. (See the discussion of William Tyndale's understanding of the national covenant in chapter 1.) In 1679 the Puritans convened a Reforming Synod that sought to correct this collapse of religious zeal. The document issued by that synod reveals the problems they sought to address.

In the first place, commerce, not religion, increasingly seized the imaginations of the children and grandchildren of the original immigrants. As the synod observed, "Farms and Merchandising" were "preferred before the things of God." This passion for the things of the world also manifested itself in fashionable clothing—and the lack thereof. The synod complained of the "Laying out of Hair, Borders, naked Necks and Arms, or, which is more abominable, naked Breasts."

Second, even though the Puritans made every effort to ensure religious uniformity in New England, they found they could not successfully fence out other kinds of Christians, especially Presbyterians, Baptists, and Quakers. Their impotence in this regard became especially apparent by the 1680s when the British revoked the original Bay Colony charter, dispatched a royal governor to the colony, and built an Anglican chapel in the heart of Boston.

Third, church membership declined in comparison to the general population, and many in the second and third generations showed little interest in fulfilling the requirements that would make them full-fledged members of the church. According to Puritan theory, only the elect—that is, those chosen by God for salvation—could be admitted fully into the church. To verify one's election, one had to relate an experience of saving grace and demonstrate the results of that grace in holy living. Without these signs, no one could be fully admitted into the church, even though one had been baptized as an infant.

The first generation of Puritan immigrants never dreamed that their children would fail to seek these signs, but many among the second and third generations were content to continue as "half-way" members of the church. They had been baptized as infants, and they thought that sufficient.

Problems emerged when these halfway church members of the second and third generations requested baptism for their own children. This request was highly irregular, since Puritan theology held that children were eligible for baptism only if their parents were among the elect and were therefore full-fledged members of the church. Now a generation that claimed neither election nor complete church membership sought baptism for their children.

This request placed the leadership of the Puritan churches in a serious quandary. If they agreed to the request that had been presented, they implicitly would abandon their insistence that the church be composed only of the elect. Soon, it seemed, the church would be filled with members who cared more for the world than for the kingdom of God. On the other hand, if the leadership rejected the request, they would virtually kill the church by denying baptism—and therefore any level of church membership—to a whole generation of children. From the 1640s into the 1660s, this issue festered. Because neither horn of the dilemma was acceptable, the leadership found it could not arrive at a resolution.

Finally, in 1662, a synod convened, determined to resolve the question. A bitter debate ensued, but when the dust finally settled, the liberals had won the day. The synod—thereafter known as the Half-Way Synod—rendered the decision that infants may be baptized, even if their parents were only halfway members who had not demonstrated the signs of their own election. True to the conservatives' predictions, the church continued its spiraling decline for the remainder of the century.

Capping all these concerns, a whole series of disasters beset New England, beginning in the 1660s. They included droughts, famines, Indian wars, fires, and finally the hysteria over witches that seized Salem Village in 1692. True to their covenant theology, the Puritans saw in these disasters the wrath of God, now poured out upon his covenant-breaking people.

As a result, Puritan preaching took on a new form as early as the 1660s. Instead of preaching traditional sermons that reinforced Puritan theology, Puritan ministers now wept for the sins of New England and warned the people to repent before God eradicated them from the land. This form of preaching is called the *jeremiad*, a term that recalls the Old Testament prophet Jeremiah, who wept over the sins of ancient Israel. In keeping with their concern that New England Christians had broken their covenant with God, the Reforming Synod asked why God would "have kindled such devouring Fires, and made such fearful Desolations in the Earth, if he had not been angry."

The decline of religious zeal that I have described here was not unique to New England. It characterized virtually all the colonies by the close of the seventeenth century. In the context of the covenant that the Puritans believed God had made with them, the righteous leaders of New England found the decline especially devastating.

THE GREAT AWAKENING

The Puritan lamentations persisted from roughly 1660 for the remainder of the century and into the next. Finally, in the 1720s, a revival began to stir. It began in small ways when a Dutchman, Theodore Frelinghuysen, arrived in New Brunswick, New Jersey, to pastor four Dutch Reformed congregations. Frelinghuysen stressed genuine conversion and his preaching produced startling results. Soon a neighboring Presbyterian preacher, Gilbert Tennent, adopted similar strategies that ignited the revival fires in his congregation. From those small beginnings, the revival spread into other colonies. In 1734 revival broke out in a Puritan congregation pastored by Jonathan Edwards in Northampton, Massachusetts.

Not until 1739, however, did these isolated revivals converge into a general spiritual awakening that swept the colonies from New England to Georgia. More than anyone else, an English revivalist named George Whitefield helped ignite those revival fires. Whitefield had been actively involved in a British revival that helped produce the Methodist movement there in the 1730s. Now, in 1739, he brought his immense oratorical and persuasive powers to the colonies.

Whitefield made several contributions to the Great Awakening. First, his persuasive powers were nothing short of astounding. In fact, some reported that he could bring an audience to tears simply by pronouncing the word *Mesopotamia*. Moreover, he could move an audience of several thousand in an outdoor setting where the voices of most speakers would dissipate into the air.

Second, Whitefield served as an important source of news for the colonies. He did so by refusing to confine his preaching to a single location. Instead, he traveled from one end of the colonies to the other, taking reports of the revival from one town to the next. By themselves, these reports helped to spread the revival wherever he went, but when he coupled his reports with stirring revivalistic preaching, the impact was even greater. In this way, Whitefield provided the spark that helped to turn a few isolated revivals into a Great Awakening that deluged the colonies with religious fervor.

The Emergence of the Millennial Nation

As time went on, the extent and power of the Great Awakening grew so impressive that many wondered whether perhaps this was not the beginning of the millennial age foretold in scripture. Jonathan Edwards, pastor of a congregation in Northampton, Massachusetts, and widely recognized as the leading theologian in the colonies, typified this viewpoint.

In 1742 Edwards wrote a treatise called "Some Thoughts Concerning the Present Revival of Religion in New England." There he made a bold prediction. "It is not unlikely," he wrote, "that this work of God's Spirit [i.e., the Awakening], so extraordinary and wonderful, is the dawning, or at least a prelude of that glorious work of God, so often foretold in scripture, which, in the progress and issue of it, shall renew the world of mankind." Indeed, Edwards argued, "We cannot reasonably think otherwise."

In part, Edwards made this case because of another theme he found in the book of Revelation. In addition to a coming golden age, Revelation seemed to predict a cosmic Battle of Armageddon (Rev. 16:16) in which the forces of Christ would finally vanquish the forces of Antichrist. Many thought that it was through this battle that Satan would be bound, thereby inaugurating the golden age. To Edwards, and to many of that generation, the Great Awakening was just such a cosmic battle. Through the power of revival, the colonists had joined hands with God to deal Satan his final defeat.

In addition to the extraordinary power of the Great Awakening, there were several other factors that led Edwards to his conclusion. First, he thought he found in Isaiah 60:9 a prediction that the millennium would begin "in some very remote part of the world." Edwards could not imagine that "any thing else can be here intended but America."

Second, Edwards viewed America as a "new world" in contrast to the "old world" back in Europe. In fact, Edwards thought that "this new world is probably now discovered, that the new and most glorious state of God's church on earth might commence there; that God might in it begin a new world in a spiritual respect, when he creates the *new heavens and new earth.*"

Third, Edwards considered America a "new world" in another respect as well. "The other continent," he declared, "hath slain Christ, and has from age to age shed the blood of the saints and martyrs of Jesus, and has often been as it were, deluged with the church's blood.—God has, therefore, probably reserved the honour of building the glorious temple to the daughter that has not shed so much blood." For this reason, Europeans "shall not have the honour of communicating religion in its most glorious state to us, but we to them."

Though Edwards thought God had chosen the "new world" for the birth of the golden age, he especially thought of New England in these terms: "If we may suppose that this glorious work of God shall begin in any part of America, I think, if we consider the circumstances of the settlement of New England, it must needs appear the most likely, of all American colonies, to be the place whence this work shall principally take its rise." For all these reasons, Edwards believed that the revival "now seen in America, and especially in New England, may prove the dawn of that glorious day."[4]

In the early 1740s, as the revival reached its crescendo, sentiments like these grew increasingly common. Then suddenly, in 1743, the revival ran out of steam and came to a grinding halt. Strikingly, the world had not changed. Evil and injustice still prevailed. In spite of the colonists' fondest hopes, it was obvious to all that the millennium was still a distant dream.

In 1754 something happened that once again stirred the millennial vision. England and France went to war in order to determine which colonial power would play what role in the North American wilderness. The conflict soon became known as the French and Indian War. In the course of the conflict, British colonists refocused their millennial vision.[5] It is easy to understand why. As Protestants, British colonists imagined themselves the agents of Christ and Catholic France the agent of Antichrist. The French and Indian War, therefore, appeared to many as a second front in the great Battle of Armageddon.

By 1759 it was apparent that the British had won the war that officially concluded in 1763 with the signing of the Peace of Paris. It also was apparent that the millennium still had not dawned. Nevertheless, the colonists continued to hope. Over the course of the eighteenth century, too many people had invested too many dreams and too much effort into the realization of a golden age for that vision to dissipate and die.

Then, in 1776, America declared its independence from Britain. The

American Revolution rapidly ensued and concluded with an American victory, ratified by the Peace of Paris, signed by all parties in 1783. By 1788 the colonies had agreed to a constitution and thereby became a new nation: the United States of America.

The point for us to grasp is this: The Revolution and the birth of the nation fanned the millennial imagination of Americans as nothing had before. Moreover, in this case the millennial vision did not fade as it had after both the Great Awakening and the French and Indian War. Instead, the vision grew stronger and stronger. Many Americans were convinced that the nation's birth had launched the golden age. If not, they believed that at the very least they were standing on its threshold.

What was it about the new nation that stimulated such exuberant millennial excitement on the part of so many American citizens? First, the land itself struck many as a Garden of Eden. It was no polluted, over-crowded landscape. Instead, here was a virgin land that seemed to have come fresh from the hand of God. As the British philosopher John Locke observed in his *Second Treatise on Government,* "In the beginning, all the world was America."

Second, the new nation guaranteed to its citizens a variety of free-doms virtually unknown in the countries from which they had come. Here, they could think as they wished to think, believe as they wished to believe, worship as they wished to worship, and speak as they wished to speak, without fear of reprisals from the government. Male citizens could even choose the president of the country and those who would represent them in the new corridors of power. Even though suffrage was limited, these developments must have seemed absolutely revolutionary to many Americans of that time.

It is hardly surprising, then, that millennial excitement abounded. It even found its way onto the Great Seal of the United States. There, an unfinished pyramid grows from arid desert sands. Inscribed on the pyra-mid's base is that notable date, 1776. Clearly, the pyramid represents the new nation. The barren desert terrain, above which the pyramid towers and from which it seems to grow, signifies all human history prior to 1776. For all their glories and achievements, past civilizations were es-sentially barren compared to the glories that would mark the new Amer-ican state. The pyramid is unfinished since the American experiment remained incomplete. Above this scene, the eye of God looks down with obvious pleasure, and the Latin inscription records his response: "annu-it coeptis," or, "he (God) has favored our undertakings." Beneath this picture stands the most critical phrase of all: "novus ordo seclorum," or, "a new order of the ages."

Many Americans living in the late eighteenth and early nineteenth centuries believed their nation to be precisely that. For them, America was no ordinary nation, corrupted by time and tradition. Instead it was radically new, a nation that would bless all the nations of the world with the glories of the long-anticipated millennial age.

One finds stirrings of this vision even before the Revolution. John Adams, for example, confided to his diary in 1765, "I always consider the settlement of America with reverence and wonder, as the opening of a grand scene and design in Providence for the illumination of the ignorant, and the emancipation of the slavish part of mankind all over the earth."[6]

After the Revolution, this vision grew more and more common. Ezra Stiles, president of Yale University, preaching before the General Assembly of the State of Connecticut in 1783, offered this:

> This great American revolution, this recent political phenomenon of a new sovereignty arising among the sovereign powers of the earth, will be attended to and contemplated by all nations. . . . That prophecy of Daniel is now literally fulfilling—there shall be an universal traveling "to and fro, and knowledge shall be increased." This knowledge will be brought home and treasured up in America: and being here digested and carried to the highest perfection, may reblaze back from America to Europe, Asia and Africa, and illumine the world with TRUTH and LIBERTY. . . . Light spreads from the day-spring in the west; and may it shine more and more until the perfect day.[7]

By the 1830s, Lyman Beecher expressed in almost classic terms the vision of the "millennial nation" that would renovate the world. Reflecting on Jonathan Edwards's claim that the millennium would begin in

America, Beecher wrote, "When I first encountered this opinion, I thought it chimerical; but all providential developments since, and all the existing signs of the times, lend corroboration to it."[8]

Any millennial vision presupposes that the moral structure of the world has deteriorated from its original perfection at the time of creation. Accordingly, in a speech he delivered in 1827, Beecher argued that "the history of the world is the history of human nature in ruins." We should not despair, he counseled, for a text from the Bible "throws light upon this dark destiny of our race. It is a voice from heaven announcing the approach of help from above: 'He that sitteth upon the throne saith, Behold, I make all things new' [Rev. 21:5]." Nor will this transformation be transient. Instead, "it is the last dispensation of Heaven for the relief of this miserable world." In this passage, Beecher reflects perfectly the message proclaimed by the Great Seal of the United States: America was a *novus ordo seclorum,* a "new order of the ages," that would usher in the final millennial dawn.

Indeed, Beecher argued, the United States would play a crucial role in this development. For the world to be made free, "a great example is required. . . . But where could such a nation be found?" Before the American Revolution, he thought, "it had no existence upon the earth." Now, "Behold what God hath wrought." God had brought forth a nation radically new in the history of the world, a nation whose institutions "recognize the equal rights of man," whose institutions "give the soil to the cultivator, and self government and the rights of conscience to the people."[9] This was the nation that would launch the millennial dawn.

In another speech delivered in 1835, Beecher made essentially the same point.

> I consider the text [Is. 66:8] as a prediction of the rapid and universal extension of civil and religious liberty, introductory to the triumphs of universal Christianity. . . . But if it is by the march of revolution and civil liberty, that the way of the Lord is to be prepared, where shall the central energy be found, and from what nation shall the renovating power go forth? What nation is blessed with such experimental knowledge of free institutions, with such facilities and resources of communication, obstructed by so few obstacles, as our own?

The United States would therefore lead the world until "the world's hope is secure. The government of force will cease, and that of intelligence and virtue will take its place; and nation after nation cheered by our example, will follow in our footsteps, till the whole earth is free."[10]

When Beecher described the process by which America would reno-vate the world, he grew almost euphoric. The light that America will send into the world, he said,

> will throw its beams beyond the waves; it will shine into darkness there and be comprehended; it will awaken desire and hope and effort, and produce revolutions and overturnings, until the world is free.
>
> From our revolutionary struggle proceeded the revolution in France and all of which has followed in Naples, Portugal, Spain, and Greece. And though the bolt of every chain has been again driven, they can no more hold the heaving mass than the chains of Xerxes could hold the Hel-lespont vexed with storms. Floods have been poured upon the rising flame, but they can no more extinguish it than they can extinguish the fires of Etna. Still it burns, and still the mountain heaves and murmurs. And soon it will explode with voices and thunderings and great earth-quakes. Then will the trumpet of Jubilee sound, and earth's debased millions will leap from the dust, and shake off their chains, and cry, "Hosanna to the Son of David."[11]

The notion that "earth's debased millions" would ultimately cry "Hosanna to the Son of David" is important, since to Beecher, the work of renovating the world was also the work of Christianizing the world. To be sure, Beecher based his hope that America would renovate the world on his belief that America was Nature's Nation. But he also based that hope on the power of the Second Great Awakening and the extent to which that revival was Christianizing the United States. "The revivals of religion which prevail in our land among Christians of all denomina-tions," he confidently proclaimed, "are without parallel in the history of the world and are constituting an era of moral power entirely new. . . . These revivals . . . seem to declare the purpose of God to employ this nation in the glorious work of renovating the earth."[12]

Beecher's vision was not unique to the early nineteenth century. Time and again since Beecher's day, Americans have predicted that Na-ture's Nation would launch the millennial dawn. In 1990, for example, when communism finally collapsed in both Eastern Europe and the So-viet Union, the American people were euphoric. The cold war had come to an end, and Soviet-style communism no longer threatened the Unit-ed States. Americans celebrated, however, not only the collapse of com-munism. They also celebrated what they viewed as the inevitable tri-umph of key American values in those far-off lands. Commentators, politicians, newscasters, and other Americans confidently predicted that nations once dominated by communism would now embrace democra-cy, capitalism, and other aspects of the American way of life.

In this context, President George Herbert Walker Bush proclaimed that a "new world order" was emerging. In part, the new world order would be a world "in which major powers worked together to ensure peace; to settle their disputes through cooperation, not confrontation." It also would be a world inspired by democratic ideals. "Today," he told the American people, "a transformed Europe stands closer than ever before to its free and democratic destiny." To a great extent, Bush explained, this new world order reflected the power of the American example: "This order gains its mission and shape not just from shared interests, but from shared ideals. And the ideals that have spawned new freedoms throughout the world have received their boldest and clearest expression in our great country the United States. Never before has the world looked more to the American example. Never before have so many millions drawn hope from the American idea."[13]

Why would Americans assume that the values of this country would fill the void where communism had reigned supreme? Why would an American president suggest that democracy was the "destiny" of these nations? And why would he proclaim the emergence of a new world order at all?

The myths of Nature's Nation and the Millennial Nation help explain why, in the popular imagination, America is a new world order. On the one hand, it reflects the values of the natural order, ordained by God himself. On the other, it heralds the dawn of a coming golden age. It heralds a golden age precisely because its values are essentially natural, uncontaminated by history or tradition. George Bush's new world order, therefore, was an idea as old as America itself.

Finally, what changed and what remained constant in the transition from the Great Awakening to the revolutionary era and the early national period? What remained constant was the expectation that a millennial age would shortly dawn. What changed was the way Americans conceptualized that age. During the Great Awakening, most thought of the millennium in terms of the sovereignty of God. That was only natural, since the majority of Christians in the colonies stood in the Reformed tradition. For centuries, Calvinists had nurtured the hope that some day God would rule over all the earth, a vision Calvin himself sought to realize in Geneva. Now in the American colonies, two hundred years later, Calvinists still nurtured that dream. They therefore hailed the Great Awakening as the dawn of the millennial age, since it seemed to promise that soon God would reign triumphant, first over America and then over all the world.

During the period of the French and Indian War, that vision changed dramatically. Now the colonists hoped not so much for the sovereignty of God as for the sovereignty of one particular expression of the Christian faith—Protestantism.

By the Revolutionary era, the colonists had invested the millennial vision with yet another meaning: "unalienable rights." They defined the golden age not so much in terms of God's sovereignty or even in terms of Protestant dominance. Instead, the golden age would be a time when all human beings would exercise their "unalienable rights" to "life, liberty, and the pursuit of happiness." Put another way, in the Revolutionary era, an affirmation of human rights largely displaced the expectation of the rule of God.

The transition from the sovereignty of God to the sovereignty of the people with their unalienable rights marked a radical shift in the thinking of the American populace. Most of all, it tells us that the old Puritan dream of a distinctly Christian state no longer controlled American expectations. In its place stood a new vision of liberty and democratic self-government, a vision generated not by Puritanism but by the Enlightenment.

But the dream of a Christian nation was by no means dead. Instead, Christian proponents of the Millennial Nation ideal argued that Christianity and the nation's "unalienable rights" were handmaidens to each other. On the one hand, they claimed, there would be no "unalienable rights" in the United States were it not for the Christian faith. On the other hand, Christianity depended on the extension of civil liberties for its own propagation. In this way, these Christian visionaries collapsed the myth of Nature's Nation and the myth of the Christian Nation into a single, unified ideal.

America's Manifest Destiny

By the mid-1840s, the United States had developed a full-blown civic faith, informed by all the myths considered to this point. Nothing more effectively marks the triumph of that faith than the doctrine of manifest destiny.[14]

The doctrine of manifest destiny meets all the requirements for the notion of myth that I laid out in the Introduction. Yet I choose not to treat manifest destiny as a foundational myth of the United States for one fundamental reason. The myths under consideration in this book are myths that have continued to define the American character since they first emerged at some particular point in American history. In contrast, the doctrine of manifest destiny served a very specific purpose—the goal of westward expansion—and therefore flourished for only a short time, namely, the second half of the nineteenth century.

What is pertinent is that manifest destiny drew on all the myths I have considered to this point and represents the absolutizing of all those myths, especially the myth of the Millennial Nation.

The term *manifest destiny* appeared for the first time in an unsigned article in the July–August 1845 issue of the *Democratic Review*, edited by John L. O'Sullivan. In the context of exploring the annexation of Texas to the United States, the article spoke of "our manifest destiny to overspread the continent allotted by Providence for the free development of our yearly multiplying millions."[15]

In using that term, the article merely gave voice to a notion that had been widely held in the United States for several years. The War of 1812 had liberated strategic Indian lands west of the Appalachian Mountains, and in the aftermath of that war, the westward movement began in earnest. Between 1810 and 1820, the white population west of the mountains more than doubled. When one adds to that the fact that so many Americans of that period believed so strongly in the United States as a divinely Chosen Nation, as Nature's Nation, as a Millennial Nation, and as a Christian Nation, a clear statement of the doctrine of manifest destiny was inevitable. Indeed, the doctrine of manifest destiny was writ large on the hearts and minds of the American people long before the term itself appeared in print.

In December 1845, in another of his papers, the *New York Morning News*, O'Sullivan himself defended American acquisition of the Oregon Territory on the same premise. He dismissed treaties and international law and argued America's claim to the Oregon territory squarely on religious grounds: "Away, away with all these cobweb tissues of rights of discovery, exploration, settlement, contiguity, etc. To state the truth at once in its naked simplicity, . . . our claim to Oregon . . . is by the right of our manifest destiny to overspread and to possess the whole of the continent which Providence has given us for the development of the great experiment of liberty and federative self-government entrusted to us." O'Sullivan concluded that editorial with the ringing affirmation that "the God of nature and of nations has marked it [the Oregon territory] for our own; and with His blessing we will firmly maintain the incontestable rights He has given, and fearlessly perform the high duties He has imposed."[16]

THE GREAT TRANSITION: FROM MILLENNIAL NATION TO MANIFEST DESTINY

In the transition from the vision of a Millennial Nation to the doctrine of manifest destiny, a significant change occurred in the way Americans understood their calling in the world. The significance of that change is almost impossible to overstate.

In the early nineteenth century, those who argued for America's millennial role in the world typically argued that America would perform that role solely through the power of example. Lyman Beecher was a case in point. "The government of force will cease," he predicted, "and nation after nation cheered by our example, will follow in our footsteps, till the whole earth is free." The Great Seal of the United States implicitly proclaimed the same vision. The pyramid that represents the United States would be complete when other nations, moved by the power of the American example, would throw off their chains and claim freedom and democratic self-government as their own inheritance.

On the other hand, those who subscribed to the doctrine of manifest destiny typically embraced a very different view of things. God, they believed, chose America not so much to exercise moral responsibility in the world as to embrace a destiny—a destiny that was "manifest," or self-evident. That destiny was "manifest" because America was both a Christian Nation, faithful to the mandates of God, and Nature's Nation, reflecting the natural order of the way things were meant to be.

Completely faithful to "the laws of Nature and Nature's God," therefore, and completely unique in the history of the world, such a nation had every right to extend its influence not only by example, but also by force—first throughout the North American continent, and then around the world. The transition from the notion of a Millennial Nation to the doctrine of manifest destiny, then, was also a transition from the belief in the power of moral example to the belief in the legitimacy of raw force to achieve America's objectives. In this way, the doctrine of manifest destiny absolutized the myth of America as the Millennial Nation.

Two examples will suffice. In the midst of the Mexican War (1845–48), when the doctrine of manifest destiny was in the very air that Americans breathed, Senator H. V. Johnson described his belief in that doctrine not in terms of moral example but in terms of military might. "War has its evils," Johnson said of that war and confessed that "in all ages it has been the minister of wholesale death and appalling desolation." Nonetheless, he maintained, "however inscrutable to us, it has also been made, by the Allwise Dispenser of events, the instrumentality of accomplishing the great end of human elevation and human happiness. . . . It is in this view, that I subscribe to the doctrine of 'manifest destiny.'"[17]

A second example comes from the period of the Spanish-American War, when America's military involvement in the Philippines struck many as unveiled, unabashed imperialism. "Did we need their [Filipinos'] consent to perform a great act for humanity?" President William McKinley asked in defense of the government's policies. "We had it in every aspiration of their minds, in every hope of their hearts."[18] McKinley could make that claim in spite of the fact that for more than two years, Emilio Aguinaldo, a Filipino freedom fighter, led a bloody popular revolution against what he viewed as American domination of his country. By the time the United States finally defeated this resistance movement, one-fifth of the entire Filipino population had died from war or disease.[19]

I wish now to explore three questions. First, I want to ask how the myths I have considered helped to shape the doctrine of manifest destiny. Second, I want to ask how the notion of the Millennial Nation and the corresponding doctrine of manifest destiny affected America's minority peoples, especially its Native American population. Finally, I want to ask how the minority peoples critiqued and responded to those themes.

Clearly, the American claim to be both a Christian Nation and a Millennial Nation undergirded the doctrine of manifest destiny in very important ways. This entire chapter has sought to demonstrate the ways in which manifest destiny found its grounding in the myth of the Millennial Nation.

As far as the idea of the Christian Nation was concerned, apologists for manifest destiny occasionally appealed to that ideal as well. Josiah Strong, for example, argued that manifest destiny rested upon America's civil liberties and "a pure spiritual Christianity." When President McKinley sought to justify America's involvement in the Philippines, he explained that the United States had sought "to educate the Filipinos, and uplift and civilize and Christianize them, and by God's grace do the very best we could by them, as our fellow-men for whom Christ also died." And Senator Albert Beveridge argued that an American retreat from the Philippines would be "a crime against Christian civilization."[20]

Still and all, most defenders of the doctrine of manifest destiny grounded that doctrine in the myths of the Chosen Nation and Nature's Nation. For this reason, I will confine the analysis that follows to those two motifs.

MANIFEST DESTINY AND THE MYTH OF THE CHOSEN NATION

From the wording of O'Sullivan's editorials, it is clear that the doctrine of manifest destiny rested squarely on the myth of the Chosen Nation. "Providence," he argued time and again, had granted the North

American continent to European Americans "for the development of the great experiment of liberty and federative self-government."

The notion of chosenness at work in mid-nineteenth-century America differed profoundly from the Puritan understanding of that same theme. For the most part, the Puritans adopted a biblical understanding of chosenness, while European Americans in the mid-nineteenth century embraced a notion of chosenness that had no serious connection with the Bible.

There are two ways to understand the difference between the Puritan understanding of chosenness and the American understanding of that theme in the mid-nineteenth century.

First, the Bible never claimed that God chose Israel as his covenant people because of Israel's innate goodness. Rather, God chose Israel for reasons altogether hidden to human reason. The most that one could say is that God chose Israel to manifest his own love and grace. But why Israel and not some other people? The answer to that question was hidden in the divine will.

The Puritan conviction that God had made them a chosen people reflected similar understandings. It is certainly true that Puritans claimed virtual perfection for their churches. Still and all, Puritans seldom made their righteousness the basis for their election. Rather, God chose them for reasons known only to himself.

By the mid-nineteenth century, however, the reasons for America's chosenness were hardly mysterious. To the contrary, the reasons were *manifest*. And because the reasons were manifest, America's destiny was manifest as well. God chose America, O'Sullivan claimed, because America stood for "liberty and federative self-government."

We can state this difference between seventeenth- and nineteenth-century understandings of chosenness in yet another way. Seventeenth-century Puritans understood that chosenness was due entirely to God's will and initiative. It was *his* call. By the nineteenth century, however, God had become a puppet in the hands of the American people who had placed on God an indisputable claim. The assumption seemed to be that God could hardly refuse to choose America, since the nation so *manifestly* exemplified God's will.

The second fundamental difference between the Puritan and the nineteenth-century understandings of chosenness is similar to the first and involved the idea of covenant. In Puritan New England, the notion of covenant duties always accompanied the notion of chosenness. This means that the blessings of the Almighty were always contingent on the extent to which God's people remained faithful to him. I noted in chapter 1, for example, that John Winthrop, the first governor of Massachusetts Bay Colony, spelled out the terms of the covenant to the Puritan immigrants before they even disembarked from the *Arbella*. He explained that "we are entered into a Covenant with him [God] for this work. . . . Now if the Lord shall please to hear us, and bring us in peace to the place we desire, then hath he ratified this Covenant and sealed our Commission."

Winthrop also explained that if the Puritans failed to conform to the terms of the covenant, they would suffer the wrath of God. If, he declared, we seek "great things for our selves and our posterity, the Lord will surely break out in wrath against us, be revenged of such a perjured people and make us know the price of the breach of such a Covenant."

Winthrop went on to explain that covenant-keeping involved, among other things, compassion and concern for one another. "The only way to avoid this shipwreck," he argued, is "to do justly, to love mercy, to walk humbly with our God. For this end, . . . we must entertain each other in brotherly affection, . . . we must delight in each other, make others conditions our own, rejoice together, mourn together, labor and suffer together."[21]

By the mid-nineteenth century, however, almost no trace of covenant remained. Because of the nature of the American experiment, most European Americans believed that God had chosen the United States for a special destiny in the world, and that was that. The sense of responsibility to others had given way to privilege and divine right.

MANIFEST DESTINY AND THE MYTH OF NATURE'S NATION

While the doctrine of manifest destiny partly rested on assumptions of American chosenness, it rested even more profoundly on the myth of Nature's Nation. By any measure, this myth was a two-edged sword. On the one hand, it argued that "unalienable rights" belonged to "all men" and grounded those rights in "Nature and Nature's God." On the other hand, it implicitly claimed that some men were more natural than others and therefore especially entitled to those unalienable rights.

How could this be? As I pointed out in chapter 2, when Americans of that period tried to define nature, they generally sought to extract from the whole of human history certain universal principles that they thought were pertinent to all human beings in all times and places. Inevitably, however, they read into nature their own experience, their own biases, and their own points of view. How could it have been otherwise?

As Carl Becker pointed out many years ago, these people were "deceiving themselves" for "they do not know that the 'man in general' they are looking for is just their own image, that the principles they are bound to find are the very ones they start out with. That is the trick they play on the dead."[22] This also was the trick they played on America's minorities, for "nature" in virtually every instance acquired a European coloration. Whoever, therefore, did not conform to European norms and standards was by definition unnatural.

The egocentric understanding of nature bore especially unfortunate consequences for America's Native American population. Native American cultures were radically different from European civilizations and European explorers almost always measured Native American cultures by European norms and found the native civilizations lacking. Worst of all, early European explorers often stereotyped all Native American populations on the basis of the worst examples they encountered.

For example, in his *Mundus Novus,* published early in the sixteenth century, Amerigo Vespucci flatly portrayed the natives of Brazil as savages and cannibals. "They eat one another," he wrote, "the victors the vanquished, and among other kinds of meat human flesh is a common article of diet with them." Vespucci told of meeting a man "who was reputed to have eaten more than three hundred human bodies." He recalled "a certain city where I saw salted human flesh suspended from beams between the houses, just as with us it is the custom to hang bacon and pork."[23] Vespucci's pamphlet circulated widely and helped create an image of Native American peoples as fundamentally unnatural.

In another report published in 1550, Juan Gines de Sepulveda described the native peoples whom Christopher Columbus encountered in the island occupied today by Haiti and the Dominican Republic. He took pains to portray these people not only as unnatural, but as fundamentally inhuman: "Now compare their [the Spanish] gifts of prudence, talent, magnanimity, temperance, humanity, and religion with those little men [homunculos] in whom you will scarcely find traces of humanity; who not only lack culture but do not even know how to write, who keep no records of their history except certain obscure and vague reminiscences of some things put down in certain pictures, and who do not have written laws but only barbarous institutions and customs."[24]

The English portrayed Native American populations precisely as had the Italians and the Spanish before them. I have already noted that white settlers in New England generally regarded Native Americans as agents of Satan. The same was true further south. After native populations wreaked

vengeance on English settlements in Virginia in 1622, for example, one poet
urged Europeans to

> consider what those Creatures are,
> (I cannot call them men) no Character
> of God in them: Soules drown'd in flesh and blood;
> Rooted in Evill, and oppos'd in Good;
> Errors of nature, of inhumane Birth,
> The very dregs, garbage, and spanne of Earth;
> Who ne're (I think) were mention'd with those creatures
> ADAM gave names to in their several natures;
> But such as coming of a later Brood,
> (Not sav'd in th' Arke) but since the generall Flood
> Sprung up like vermine of an earthy slime,
> And so have held b' intrusion to this time.[25]

Roger Williams explained in 1643 that when English colonists spoke of
Native American populations, they routinely described them with names
like *"Natives, Salvages, Indians, Wild-men, . . . Abergeny men, Pagans,
Barbarians, Heathen."*[26]

By the time of the American Revolution and the founding of the
United States, these images still held. Most whites still thought of the
natural order in terms of European civilizations. The natural order therefore meant settled communities, roads, schools, books, parliaments, factories, and the Christian religion. Typically, Native American cultures
had none of these. Most whites therefore continued to view native populations as fundamentally unnatural and less than human. Further, because of their presence on the land, Native Americans blocked the path
to American "progress."

Accordingly, even Thomas Jefferson—the man who claimed that
according to "Nature and Nature's God, . . . all men are created equal"—
even Jefferson argued that the American government should "pursue [the
Indians] to extermination, or drive them to new seats beyond our reach."
In fact, after a careful reading of Jefferson's works, one historian concluded
that his "writings on Indians are filled with the straightforward assertion
that the natives are to be given a simple choice—to be 'extirpate[d] from
the earth' or to remove themselves out of the Americans' way."[27]

Why should this be surprising if, according to the popular sentiment
of that age, Native Americans were neither natural nor fully human?
Here, in Jefferson's Indian policy, therefore, one finds perhaps the most
poignant example of the clash between an absolutized American myth,
on the one hand, and the American Creed, on the other.

In the early nineteenth century, two characteristics of the supposed "natural order" dominated the thinking of American whites. First, whites routinely ascribed to the natural order a characteristic that one historian describes as "geographical predestination."[28] In other words, European Americans believed that God had placed natural boundaries for all the nations of the earth. It became America's duty and destiny, therefore, to extend its domain until its borders coincided with the divinely placed natural boundaries.

Representative David Trimble argued for the acquisition of Texas on just these grounds. Speaking of the Rio Grande and the mountains to the west, Trimble declared, "The great Engineer of the Universe has fixed the natural limits of our country. . . . To that boundary we shall go; 'peaceably if we can, forcibly if we must.'"[29] In time, European Americans employed the same argument to justify the march of their civilization to the Pacific Ocean.

Often, European Americans combined the argument based on "natural" use of the land with the argument based on "natural boundaries" and thereby made what they regarded as an irrefutable claim to North American lands. For example, an 1829 editorial in the *Nashville Republican* explained why the Rio Grande "seems to be marked out for a boundary": "On this side of the Rio Grande, the country is seasonable, fertile, and every way desirable to the people of the United States. On the other side the lands are unproductive, crops cannot be matured without irrigation; in short they are entirely calculated for a lazy, pastoral, mining people like the Mexicans."[30]

Second, whites routinely argued that settlement, cultivation, and improvement of the land stood at the very heart of the natural order. They justified this conviction on the grounds that God, at the creation itself, had given humanity the charge "Fill the earth and subdue it" (Gen. 1:28). From the white perspective that was precisely what Native American populations had never done.

In 1845, the year that O'Sullivan proclaimed his doctrine of manifest destiny, a writer in O'Sullivan's paper, the *New York Morning News*, made this point crystal clear. "There is in fact," he wrote, "no such thing as title to the wild lands of the new world, except that which actual possession gives. They belong to whoever will redeem them from the Indian and the desert, and subjugate them to the use of man."[31] One must note in this statement not only the appeal to possession and redemption of the land, but also the implicit judgment, rendered here offhandedly, that Native Americans were not men. That, of course, was precisely the assumption that many European Americans made.

Throughout the century, many whites took up the refrain that those who subdued the earth were entitled to own the land. Senator Thomas Hart Benton of Missouri, for example, argued that the claim that white settlers placed on the land was far superior to all other claims since whites "used it according to the intentions of the CREATOR." Likewise, William Henry Harrison, a noted Indian fighter, governor of the Indiana Territory, and finally president of the United States (1841), pointedly asked, "Is one of the fairest portions of the globe to remain in a state of nature, the haunt of a few wretched savages, when it seems destined by the Creator to give support to a large population and to be the seat of civilization, of science, and of true religion?"[32] Horace Greeley concurred and in 1859 decreed extinction for Native Americans precisely on this ground:

> As I passed over those magnificent bottoms of the Kansas which form reservations of the Delawares, Potawatamies, etc., constituting the very best corn lands on earth, and saw their owners sitting round the floors of their lodges in the height of the planting season, and in as good, bright planting weather as sun and soil ever made, I could not help saying, "These people must die out—there is no help for them. God has given this earth to those who will subdue and cultivate it, and it is vain to struggle against His righteous decree."[33]

And die they did.

Fruits of the Doctrine of Manifest Destiny

Manifest destiny ultimately meant the virtual extermination of Native American peoples, and no one contributed more to that process than Andrew Jackson, president of the United States from 1829 to 1837. Long before he became president, Jackson had made a name for himself as an Indian fighter. In the Battle of Horseshoe Bend in 1814, Jackson's troops killed eight hundred Creeks. According to historian David E. Stannard, Jackson personally "supervised the mutilation of [their] corpses—the bodies of men, women, and children that he and his men had massacred—cutting off their noses to count and preserve a record of the dead, slicing long strips of flesh from their bodies to tan and turn into bridle reins."[34] Another historian, Howard Zinn, reports that Jackson then "got himself appointed treaty commissioner and dictated a treaty which took away half the land of the Creek nation."[35] Then, in 1818, Jackson's troops inflicted a devastating defeat on the Seminoles (Creek refugees), thereby preparing the way for Florida to become a territory of the United States in 1821.

Once in the presidency, Jackson announced a virtual war on Native Americans everywhere, and Congress immediately approved the Indian

Removal Act. Under Jackson's leadership, the United States entered into some ninety-four removal treaties with various tribes. By 1835, Jackson announced that Indian removal was well under way and, in many instances, practically complete.

When he learned of Jackson's policy of Indian removal, an aged Cherokee named Speckled Snake responded: "Our great father . . . said much; but it all meant nothing, but 'move a little farther; you are too near me.' I have heard a great many talks from our great father, and they all begun and ended the same."[36]

It must be granted that all this occurred several years before O'Sullivan gave the doctrine of manifest destiny a quasi-official status through his editorials in the *New York Morning News* and the *Democratic Review*. Because of the power of the myths discussed so far and because westward expansion seemed so inevitable, the doctrine of manifest destiny was written on the hearts of most white Americans long before O'Sullivan put the doctrine into words.

In that context, two clashes between whites and Native Americans are especially noteworthy. The first such clash, the Black Hawk War, occurred in the State of Illinois and the Wisconsin Territory. Shortly after the War of 1812, white settlers flooded into those regions. Many Sauk and Fox fled west, but one Native American leader, Chief Black Hawk, refused to run. In time, he established alliances with other tribes and, together, they waged war on the expanding white settlements. The tribes who joined Black Hawk in this effort were the Winnebagos, the Potawatomis, and the Kickapoos.

When Andrew Jackson and the United States Congress sought to drive these tribes from their lands in the early 1830s, they naturally resisted. The resulting Black Hawk War raged from April to August 1832. When finally they were unable to continue their resistance, the Indians fled into Wisconsin Territory with the U.S. Army in hot pursuit. When the Indians attempted to cross the Mississippi River, the army massacred warriors, women, and children, thereby ending the Black Hawk War.

Another important clash occurred between whites and the Cherokee nation in Georgia and North Carolina. The Cherokees believed that if they adopted the ways of the whites, their homes would be safe. Accordingly, they built settlements that resembled towns of white people, adopted ownership of private property, became artisans and craftspersons, invented a written language, adopted a written constitution, established a formal government that resembled that of the whites, welcomed Christian missionaries, and published a newspaper called the *Cherokee Phoenix*. They even adopted the practice of owning black slaves, thereby confirming the lament of Black Hawk that "we were becoming like them [the whites]" in ways that Native Americans would later regret.

When gold was discovered on Cherokee lands, none of their efforts made any difference. Perhaps 40,000 white settlers initially swarmed over Cherokee lands.[37] They confiscated farms and killed the game. Soon the Cherokees faced mass starvation. Still, the Cherokees determined to resist. They appealed to a 1791 treaty with the United States, placing the Cherokees under the protection of the federal government and stipulating that whites would never hunt on their lands or even enter their country without a passport. For all practical purposes, they claimed, theirs was an independent nation whose rights were being violated.

President Jackson responded by pointing out to the Cherokees the advantages of their removal to western lands. For whites, he said, their removal "will place a dense and civilized population in large tracts of country now occupied by a few savage hunters." For the Cherokees, it will "perhaps cause them, gradually, under the protection of the Government and through the influence of good counsels, to cast off their savage habits and become an interesting, civilized, and Christian community."[38] Here was the doctrine of manifest destiny, couched in religious language and articulated long before John L. O'Sullivan made the term a household word.

The truth is, in an effort to dispossess the Cherokees, the government had encouraged white settlers and gold diggers to squat on Cherokee lands. Soon the state of Georgia passed its own laws, severely restricting the Cherokee people. The law provided for confiscation of Cherokee lands, it put an end to the independent government the Cherokees had created, it barred any Cherokee from testifying in court against any white person, and it prohibited the Cherokees from mining any gold found on their own land.

When three white Christian missionaries took the side of the Cherokees and protested plans for their removal, state troops arrested them. The missionaries appealed their case to the Supreme Court of the United States. The court, led by Chief Justice John Marshall, ruled that Georgia laws violated the Cherokees' treaty with the United States. When Andrew Jackson learned of the court's ruling, he remarked, "John Marshall has made his decision, now let him enforce it."[39] Obviously, the court had no power to enforce its own decisions. In effect, President Jackson had granted whites the right to continue their illegal incursion into Cherokee lands.

The federal government then drew up a treaty. Federal officials knew that none of the Cherokee leaders would sign a treaty that would virtually give away their lands. So they arrested tribal leaders and held them in jail while negotiating with a small group of compliant Cherokees.

Finally, the "Trail of Tears" began, a trail that led to Indian Territory in what would eventually become the state of Oklahoma. General Winfield Scott directed the operation. James Mooney later interviewed participants in that operation and wrote the following description.

> Under Scott's orders the troops were disposed at various points throughout the Cherokee country, where stockade forts were erected for gathering in and holding the Indians preparatory to removal. From these, squads of troops were sent to search out with rifle and bayonet every small cabin hidden away in the coves or by the sides of mountain streams, to seize and bring in as prisoners all the occupants, however or wherever they might be found. Families at dinner were startled by the sudden gleam of bayonets in the doorway and rose up to be driven with blows and oaths along the weary miles of trail that led to the stockade. Men were seized in their fields or going along the road, women were taken from their wheels and children from their play. In many cases, on turning for one last look as they crossed the ridge, they saw their homes in flames, fired by the lawless rabble that followed on the heels of the soldiers to loot and pillage. . . . A Georgia volunteer, afterward a colonel in the Confederate service, said: "I fought through the civil war and have seen men shot to pieces and slaughtered by thousands, but the Cherokee removal was the cruelest work I ever knew."[40]

David Stannard describes in numerical terms the results of the assault on the Cherokee civilization:

> All told, by the time it was over, more than 8000 Cherokee men, women, and children died as a result of their expulsion from their homeland. That is, about half of what then remained of the Cherokee nation was liquidated under Presidential directive, a death rate similar to that of other southeastern peoples who had undergone the same process—the Creeks and the Seminoles in particular. . . . And all these massacres of Indians took place, of course, only after many years of preliminary slaughter, from disease and military assault, that already had reduced these peoples' populations down to a fragment of what they had been prior to the coming of the Europeans.[41]

Andrew Jackson's Indian Removal Act of 1830 was only the beginning of the organized assault on Native American populations, informed by the premises of manifest destiny. In 1861 General James Carleton finally subdued the Navajos of the American Southwest. Reflecting on their removal, Carleton gloated

The exodus of this whole people from the land of their fathers is not only an interesting but a touching sight. They have fought us gallantly for years on years; they have defended their mountains and their stupendous canyons with a heroism which any people might be proud to emulate; but when at length, they found it was their destiny, too, as it had been that of their brethren, tribe after tribe, away back toward the rising of the sun, to give way to the insatiable progress of our race, they threw down their arms, and, as brave men entitled to our admiration and respect, have come to us with confidence in our magnanimity.[42]

Systematic attempts to subdue Native American populations continued throughout the nineteenth century. Finally, in 1890, at Wounded Knee, South Dakota, a tragedy occurred that marked their final defeat. A young Paiute named Wovoka, living in western Nevada, announced in 1888 a new religion that focused on a special ritual called the Ghost Dance. According to Wovoka, if Indians danced the Ghost Dance long enough and hard enough, the Messiah would come, whites would die, Indian ancestors would rise from their graves, and the land would be as it was before the whites ever arrived.

Nothing in the Ghost Dance religion suggested violence. In fact, proponents of this new faith taught just the opposite. The dance made guns, knives, and weapons of all kinds superfluous. Further, Wovoka taught that if the dancers wore certain sacred garments, they would be protected from all harm, including the bullets fired from the guns of the whites.

Nonetheless, government officials saw the Ghost Dance as a major threat, especially when Ghost Dance fever seized the imaginations of Native Americans throughout the west, especially the Sioux. The government therefore dispatched soldiers to disarm the Indians and to put a stop to the dance.

They arrested Big Foot, a Sioux suspected of promoting interest in the dance and disturbing the peace. They took Big Foot, along with 120 men and 230 women and children to a cavalry tent camp on Wounded Knee Creek. There they began to disarm the Indians. When one of the Sioux accidentally fired his rifle, nervous soldiers repeatedly fired into the crowd of Indians, killing 350 Sioux men, women, and children. Many died instantly. Others died from their wounds only later.

The soldiers took the bodies of the dead and the wounded to an Episcopal mission. As Dee Brown tells the story, "It was the fourth day after Christmas in the Year of Our Lord 1890. When the first torn and bleeding bodies were carried into the candlelit church, those who were conscious could see Christmas greenery hanging from the open rafters. Across the chancel from above the pulpit was strung a crudely lettered banner: PEACE ON EARTH, GOOD WILL TO MEN."[43]

A Minority Response to the Doctrine of Manifest Destiny

Black Elk, a Sioux who witnessed these events, later reflected on what his people had lost.

> You have noticed that everything an Indian does is in a circle, and that is because the Power of the World always works in circles, and everything tries to be round. In the old days when we were a strong and happy people, all our power came to us from the sacred hoop of the nation, and so long as the hoop was unbroken, the people flourished. . . . But the Wasichus (whites) have put us in these square boxes. Our power is gone and we are dying, for the power is not in us any more.
>
> I did not know then how much was ended. When I look back now from this high hill of my old age, I can still see the butchered women and children lying heaped and scattered all along the crooked gulch as plain as when I saw them with eyes still young. And I can see that something else died there in the bloody mud, and was buried in the blizzard. A people's dream died there. It was a beautiful dream . . . the nation's hoop is broken and scattered. There is no center any longer, and the sacred tree is dead.[44]

Other Native Americans reflected on comparable events. After federal troops had subdued the Native American alliance in the Black Hawk War, Chief Black Hawk made a speech. He spoke of the "last sun that shone on Black Hawk."

> He is now a prisoner to the white men. . . . He has done nothing for which an Indian ought to be ashamed. He has fought for his countrymen, the squaws and papooses, against white men, who came, year after year, to cheat them and take away their lands. You know the cause of our making war. It is known to all white men. They ought to be ashamed of it. The white men despise the Indians, and drive them from their homes. But the Indians are not deceitful. The white men speak bad of the Indian and look at him spitefully. But the Indian does not tell lies; Indians do not steal.
>
> An Indian, who is as bad as the white men, could not live in our nation; he would be put to death, and eat up by the wolves. The white men . . . deal in false actions. . . . We told them to let us alone, and keep away from us; but they followed on, and beset our paths, and they coiled themselves among us, like the snake. They poisoned us by their touch. We were not safe. We lived in danger. We were becoming like them, hypocrites and liars, adulterers, lazy drones, all talkers, and no workers. . . .

The white men do not scalp the head; but they do worse—they poi-
son the heart. . . . Farewell, my nation! Black-hawk tried to save you.
. . . He can do no more. He is near his end. His sun is setting, and he will
rise no more. Farewell to Black Hawk.[45]

In 1854 a Mahican named John Quinney addressed the citizens of
Reidsville, New York, in a speech reminiscent of Frederick Douglass's ora-
tion, "What, to the Slave, Is the Fourth of July?" delivered two years earlier. "It may appear . . . a singular taste for me, an Indian," Quinney began,

> to take an interest in the triumphal days of a people who occupy, by
> conquest or have usurped, the possessions of my fathers and have laid
> and carefully preserved a train of terrible miseries to end when my race
> ceased to exist. . . .
>
> It is curious, the history of my tribe, in its decline, in the last two
> centuries and a half. Nothing that deserved the name of purchase was
> made. . . .
>
> The Indians were informed, in many instances, that they were selling
> one piece of land when they were conveying another and much larger
> limits. Should a particular band, for purposes of hunting or fishing, for a
> time leave its usual place of residence, the land was said to be abandoned,
> and the Indian claim extinguished. To legalize and confirm titles thus
> acquitted, laws and edicts were subsequently passed, and these laws were
> said then to be, and are now called, justice.
>
> Oh, what mockery to confound justice with law! . . .
>
> Let it not surprise you, my friends, when I say that the spot upon which
> I stand has never been rightly purchased or obtained. . . .
>
> My friends, your Holy Book, the Bible, teaches us that individual of-
> fenses are punished in an existence—when time shall be no more—and
> the annals of the earth are equally instructive that national wrongs are
> avenged, and national crimes atoned for in this world to which alone the
> conformation of existence adapts them.
>
> For myself and for my tribe I ask for justice—I believe it will sooner
> or later occur, and may the Great Spirit enable me to die in hope.[46]

It is telling that many African Americans made common cause with
Native Americans in their struggle against America's manifest destiny.
After all, having been denied their "unalienable rights" for so many years,
blacks were uniquely situated to unmask the "myths America lives by"
and the doctrine of manifest destiny that those myths had helped produce.

After the Sioux and their Cheyenne allies completely annihilated
Colonel George A. Custer and his men at the Battle of Little Big Horn
on June 25, 1876, few blacks in the country felt remorse. Only three weeks
after that event, black Christians gathered at Bethel Church in Philadelphia and heard the Reverend B. T. Tanner rebuke not only Custer but also

the United States government. "By the sacred obligation of treaty," Tanner began, "no white man had any right or business to the Black Hill country. It belongs to the Sioux, and is guaranteed him by the nation." As a result, Tanner thought, making war on the Sioux made no sense at all. "The thing to do is not to fight him, but to secure him his rights."

Regarding Custer, Tanner said

> Of all our military captains, [he] was the one who took pleasure in the sword. He was the *beau sabreur* of our Army and with joy did he unsheathe it to strike down the "red nagurs" of the Far West—the "red nagurs," as the men of his command felt free to call the Indians in his presence. Custer hated the Indians, as he hated any man of color. . . .
>
> Of course, we gathered here today do not feel as the nation feels, nor can we—nor can any Negro. Does one say he does? He is either a fool or hypocrite. . . . Have we tears to shed—and we have—we shed them for the scores and hundreds of our people who die violently every day in the South. Have we a heart to bleed, it is rather for our brothers cowardly assaulted and more cowardly riddled with Southern bullets. It cannot be that all the blood shedding is to be on one side.[47]

Twenty-three years later, another African American reflected on another military campaign prompted in large part by the doctrine of manifest destiny: the Spanish-American War. African Americans were able to expose the myths that sustained that war just as they had exposed the myths that sustained the policy of Indian removal.

In an address delivered in 1899 to the New England Conference of the African Methodist Episcopal Church, D. P. Brown roundly criticized America's involvement in the war. The United States fought the war, he said, "not so much in the interest of humanity as . . . for territorial expansion—a war to open up to this country greater commercial interest and advantages." Brown thought it hard to believe "that a government which had shown so little concern for the lives and liberties of ten millions of its most loyal citizens should so suddenly become interested in and imbued with a love of liberty for our brothers in black in another country."

Brown issued a call for resistance:

> Let us speak out, in no uncertain language, and enter our protest against this further murdering of an inoffensive people in the Philippines, struggling for their independence. Let us protest against this sham of taking to these people the Christian religion and civilization, with the Bible in one hand, and the bayonet and torch in the other. Until this government shall have demonstrated its ability or willingness to protect the humblest of its citizens at home, in all the enjoyment of all his rights under the

law, it is the duty of every black man to protest, even with his vote, against any further expansion or extending its weakness over other black people beyond the seas.[48]

Conclusions

This rather lengthy chapter began with a consideration of the fourth American myth—the myth of the Millennial Nation. It is clear that apart from the other myths I have considered in this book, the notion of America as a millennial nation had no meaning at all. Put another way, the myths of America as Chosen Nation, Nature's Nation, and Christian Nation gave to the millennial vision whatever content it had.

The millennium, therefore, would be a time when God's chosen people would liberate and enlighten all the peoples of the earth, when Protestant Christianity would reign supreme, and when all things would be conformed to the standards of "Nature and Nature's God." Though Americans imagined it a universal vision, they nonetheless understood it in distinctly Eurocentric terms.

This call to renovate the world quickly transformed itself into the doctrine of manifest destiny, also understood in distinctly Eurocentric terms. Perhaps nowhere is the link clearer between the myth of the Millennial Nation and the doctrine of manifest destiny than in the thought of Alexander Campbell, a prominent religious leader in the first half of the nineteenth century. Founder of a religious movement that spawned the Disciples of Christ, the Independent Christian Churches, and the Churches of Christ, Campbell firmly believed that the world stood at the millennial dawn. In fact, from 1830 until his death in 1866, he edited a journal that he called the *Millennial Harbinger*.

In 1849, in the aftermath of the annexation of Mexican territories to the United States and as Indian removal continued throughout the west, Campbell explained for his readers the various forces that, in his judgment, would hasten the millennium, and what that golden age would look like when it finally dawned. It would be a period of universal peace, to be sure, but it would also be a period dominated by Anglo-American culture and civilization. In framing the issue in this way, Campbell completely collapsed the myth of the Millennial Nation and the doctrine of manifest destiny into a single grand vision. Here is Campbell in his own words:

> The Lord Almighty, who has now girdled the earth from east to west with the Anglo-Saxon people, the Anglo-Saxon tongue, sciences, learning and civilization, by giving a colossal power and grandeur to Great Britain and

the United States over the continents and oceans of the earth, will continue to extend that power and magnificence until they spread from north to south, as they have already from east to west, until, in one vernacular, in one language and with one consent they shall, in loud acclaim and in hallowed concert, raise their joyful and grateful anthem, pealing over all lands and from shore to shore, from the Euphrates to the ends of the earth. Then will "they hang their trumpet in the hall, and study war no more." Peace and universal amity will reign triumphant. For over all the earth there will be but one Lord, one faith, one hope and one language.[49]

Of Alexander Campbell, Ernest Tuveson wrote, "No other preacher more completely fused the religious and secular elements of the millennial utopia."[50] In so many ways, Campbell typified the sentiments of an entire generation of Americans. For those Americans, the millennium would be a golden age of peace and tranquility precisely because Anglo-American civilization, the Christian faith, and the English language would dominate it.

I turn next to the notion that free enterprise capitalism is a sacred economic system, fully natural, and designed by God himself.

Notes

1. The standard account of the millennial role of the United States is Ernest Lee Tuveson, *Redeemer Nation: The Idea of America's Millennial Role* (Chicago: University of Chicago Press, 1968).

2. Paul Boyer has documented the modern American preoccupation with end times in his book *When Time Shall Be No More: Prophecy Belief in Modern American Culture* (Cambridge, Mass.: Belknap Press, 1992).

3. Before the eighteenth century, many Christians embraced an *amillennial* understanding of end times, that is, a view of the end that has no place for the millennium at all.

4. Jonathan Edwards, "Some Thoughts Concerning the Present Revival of Religion in New England" (New York: S. Converse, 1830), 128–33.

5. Nathan O. Hatch, *The Sacred Cause of Liberty: Republican Thought and the Millennium in Revolutionary New England* (New Haven, Conn.: Yale University Press, 1977), 29–54.

6. Tuveson, *Redeemer Nation*, 25.

7. Ezra Stiles, "The United States Elevated to Glory and Honour" (1783), in *God's New Israel: Religious Interpretations of American Destiny*, rev. ed., ed. Conrad Cherry (Chapel Hill: University of North Carolina Press, 1998), 90.

8. Lyman Beecher, "A Plea for the West" (1835), in Cherry, *God's New Israel*, 123.

9. Lyman Beecher, "The Memory of Our Fathers" (Dec. 22, 1827), in *Nationalism and Religion in America*, ed. Winthrop Hudson (New York: Harper and Row, 1970), 99, 101–2.

10. Lyman Beecher, "A Plea for the West" (1835), in Cherry, *God's New Israel*, 122–23, 130.

11. Beecher, "Memory of Our Fathers," 104–5.

12. Ibid., 104.

13. George H. W. Bush, "The Possibility of a New World Order," *Vital Speeches of the Day* 57 (May 15, 1991): 450–52. The war with Iraq that Americans called Desert Storm also provided a context for Bush's proclamation of a "new world order." Bush was particularly struck by the fact that that war had drawn together diverse nations "in common cause, to achieve the universal aspirations of mankind: peace and security, freedom and the rule of law" (State of the Union address, January 29, 1991, as reported in *Los Angeles Times*, January 30, 1991, A11).

14. On manifest destiny, see Albert K. Weinberg, *Manifest Destiny: A Study of Nationalist Expansionism in American History* (1935; reprint, Chicago: Quadrangle Books, 1963); Frederick Merk, *Manifest Destiny and Mission in American History* (New York: Alfred A. Knopf, 1963); and Anders Stephanson, *Manifest Destiny: American Expansion and the Empire of Right* (New York: Hill and Wang, 1995).

15. "Annexation," *Democratic Review* (New York), July–August 1845, 5.

16. John L. O'Sullivan, quoted in *New York Morning News*, December 27, 1845.

17. H. V. Johnson, *Congressional Globe*, 30th Cong., 1st sess. (Washington, D.C.: Blair and Rives, 1848), appendix, 379.

18. William McKinley quoted in *Congressional Record*, 55th Cong., 3d sess., 2518, cited in Weinberg, *Manifest Destiny*, 294.

19. Emily S. Rosenberg, *Spreading the American Dream: American Economic and Cultural Expansion, 1890–1945* (New York: Hill and Wang, 1982), 44.

20. Josiah Strong cited in Cherry, *God's New Israel*, 119; Charles S. Olcott, *The Life of William McKinley* (Boston: Houghton Mifflin, 1916), 2:109–11; Albert Beveridge, "For the Greater Republic, Not for Imperialism" (Feb. 15, 1899), in Hudson, *Nationalism and Religion in America*, 117–19.

21. John Winthrop, "A Modell of Christian Charity" (1630), in Cherry, *God's New Israel*, 37–41.

22. Carl L. Becker, *The Heavenly City of the Eighteenth-Century Philosophers* (New Haven, Conn.: Yale University Press, 1932), 103–4.

23. George T. Northrup, trans., *Vespucci Reprints, Texts, and Studies*, vol. 5 (Princeton, N.J.: Princeton University Press, 1916).

24. Cited in Lewis Hanke, *All Mankind Is One: A Study of the Disputation between Bartolome de Las Casas and Juan Gines de Sepulveda in 1550 on the Intellectual and Religious Capacity of the American Indians* (DeKalb: Northern Illinois Press, 1974), 85.

25. Christopher Brooke, *A Poem on the Late Massacre in Virginia, with Particular Mention of Those Men of Note That Suffered in That Disaster* (London, 1622), 22–23.

26. Roger Williams, *A Key into the Language of America* (1643), ed. John Teunissen and Evelyn J. Hinz (Detroit: Wayne State University Press, 1973), 84–85.

27. David Stannard, *American Holocaust: Columbus and the Conquest of the New World* (New York: Oxford University Press, 1992), 120.

28. Weinberg, *Manifest Destiny*, 43–71.

29. David Trimble in *The Debates and Proceedings in the Congress of the United States*, 16th Cong., 1st sess. (Washington, D.C.: Gales and Seaton, 1855), col. 1768.

30. *Nashville Republican and State Gazette*, as reprinted in *St. Louis Beacon*, September 9, 1829, and cited in Weinberg, *Manifest Destiny*, 58.

31. *New York Morning News*, Nov. 15, 1845.

32. For Benton, see *Congressional Globe*, 27th Cong., 3d sess. appendix, 74; for Harrison, see John F. Cade, "Western Opinion and the War of 1812," *Ohio Archaeological and Historical Society Publications* 33 (1924): 435–36, cited in Weinberg, *Manifest Destiny*, 79.

33. Horace Greeley, letter in *New York Tribune,* June 1859, reprinted in James Parton, *Life of Andrew Jackson* (New York: Mason Brothers, 1861), 1:401n.

34. Stannard, *American Holocaust,* 121.

35. Howard Zinn, *A People's History of the United States* (New York: Harper Colophon, 1980), 127.

36. Speckled Snake (Cherokee), "Response to a Message from President Andrew Jackson Concerning Indian Removal" (1830), in *Great Documents in American Indian History,* ed. Wayne Moquin and Charles Van Doren (New York: Praeger, 1973), 149.

37. Stannard, *American Holocaust,* 122.

38. Cited in Zinn, *People's History,* 139.

39. Cited in Stannard, *American Holocaust,* 122.

40. Cited in ibid., 123.

41. Ibid., 124–25.

42. Cited in Dee Brown, *Bury My Heart at Wounded Knee: An Indian History of the American West* (New York: Bantam, 1972), 31.

43. Ibid., 418.

44. John G. Neihardt, *Black Elk Speaks* (New York: Washington Square Press, 1932), 230.

45. Black Hawk (Sac-Potawatomi), "Farewell Speech at Prairie Du Chien, Wisconsin, at the End of the Black Hawk War" (August 1835), in Moquin and Van Doren, *Great Documents in American Indian History,* 154–55.

46. John Quinney (Mahican), "Fourth of July Address at Reidsville, New York" (1854), in Moquin and Van Doren, *Great Documents in American Indian History,* 166–70.

47. B. T. Tanner, "The Sioux's Revenge" (1876), in *Lift Every Voice: African American Oratory, 1787–1900,* ed. Philip S. Foner and Robert James Branham (Tuscaloosa: University of Alabama Press, 1998), 577–78.

48. D. P. Brown, "The State of the Country from a Black Man's Point of View" (1899), in Foner and Branham, *Lift Every Voice,* 891, 896.

49. Alexander Campbell, "Address on the Anglo-Saxon Language," in Campbell, *Popular Lectures and Addresses* (St. Louis: John Burns, 1861), 44.

50. Tuveson, *Redeemer Nation,* 217.

5 The Mythic Dimensions of American Capitalism

THE GILDED AGE

Like the doctrine of manifest destiny, capitalism is not one of the foundational myths under consideration in this text. The relevance is that, as capitalism entrenched itself in American life, it drew its legitimacy from all the myths I have considered in this book.

Capitalism and the Myths America Lives By

NATURE'S NATION

Americans who benefited from the capitalist system could hardly imagine viable alternatives. Because it seemed so natural, so thoroughly in keeping with "the way things were meant to be," it was easy to imagine that the capitalist system was rooted squarely in the self-evident patterns of "Nature and Nature's God." The myth of Nature's Nation, therefore, probably did more to legitimate American capitalism than any other single factor.

In line with that assumption, D. S. Gregory affirmed in a popular ethics textbook of the 1880s, "The Moral Governor has placed the power of acquisitiveness in man for a good and noble purpose." William Lawrence, the Episcopal bishop of Massachusetts, also placed capitalism in the context of "Nature and Nature's God." "To seek for and earn wealth is a sign of a natural, vigorous, and strong character," he proclaimed. "The search for material wealth is therefore as natural and necessary to the man as is the pushing out of its roots for more moisture and food to the oak." And Charles Conant, the leading economic adviser to the State Department during that same period, judged as fundamentally natural the "irresistible tendency to expansion" that was part and parcel of the capitalist ethos. "Seeking new outlets for American capital and new opportunities for American enterprise," he wrote, was simply "a natural law of economic and race development."[1]

Here one finds a classic example of Carl Becker's claim—noted often in this book—that those who appealed to "Nature and Nature's God" typically found in nature precisely what they wished to find. In the first place, the myth of Nature's Nation was so pervasive and so powerful that virtually every key element of American culture seemed to reflect some self-evident truth. There is more, for the late nineteenth century was the period of the "barons of industry" who engaged in unrestrained and unregulated laissez-faire capitalism and thereby accumulated immense fortunes, often at the expense of their workers. It is little wonder that these barons of industry and those who admired them grounded their defense of capitalism in "Nature and Nature's God."

The myth of Nature's Nation sustained American capitalism in other ways as well, and I shall return to this theme later in this chapter. But for now, I must explore the myth under which American capitalism first took shelter.

THE CHOSEN NATION

In the beginning—especially in the years immediately after the American Civil War—American capitalism found its justification in the myth of the Chosen Nation that had struck a covenant relationship with its God. The context for this development was the Civil War itself.

Both North and South entered the Civil War convinced that it was God's chosen people, standing in covenant relationship with the Almighty. If its cause was just—and each side believed that it was—then God would surely grant the victory. When the war was over, the North had won the war. Even more important for the purposes of this book, the war had brought to the northern states burgeoning cities, humming factories, and enormous wealth. On the other hand, it brought to the South not only defeat but also grinding poverty that would haunt the South for years to come. In the context of the national covenant, many northerners interpreted both victory and material prosperity as blessings that God had bestowed upon the North, confirming the righteousness of their cause.

At the very same time, two other developments were occurring that have an enormous bearing on this story. First, a few Americans took advantage of the growing industrialization and wealth of the North and amassed immense fortunes—men like J. Pierpont Morgan, Andrew Carnegie, John D. Rockefeller, Cornelius Vanderbilt, Leland Stanford, and Henry Huntington. We know these men—and others like them—as the "barons of industry," the men who formed the vanguard of the Gilded Age.

Second, between the Civil War and 1900, 13.5 million impoverished immigrants came to these shores, where they often faced desperate economic conditions. In order to earn any livelihood at all, they typically accepted factory positions in which they worked long hours for subsistence wages under extraordinarily poor working conditions. Often, the factories were owned by one of the barons of industry. There was developing in America during this period, then, a great disparity between the few who were extraordinarily wealthy and the masses who were extremely poor and who found themselves dependent on the rich for their very existence.

THE GOSPEL OF WEALTH

If many northerners viewed the wealth of the northern states as God's reward for national righteousness, it was a very short step to apply that understanding to the wealth of individuals. Many, therefore, came to view the wealth of the barons of industry as God's reward for individual righteousness. Likewise, if many viewed southern poverty as God's curse on the South for the institution of slavery, they also came to view the poverty of the masses in northern cities as God's curse for laziness and immorality.

Put another way, an ideology was rapidly developing in the northern states that equated wealth with righteousness and poverty with sin. In the context of the national myths described in this book, how could it have been otherwise? If America offered everyone an equal opportunity, as was widely believed, and if capitalism was ordained of God and rooted in nature, then those who failed to excel in this system had only themselves to blame. This ideology formed the substance of the gospel of wealth that dominated the thinking of privileged people in the northern states from the close of the Civil War to roughly 1900.

Of the thousands of examples that might be offered depicting that sort of thinking, none is more pointedly clear than a sermon preached in

1901 by the Reverend William Lawrence, the Episcopal bishop of Massachusetts. In it, Lawrence made this judgment:

> In the long run, it is only to the man of morality that wealth comes.
> . . . Put two men in adjoining fields, one man strong and normal, the other
> weak and listless. One picks up his spade, turns over the earth, and works
> till sunset. The other turns over a few clods, gets a drink from the spring,
> takes a nap, and loafs back to his work. In a few years one will be rich
> for his needs, and the other a pauper dependent on the first, and growl-
> ing at his prosperity.
>
> Put ten thousand immoral men to live and work in one fertile valley
> and ten thousand moral men to live and work in the next valley, and the
> question is soon answered as to who wins the material wealth. Godli-
> ness is in league with riches.[2]

Other ministers made the same judgment. Russell Conwell, a prominent Baptist preacher from Philadelphia, delivered his classic sermon,
"Acres of Diamonds," more than five thousand times throughout the
country and saw it issued in print time and again. Among the best-known
apologists for the gospel of wealth, Conwell advised his listeners, "I say
that you ought to get rich, and it is your duty to get rich. How many of
my pious brethren say to me, 'Do you, a Christian minister, spend your
time going up and down the country advising young people to get rich,
to get money?' 'Yes, of course I do.' They say, 'Isn't that awful! Why don't
you preach the gospel instead of preaching about man's making money?'
'Because to make money honestly is to preach the gospel.' That is the
reason." Conwell then concluded with a line that reflected the very essence of the gospel of wealth: "The men who get rich may be the most
honest men you find in the community."[3]

Only five years after the Civil War, the noted preacher Henry Ward
Beecher—son of the famed Lyman Beecher and the man whom Sidney
E. Mead described as "that magnificent weathervane of respectable
opinion"[4]—preached a sermon that turned the traditional Christian
message upside down. Many Christians believe, Beecher affirmed, that
virtue requires having and using little. "Far from it. As you go toward
the savage state, you go away from complexity, from multitudinous
power, down toward simplicity, and when you come to the lowest state—
to the simplicity of men that wear skins and leather apparel, and live in
huts and caves—you come to the fool's ideal of prosperity."

In Beecher's judgment, the creation of wealth was not incompatible
with genuine Christianity; to the contrary, the two went hand in hand:
"I affirm that the preaching of the Gospel to the heathen will be invalid

and void if it does not make them active workmen, and teach them how to make money. And although the evidences of the conversion of the individual are not that he knows how to make money; yet in a nation no religion is a good religion that does not teach industry, and the thrift which comes from industry." For all these reasons, Beecher advised his audiences in this way:

> So then, I am not afraid to rejoice. Get rich, if you can. . . . And when you shall have amassed wealth, it will be God's power, if you are wise to use it, by which you can make your home happier, the community more refined, and the whole land more civilized.
>
> And, on the whole, the general tendency of wealth is such as to lead me today to thank God for the increasing wealth of America. May it ever be sanctified. May it ever learn nobler uses, and aspire higher and higher, until the symbolism of the heavenly state, where the very streets are paved with gold, shall be reproduced in the realities and actualities of our life here on earth.[5]

Beecher summed up his philosophy, and that of thousands of his peers, with this simple judgment: "The general truth will stand, that no man in this land suffers from poverty unless it be more than his fault—unless it be his sin."[6]

All these passages reflect the same fundamental assumption: the righteousness of a single individual will win God's favor in the form of material blessings, while laziness, drunkenness, and immorality on the part of a single individual will earn God's curse in the form of poverty.

One finds here a radical transformation of the myth of the Chosen Nation. The older myth spoke of covenant for the *entire nation.* The newer myth spoke of covenant for the *individual.* The older myth persisted, to be sure, but was now supplemented by a radically individualized understanding. In the context of capitalism and the accumulation of wealth, therefore, we can rightly speak of the myth of Chosen People as opposed to the myth of the Chosen Nation.

SOCIAL DARWINISM

The myth of Chosen People underwent another modification as well, this time in the context of Darwin's theory of evolution. Darwin published his *Origin of Species* in 1859, arguing that nature operates on the principle of the survival of the fittest. Fascinated by this idea, an Englishman named Herbert Spencer became "the greatest popularizer of Darwinian notions in both Britain and America."[7]

For my purposes, it is important to understand that as Spencer popularized Darwin's theory of evolution, he did so with an important twist. If Darwin had advocated *biological* evolution, Spencer advocated *social* evolution, or what commentators often call *social Darwinism*. Just like biological organisms, Spencer said, society also passes through the process of natural selection. And the principle of "the survival of the fittest" applies to cultures and classes of people just as it applies to biological entities.

No one in America took over the theme of social Darwinism more effectively than did Andrew Carnegie, a man who had risen from the post of bobbin boy to become one of the most powerful of all the barons of industry in the late nineteenth century. In 1889 Carnegie published in the *North American Review* an important article that he entitled simply "Wealth." There he employed the Spencerian theme of "survival of the fittest" to justify "great inequality of environment [and] the concentration of business in the hands of a few."

Carnegie's essay was influential, to be sure, but to a large extent, his essay only reflected and put into words a set of perspectives already assumed by many in the privileged classes in the United States. For this reason, we should hear him at length:

> It is . . . essential for the progress of the race, that the houses of some should be homes for all that is highest and best in literature and the arts, and for all the refinements of civilization, rather than that none should be so. . . .
>
> While the law [of competition] may be sometimes hard for the individual, it is best for the race, because it insures the survival of the fittest in every department. We accept and welcome, therefore, as conditions to which we must accommodate ourselves, great inequality of environment [and] the concentration of business . . . in the hands of a few. . . .
>
> The Socialist or Anarchist who seeks to overturn present conditions is to be regarded as attacking the foundation upon which civilization itself rests. . . . One who studies this subject will soon be brought face to face with the conclusion that upon the sacredness of property civilization itself depends. . . .
>
> Individualism will continue, but the millionaire will be but a trustee for the poor; intrusted for a season with a great part of the increased wealth of the community, but administering it for the community far better than it could or would have done for itself. . . .
>
> Such, in my opinion, is the true Gospel concerning Wealth, obedience to which is destined some day to solve the problem of the Rich and the Poor, and to bring "Peace on earth, among men Good Will."[8]

Central to Carnegie's analysis was his contention regarding the "sacredness of property"—clearly a way of claiming that capitalism was divinely ordained. Beyond this, he grounded his assessment in a number of the myths I have already considered in this book. First, the myth of Chosen People is obviously at work here, since, as Carnegie put it, "it is . . . essential for the progress of the race, that the houses of some should be homes . . . for all the refinements of civilization, rather than that none should be so."

Second, the myth of Nature's Nation is fundamental to Carnegie's assessment on two counts. First, he speaks of capitalism as if it were grounded in an immutable law of nature that he calls the "law of competition." At this point, his analysis of this law of competition is worth hearing: "The price which society pays for the law of competition, like the price it pays for cheap comforts and luxuries, is . . . great; but the advantages of this law are also greater still, for it is to this law that we owe our wonderful material development, which brings improved conditions in its train. But, whether the law be benign or not, we must say of it: It is here; we cannot evade it; no substitutes for it have been found."

The myth of Nature's Nation is fundamental to Carnegie's analysis in another way as well, for he speaks of the doctrine of the "survival of the fittest" as if it also were an immutable law of nature. Indeed, Carnegie collapsed the myth of Nature's Nation into the myth of Chosen People, since those chosen by wealth were chosen not only by God but also by nature, that is, by the process of natural selection and the principle of the survival of the fittest.

Third, Carnegie's assessment reaches deeply into the longstanding notion of America as a Millennial Nation, although Carnegie's statement contains an important modification of that myth.

During the Great Awakening, the emergence of the millennial age depended on faithfulness to the sovereignty of God. During the French and Indian War, it depended to a very great extent on the sovereignty of Protestantism. During the Revolutionary period, it depended on the sovereignty of the people with their "unalienable rights." Now, in the period of the gospel of wealth, it depended on the principle of competition, which stood at the heart of the capitalist system, on "the survival of the fittest in every department," and on "the concentration of business in the hands of a few."

Obedience to these principles, Carnegie believed, would "solve the problem of the Rich and the Poor" and "bring 'Peace on earth, among men Good Will.'" It is clear that Carnegie anticipated a millennium or a golden age yet to come. The millennium he anticipated, however, was a secular millennium, now divorced from the Christian faith and completely dependent instead on sound business strategies.

Carnegie's statement, then, expresses the full meaning of the gospel of wealth as it emerged in the late nineteenth century. The rich were chosen for privilege and for wealth, and they were chosen twice, not once: God had chosen them because they were virtuous, while nature had chosen them because they were fit. At the same time, the poor received a double curse: God had cursed them for their immorality while nature had cursed them because of their inability to compete in the arena of American capitalism.

This understanding of the gospel of wealth also held great implications for the doctrine of manifest destiny. The gospel of wealth, interpreted through the lens of social Darwinism, now served to justify American expansion around the globe at the expense of the smaller and less well developed nations of the earth.

MANIFEST DESTINY IN THE THOUGHT OF JOSIAH STRONG

No one articulated this vision more cogently than Josiah Strong in his best-selling text *Our Country*, published in 1885:

> The unoccupied arable lands of the earth are limited and will soon be taken. . . . Then will the world enter upon a new stage of its history—*the final competition of races, for which the Anglo-Saxon is being schooled.* . . . Then this race of unequaled energy, with all the majesty of numbers and the might of wealth behind it—the representative, let us hope, of the largest liberty, the purest Christianity, the highest civilization—having developed peculiarly aggressive traits calculated to impress its institutions upon mankind will spread itself over the earth. . . . Can anyone doubt that the result of this competition of races will . . . be "the survival of the fittest"? . . . Nothing can save the inferior race but a steady and pliant assimilation. . . . The contest is not one of arms, but of vitality and civilization. . . . Is there reasonable room for doubt that this race . . . is destined to dispossess many weaker races, assimilate others, and mold the remainder, until in a very true and important sense it has Anglo-Saxonized mankind?[9]

In this passage, Strong affirms the major premise of manifest destiny. He tells us that the Anglo-Saxon heritage—and by implication, America as the bearer of that heritage—embodies "the largest liberty, the purest Christianity, [and] the highest civilization." For this reason, it will soon "impress its institutions upon mankind" and "spread itself over the earth."

This is not the doctrine of manifest destiny as John L. O'Sullivan might have defined it forty years before. Rather, now in 1885, in the light of the evolutionary theories of Darwin and Spencer, Strong has grounded the doctrine of manifest destiny squarely in his convictions on the survival of the fittest. "Can anyone doubt," he asks, "that the result of this competition [of races] will . . . be 'the survival of the fittest'?" And because he believes so strongly in the survival of the fittest, he is able to affirm his belief in the inevitable destiny of the Anglo-Saxon people. "Is there reasonable room for doubt that this race . . . is destined to dispossess many weaker races, assimilate others, and mold the remainder, until in a very true and important sense it has Anglo-Saxonized mankind?"

Shortly, I shall explore the very concrete ways in which this vision played itself out beyond the borders of the United States. But in the interest of clarity, I must now summarize what I have attempted to say thus far about the mythic dimensions of American capitalism.

In the late nineteenth century, capitalism became shrouded in myth and linked to other mythical dimensions of American culture. First, Americans imagined capitalism ordained of God and grounded squarely in the natural order of things. Second, because of their virtue, God had chosen some to succeed on the capitalist playing field, and because of their sinfulness, he had chosen others to fail. Third, because they were fit, nature had decreed that some would survive in the context of capitalist competition, and because they were "weak and listless," as William Lawrence put it, nature had decreed that others would simply die away. Finally, fidelity to the principle of competition that stood at the heart of the capitalist system would usher in the final golden age and bring peace on earth, good will to men.

This constellation of myths provided privileged and wealthy Americans of the late nineteenth century a virtual mandate to extend their power not only throughout the lands that belonged to the United States, but also throughout the world.

INTERNATIONAL AMERICAN BUSINESS

During the closing years of the nineteenth century, America fought the Spanish-American War, ostensibly designed to liberate Cuba and the Philippines from the cruel tyranny of the Spanish. Senator James Henderson Berry, however, charged on the floor of the Senate that America had fought the war "on the pretense, it may be, of humanity and Christianity, but behind it all . . . is the desire for trade and commerce."[10]

If anything, Berry understated his case. A desire for trade and commerce was fully evident in American life, to be sure. There was also a growing desire on the part of many Americans to dominate the world economically. Senator Albert Beveridge, for example, proclaimed that "we are enlisted in the cause of American supremacy, which will never end until American commerce has made the conquest of the world." Likewise, J. G. Kitchell observed in his book *American Supremacy* (1901), "Commercially we are breaking into every market in the world. It is a part of our economic development. We are marching fast to the economic supremacy of the world."[11]

The problem with this kind of talk was that it sounded so singularly un-American. How could Americans speak of "the conquest of the world" and remain faithful to the American Creed? How could they speak of "American supremacy" and affirm at the very same time the equality and unalienable rights that nature had bestowed on *all* human beings?

Americans clearly needed a policy that would promote global expansion and, at the very same time, allow Americans to believe that they were not imperialists but rather the benefactors of all humankind. The truth is, that strategy was close at hand.

Indeed, it was part and parcel of the kind of expansion Americans had in mind: economic expansion. An economic conquest of the world depended upon the private sector, not upon government or the military. Government would facilitate commercial expansion by providing financial assistance, by negotiating a reduction of foreign restrictions, and by making it clear to all parties that the American military stood ready to intervene if its business interests should be threatened. America could always defend a military action of this kind as defensive rather than aggressive.[12] In all these ways, the private sector became the vehicle by which the doctrine of manifest destiny was implemented beyond the borders of the United States.

We should not imagine, however, that Americans of that period thought themselves duplicitous in any sense at all. On the one hand, circumstances seemed to demand this sort of economic expansion. As State Department adviser Charles Conant put it in 1900, "The United States have actually reached, or are approaching, the economic state where . . . outlets are required outside their own boundaries, in order to prevent business depression, idleness, and suffering at home."[13]

On the other hand, the myths that dominated American culture in that period also seemed to justify this sort of expansion. Those myths were implicit both in the doctrine of manifest destiny and in the mandates of American capitalism. Thus, if God had singled out America as his chosen instrument among all the nations of the earth, then America had every right to engage in economic expansion. If God blessed the righteous with wealth and cursed sinners with poverty, then it stood to reason that God *required* economic expansion. If capitalism was rooted in the natural order of things, then American economic expansion partook of the natural order as well. If America was a Christian nation, then the work of economic expansion was an act of Christian charity. And if part of the American mission was to hasten the redemption of the world and the final golden age, then economic expansion was, in all likelihood, a significant part of the redemptive process.

Driven by circumstance and justified by myth, therefore, America threw its full weight behind a massive economic expansion that relied almost entirely on the private sector for implementation. As Emily Rosenberg has pointed out,

> Singer produced a huge plant in Scotland, producing machines there for Europe, and set up smaller branches in Canada and Australia. American Tobacco moved into Australia, Japan and Germany to avoid being shut out by tariffs. Western Electric manufactured equipment in Japan after the termination of the unequal treaties in 1899 and the adoption of a protective tariff in 1911. General Electric established associates or subsidiaries in Europe, South Africa, Canada, and Mexico. Westinghouse built huge plants in Russia and Western Europe. Food companies and meat packers such as J. F. Heinz, Armour, Swift, and American Tobacco increasingly processed abroad—closer to potential markets . . . [and] Parke Davis and other drug companies established plants abroad in order to supply foreign markets unhampered by domestic regulation.

Rosenberg goes on to note that "from 1897 to 1914, American direct investments abroad more than quadrupled, rising from an estimated $634 million to $2.6 billion."[14] In this way, America did precisely what Albert Beveridge had predicted. It embarked upon the economic conquest of the world.

Voices of Protest and Dissent

In the late nineteenth century, therefore, unregulated, laissez-faire capitalism stood at the center of two powerful forces in American life. By virtue of the gospel of wealth, Americans sought to justify concentration of both business and riches in the hands of a few. By virtue of the doctrine of manifest destiny, Americans embarked upon the economic conquest of the world. Americans who led lives of privilege typically supported both these developments as well as the capitalist system upon which they fed. On the fringes of that support, however, significant voices of dissent began to be heard.

A LABOR CRITIQUE

As early as 1840, the New England social crusader Orestes A. Brownson lamented the inequalities that industrial capitalism had brought to American life. Arthur M. Schlesinger tells us that, in Brownson's judgment, "the injustices of capitalism now exceeded those of slavery." For this reason, Brownson worried about the possibility of the "most dreaded of all wars, the war of the poor against the rich."[15]

Had Brownson lived another half-century, he would have witnessed the war that he so much feared. In 1886, the American Federation of Labor called on workers to strike throughout the United States against any company that refused to grant the eight-hour workday. Some 350,000 workers in 11,562 business concerns responded and essentially shut down the country.

The proposal for an eight-hour day was not new. The previous year, in 1885, Albert Parsons and August Spies, anarchist leaders of the Central Labor Union, expressed their frustration with the capitalists who had systematically refused to accommodate labor on this point and called for revolution. "Be it Resolved," they wrote, "That we urgently call upon the wage earning class to arm itself in order to be able to put forth against their exploiters such an argument which alone can be effective: Violence. . . . Our war-cry is 'Death to the foes of the human race.'"

In May 1886 police fired into a crowd of strikers who were manning the picket lines at McCormick Harvester Works. The next day, some 3,000 working men and women gathered at Chicago's Haymarket Square. Before the meeting ended, 180 policemen arrived and commanded the crowd to disperse. Suddenly, a bomb exploded. Sixty-six policemen were wounded. Of that number, seven died. With no evidence except their literature and their spoken ideas, the police arrested eight anarchists, four of whom were hanged.[16]

John Commons reports that the year 1886—the year of the McCormick Harvester strikes and the Haymarket riots—was a signal year in the history of labor-capital relations in the United States. The 1,400 strikes that occurred that year signaled to Commons "the signs of a great movement by the class of the unskilled, which had finally risen in rebellion. . . . The movement bore in every way the aspect of a social war."[17]

The next several years witnessed what did, indeed, amount to a bloody war between labor and capital in the United States, involving perhaps millions of workers in thousands of strikes, including the strike at the Carnegie Steel plant at Homestead, Pennsylvania, in 1892 and the strike against the Pullman Palace Car Company just outside Chicago in 1894.

These events speak to us today more loudly than any statement we might invoke from any of the working people of that period. The depth and breadth of those strikes clearly proclaimed that, from the perspective of working people, the "law of competition" was neither sacred nor grounded in the natural order. Far from "solving the problem of the rich and the poor" and bringing in a golden age of peace and justice, unregulated capitalism had created for these workers extraordinary suffering and deprivation.

Many working people especially objected to the "sacredness of private property"—a slogan that Andrew Carnegie had invoked in "Wealth." The workers leveled this objection, not so much in principle, but rather when the capitalists seemed to place property rights above human rights.

In a speech that Jack White made to the judge in a San Diego courtroom in 1912, one can practically feel the pent-up frustration over the issue. A member of the Industrial Workers of the World, White was involved in a free-speech fight and was subsequently arrested. The judge sentenced him to six months in jail on a bread-and-water diet. When the judge asked White whether he wished to address the court, White said this:

> The prosecuting attorney, in his plea to the jury, accused me of saying on a public platform at a public meeting, "To hell with the courts, we know what justice is." He told a great truth when he lied, for if he had searched the innermost recesses of my mind he could have found that thought, never expressed by me before, but which I express now, "To hell with your courts, I know what justice is," for I have sat in your court room day after day and have seen members of my class pass before this, the so-called bar of justice. I have seen you, Judge Sloane, and others of your kind, send them to prison because they dared to infringe upon the sacred rights of property. You have become blind and deaf to the rights of man to pursue life and happiness, and you have crushed those rights so that the sacred right of property shall be preserved. Then you tell me to respect the law. I do not. I did violate the law, as I will violate every one of your laws and still come before you and say, "To hell with the courts." . . .
>
> The prosecutor lied, but I will accept his lie as a truth and say again so that you, Judge Sloane, may not be mistaken as to my attitude, "To hell with your courts, I know what justice is."[18]

THE SOCIAL GOSPEL

In the late nineteenth century, in spite of the power of the gospel of wealth, voices of dissent emerged from within the churches themselves, both Catholic and Protestant. On the Catholic side, no one pled the rights of workers more forcefully than James Cardinal Gibbons, archbishop of Baltimore. In particular, he argued that workers should have the right to organize in order to challenge domination and exploitation by owners and entrepreneurs.

The first national labor union, the Knights of Labor, boasted a majority of Catholic immigrant members from its inception. Uriah Stevens founded the Knights of Labor in 1869, and Terrence Powderly, Roman Catholic mayor of Scranton, Pennsylvania, began to lead that organization in 1878.

Many, however, thought labor unions inimical both to the principle of private property and to the tenets of the Christian faith. The question arose, therefore, whether Catholics should participate in labor unions at all. It was in that context that Rome, in 1884, upheld a judgment by the Canadian hierarchy that condemned the Knights of Labor. In 1887, however, James Cardinal Gibbons successfully lobbied Rome to exempt the Knights of Labor from that condemnation, clearing the way for Catholic workers to actively participate in labor organizations.

On the Protestant side, a variety of voices in the late nineteenth and early twentieth centuries challenged the gospel of wealth as a phenomenon fundamentally alien to the spirit of the Christian faith and launched a countermovement that came to be known as the social gospel. While one can point to several leading figures of the social gospel, among them Washington Gladden of Columbus, Ohio, Walter Rauschenbusch clearly stands as the preeminent prophet of that movement.

Rauschenbusch witnessed firsthand the disastrous effects of the gospel of wealth on the urban poor when he pastored a small church of German immigrants in New York City in the late nineteenth century. In 1897 he began teaching at Rochester Seminary in New York and there developed a theological rationale for the social gospel in several books, among them *Christianity and the Social Crisis* (1907) and *A Theology for the Social Gospel* (1917).

In the first of those two books, Rauschenbusch charged that Christian advocates of the gospel of wealth were "religious men" who had been "cowed by the prevailing materialism and arrogant selfishness of our business world." There were alternatives, he said. "The spiritual force of Christianity should be turned against the materialism and mammonism of our industrial and social order."[19] In practical terms, his statement meant that Christian churches should reject the gospel of wealth and embrace instead a massive effort to minister to the poor and the dispossessed with food, clothing, and medical care.

No one articulated this vision for the white churchgoing masses more effectively than Charles Sheldon, whose best-selling novel, *In His Steps*, first appeared in 1897. In it, Sheldon tells the story of the Reverend Henry Maxwell, pastor of a fashionable church that, implicitly at least, was devoted to the principles of the gospel of wealth. In time, Maxwell caught the vision of the social gospel and challenged members of his church to deal with the social crisis of that time by responding in positive ways to the simple question, "What would Jesus do?"

> What would Jesus do in the matter of wealth? How would He spend it? What principles would regulate His use of money? Would He be likely to live in great luxury and spend ten times as much on personal adornment and entertainment as He spent to relieve the needs of suffering humanity? . . . What would Jesus do about the great army of unemployed and desperate who tramp the streets and curse the church? . . . Would Jesus care nothing for them? Would He go His way in comparative ease and comfort? Would He say it was none of His business? Would He excuse Himself from all responsibility to remove the causes of such a condition?[20]

In the novel, that simple question, "What would Jesus do?" helped transform Maxwell's church from a bastion of the gospel of wealth into a congregation driven by the mandates of the social gospel on behalf of the poor, the disenfranchised, and the dispossessed. Because of its vast popularity, Sheldon's book helped popularize the principles of the social gospel throughout the United States.

AN AFRICAN AMERICAN CRITIQUE

Black Americans—whether in the ranks of labor or not—also reflected on this period and what it meant for them. Blacks, of course, were victims of intense racial discrimination in the late nineteenth century. Moreover, their sufferings stand out in stark relief in light of the promises and prosperity of the Gilded Age.

Albert Parsons was one of the eight anarchists who were arrested at the Haymarket Square riots in Chicago in 1886. He was the coleader of the Central Labor Union who raised his voice on behalf of revolution if the capitalists refused to accommodate the needs of America's working people. After Albert was convicted and sentenced to death, his wife Lucy embarked on a seven-week speaking tour with two objectives: to raise public awareness of the plight of poor and working people and to generate enough money to appeal Albert's case to the Illinois Supreme Court. In the course of that tour, she delivered more than forty speeches in seventeen states. In spite of all her efforts on her husband's behalf, he was hanged in November 1887.

Lucy was born, perhaps in slavery, in Waco, Texas, in 1853. After Albert was shot for helping register blacks to vote, the couple moved to Chicago in 1873. As Philip Foner and Robert Branham put it, she "was quite literally a revolutionary woman" and "the only woman to address the founding convention of the Industrial Workers of the World (Wobblies) in 1905."[21] On December 20, 1886, she addressed a meeting of socialists in Kansas City, Missouri. There she spoke these words:

> Do you wonder why there are anarchists in this country, in this grand land of liberty, as you love to call it? Go to New York. Go through the byways and alleys of that great city. Count the myriads starving; count the multiplied thousands who are homeless; number those who work harder than slaves and live on less and have fewer comforts than the meanest slaves. You will be dumbfounded by your discoveries, you who have paid no attention to these poor, save as objects of charity and commiseration. They are not objects of charity, they are the victims of the rank injustice that permeates the system of government, and of political economy that holds sway from the Atlantic to the Pacific. . . . But almost [their] equal is found among the miners of the West, who dwell in squalor and wear rags, that the capitalists, who control the earth, that should be free to all, may add still further to their millions. Oh, there are plenty of reasons for the existence of anarchists.[22]

Only days before the infamous events of May of 1886—the nationwide strikes and the violence at Haymarket Square—a black man named T. Thomas Fortune delivered a stunning commentary on labor-capital relations before the Brooklyn Literary Union. Like Frederick Douglass, Fortune had been born in slavery and had received virtually no formal education. He was, however, acquainted with the printer's trade and after arriving in New York in 1879 became a noted journalist. The newspaper he edited and jointly owned, the *Globe,* evolved to become the *Freeman* and later the *New York Age.*[23]

In his speech, Fortune condemned out of hand "the iniquity of privileged class and concentrated wealth [that] has become so glaring and grievous" to poor and working people. He affirmed that every man had a natural right to the necessities of life—food, air, water, and shelter. "These," he said, "are self-evident propositions," grounded in the laws of nature. Unfortunately, he said, the capitalists had abrogated these basic rights for poor and working people, and "the moment you deny to a man the unrestricted enjoyment of all the elements upon which the breath he draws is dependent, that moment you deny to him the inheritance to which he was born."

With this judgment as his premise, he maintained, "Organized soci-

ety, as it obtains today . . . is an outrageous engine of torture and an odi-
ous tyranny." If it were not for the laws that support them, the capitalists "would otherwise be powerless to practice upon the masses of society the gross injustice which everywhere prevails." In fact, for many
centuries past, "the aim and scope of all law have been to more securely
hedge about the capitalist and the landowner and to repress labor within
a condition wherein bare subsistence was the point aimed at."

If Andrew Carnegie thought it "essential for the progress of the race,
that the houses of some should be homes . . . for all the refinements of
civilization," and that "we must accommodate ourselves [to] great inequality of environment [and] the concentration of business . . . in the
hands of a few," Fortune flatly disagreed. "The social and material differences which obtain in the relations of mankind are the creations of
man, not of God," he said. "God never made such a spook as a king or a
duke; he never made such an economic monstrosity as a millionaire; he
never gave John Jones the right to own a thousand or a hundred thousand
acres of land, with their complement of air and water. These are the conditions of man, who has sold his birthright to the Shylocks of the world
and received not even a mess of pottage for his inheritance."[24]

One might imagine that the gospel of wealth, born as it was of northern experience, never exerted much influence on the American South,
much less on the southern Negro. That judgment is false, thanks mainly to influential white southerners who sought to coax northern entrepreneurs to invest in the South in the years after the Civil War.

Henry W. Grady, the young editor of the *Atlanta Constitution* in the
late nineteenth century, was a notable case in point. In 1886 Grady spoke
to the New England Society of New York and essentially announced to
that august body the emergence of a "New South" with "new conditions,
new adjustments and . . . new ideas and aspirations. . . . We have sowed
towns and cities in the place of theories and put business above politics."
Moreover, he extended a broad invitation to his northern entrepreneur-
ial hosts. "We have smoothed the path to southward, wiped out the place
where Mason and Dixon's line used to be, and hung our latch-string out
to you and yours."[25]

By 1903 the black intellectual who helped found the National Association for the Advancement of Colored People, W. E. B. Du Bois, worried that the "dream of material prosperity" was emerging in the South
as the "touchstone of all success." That vision, he said, "is replacing the
finer type of Southerner with vulgar money-getters; it is burying the
sweeter beauties of Southern life beneath pretense and ostentation."[26]

In order to see the influence of the northern apostles of the gospel of wealth in the American South, Du Bois had to look no further than The Tuskegee Institute, founded by Booker T. Washington in Tuskegee, Alabama, in 1881. In 1901, Washington published his classic text, *Up from Slavery*, where he told of his attempts to get funding for Tuskegee Institute from America's barons of industry. In that context, Washington offered a justification for the gospel of wealth that could easily have come from the pen of an Andrew Carnegie or a Henry Ward Beecher. "My experience in getting money for Tuskegee," he wrote, "has taught me to have no patience with those people who are always condemning the rich because they are rich, and because they do not give more money to objects of charity. In the first place, those who are guilty of such sweeping criticisms do not know how many people would be made poor, and how much suffering would result, if wealthy people were to part all at once with any large proportion of their wealth in a way to disorganize and cripple great business enterprises."

Then, echoing Russell Conwell's affirmation that "the men who get rich may be the most honest men you find in the community," Washington described his wealthy northern donors as "some of the best people in the world—to be more correct, I think I should say *the best* people in the world."[27] In *Up from Slavery*, Washington specifically mentioned several of these benefactors and friends, including Andrew Carnegie, John D. Rockefeller, and the Right Reverend William Lawrence, Episcopal bishop of Massachusetts,[28] who had argued in 1901 that "it is only to the man of morality that wealth comes" and that "godliness is in league with riches."

Perhaps that context helps us better understand Washington's "Atlanta Exposition Address" of 1895, in which he told a largely white audience that if blacks wished to improve themselves, they must understand that "it is at the bottom of life we must begin, and not at the top." He assured his audience that "in all things that are purely social we [blacks and whites] can be as separate as the fingers, yet one as the hand in all things essential to mutual progress." "The wisest among my race," he said, "understand that the agitation of questions of social equality is the extremest folly." For that reason, he routinely advised blacks to "cast down your bucket where you are."[29]

W. E. B. Du Bois attacked that speech unmercifully, calling it "the Atlanta Compromise." As Du Bois saw it, the compromise was rooted in that fact that Washington had so "intuitively grasped the spirit of the age which was dominating the North" and had thoroughly learned "the speech and thought of triumphant commercialism and the ideals of material prosperity."[30]

Indeed, Du Bois satirized "triumphant commercialism" and its chief spokesperson, Andrew Carnegie, when he wrote that "all honorable men" will eventually come to see "that in the future competition of races the survival of the fittest shall mean the triumph of the good, the beautiful, and the true; that we may be able to preserve for future civilization all that is really fine and noble and strong, and not continue to put a premium on greed and impudence and cruelty."[31]

Finally, Du Bois pointed out that the Gilded Age with its gospel of wealth had brought nothing to the Negro except further suffering:

> Despite compromise, war, and struggle, the Negro is not free. In the backwoods of the Gulf States, for miles and miles, he may not leave the plantation of his birth; in well-nigh the whole rural South the black farmers are peons, bound by law and custom to an economic slavery, from which the only escape is death or the penitentiary. In the most cultured sections and cities of the South the Negroes are a segregated servile caste, with restricted rights and privileges. Before the courts, both in law and custom, they stand on a different and peculiar basis. Taxation without representation is the rule of their political life.[32]

Du Bois concluded that America was "a land whose freedom is to us a mockery and whose liberty a lie."[33] By 1961, when Du Bois was ninety-three years old, he was thoroughly discouraged over America's failure to implement the promise of the American Creed for African Americans. He therefore joined the American Communist party and moved to Ghana, where he died two years later.

In the waning years of the nineteenth century, Frederick Douglass—the man who had emerged before the Civil War as the country's most powerful voice for abolition of slavery—now devoted himself to defending his people from the dark side of America's Gilded Age. Accordingly, Douglass described the system of tenant farming that controlled the lives of southern blacks.

> The same class that once extorted his labor under the lash now gets his labor by a mean, sneaking, and fraudulent device. That device is a trucking system which never permits him [the black tenant farmer] to see or to save a dollar of his hard earnings. . . . The highest wages paid him is eight dollars a month, and this he receives only in orders on the store, which, in many cases, is owned by his employer. The scrip has purchasing power on that one store, and that one only. . . . The laborer is by this arrangement . . . completely in the power of his employer. He can charge the poor fellow what he pleases and give what kind of goods he pleases, and he does both. His victim cannot go to another store and buy, and this the storekeeper knows. The only security the wretched Negro has un-

der this arrangement is the conscience of the storekeeper—a conscience educated in the school of slavery, where the idea prevailed in theory and practice that the Negro had no rights which men were bound to respect.

One might wish that the federal government would protect the Negro, Douglass said, but this was an idle dream: "The true object for which governments are ordained among men is to protect the weak against the encroachments of the strong, to hold its strong arm of justice over all the civil relations of its citizens and to see that all have an equal chance in the race of life. Now, in the case of the Negro citizen, our national government does precisely the reverse of all this. Instead of protecting the weak against the encroachments of the strong, it tacitly protects the strong in its encroachments upon the weak."[34]

In 1896 the Supreme Court of the United States handed down its judgment on segregation in *Plessy* v. *Ferguson.* The court ruled that it was entirely legal to segregate black Americans from white Americans if the facilities were equal.

Little wonder that D. P. Brown, in a speech to the New England Conference of the African Methodist Episcopal Church in 1899, dismissed the gospel of wealth, the elaborate projections for what capitalism might achieve in American life, and even the gains some workers had made by the century's end:

> What does the greatness or prosperity of our country amount to, to us as a race, if at the same time it shows to the civilized world either its weakness or unwillingness to protect ten millions of its most loyal citizens in the enjoyment of the simplest rights set forth in the Declaration of Independence . . . ? What is it to us if the wages of the factory employees are increased, if over the door of each of them the sign hangs out, "No Black Man Wanted Here" . . . ? Why should we shout for prosperity that means much to the white man and but little to his brother in black, when we know that it is the fixed purpose and determination to drive us from every favored avenue where we may earn our daily bread?[35]

The period of the gospel of wealth also coincided with a level of violence against blacks that, during the final years of the nineteenth century, was "greater than at any other period in American history," according to historian Gayraud Wilmore. Wilmore reports "unprecedented mob violence and terrorism perpetrated against Negro citizens between 1890 and 1914. Between 1885 and 1915, 3,500 Blacks were the known victims of lynch mobs, with 235 lynchings in the year 1892 alone."[36]

No one did more during that period to protest the lynching of black people than Ida B. Wells, the editor and part owner of the *Memphis Free*

Speech, a newspaper serving the black community in and around Memphis, Tennessee. Wells edited that paper for three years, beginning in 1889. Then, in 1892, a mob destroyed the newspaper office in retaliation for an editorial in which Wells exposed the true motive of a white mob that had viciously murdered three black entrepreneurs. Using the capitalist system to their advantage, these three entrepreneurs had competed successfully with neighboring whites in a comparable business—an offense that led to their execution.

Time and again, Wells placed before the public the murders that whites routinely inflicted on blacks in the American South during the period of the gospel of wealth. She took particular pains to refute the claim—typically offered by southern whites—that whites lynched blacks who had raped white women. In 1909 she pointedly asked, "Why is mob murder permitted by a Christian nation? What is the cause of this awful slaughter? This question is answered almost daily—always the same shameless falsehood that 'Negroes are lynched to protect womanhood.' . . . This is the never varying answer of lynchers and their apologists. All know that it is untrue. The cowardly lyncher revels in murder, then seeks to shield himself from public execration by claiming devotion to woman."[37]

Wells also brought to light the fact that many blacks were burned at the stake during this period. "Twenty-eight human beings burned at the stake, one of them a woman and two of them children, is the awful indictment against American civilization," she reported. She added, "No other nation, civilized or savage, burns its criminals; only under the stars and stripes is the human holocaust possible."[38]

In a speech presented in Boston in 1893, Wells highlighted two particular examples of this practice, one in Texarkana in 1892 and another in Paris, Texas, in 1893. "The Texarkana man, Ed Coy, was charge[d] with assaulting a white woman. A mob pronounced him guilty, strapped him to a tree, chipped the flesh from his body, poured coal oil over him and the woman in the case set fire to him." In the Paris, Texas, burning,

> The man [Henry Smith] was drawn through the streets on a float, as the Roman generals used to parade their trophies of war, while the scaffold ten feet high, was being built, and irons were heated in the fire. He was bound on it, and red-hot irons began at his feet and slowly branded his body, while the mob howled with delight at his shrieks. Red hot irons were run down his throat and cooked his tongue; his eyes were burned out, and when he was at last unconscious, cotton seed hulls were placed under him, coal oil poured all over him, and a torch applied to the mass. When the flames burned away the ropes which bound Smith and scorched his flesh, he was brought back to sensibility and burned and maimed and sightless

as he was, he rolled off the platform and away from the fire. His half-cooked body was seized and trampled and thrown back into the flames while a mob of twenty thousand persons who came from all over the country howled with delight, and gathered up some buttons and ashes after all was over to preserve for relics.[39]

Wells puzzled over the fact that "this Christian nation, the flower of the nineteenth century civilization, says it can do nothing to stop this inhuman slaughter. The general government is willingly powerless to send troops to protect the lives of its black citizens, but the state governments are free to use state troops to shoot them down like cattle, when in desperation the black men attempt to defend themselves, and then tell the world that it was necessary to put down a 'race war.'"[40]

In spite of the burnings, the lynchings, and the economic injustices wreaked on American blacks during the period of the gospel of wealth, the wonder is that so many blacks still kept faith in the promise of America. Ida B. Wells is a case in point. She longed for the day when

> mob rule shall be put down and equal and exact justice be accorded to every citizen of whatever race, who finds a home within the borders of the land of the free and the home of the brave.
>   Then no longer will our national hymn be sounding brass and a tinkling cymbal, but every member of this great composite nation will be a living, harmonious illustration of the words, and all can honestly and gladly join in singing:
>   My country! 'tis of thee,
>   Sweet land of liberty
>   Of thee I sing.
>   Land where our fathers died,
>   Land of the Pilgrim's pride,
>   From every mountain side
>   Freedom does ring.[41]

Indeed, Wells lamented the attacks on blacks as "attacks on distinctive American institutions" that she, for one, hoped to preserve.[42]

The educator and activist Anna J. Cooper concurred. In 1902 she told the Friends General Conference, meeting in Asbury Park, New Jersey, of her conviction "that America is the land of destiny for the descendants of the enslaved race, that here in the house of bondage are the seeds of promise for their ultimate enfranchisement and development."[43]

Sixteen years before, in 1886, she had made a similar point:

> Our satisfaction in American institutions rests not on the fruition we now enjoy, but springs rather from the possibilities and promise that are inherent in the system, though as yet, perhaps, far in the future. . . . We

have not yet reached our ideal in American civilization. The pessimists even declare that we are not marching in that direction. But there can be no doubt that here in America is the arena in which the next triumph of civilization is to be won; and here too we find promise abundant and possibilities infinite.[44]

The fact that blacks could suffer such extraordinary injustices and yet keep faith in the American system underscores the paradox that stands at the center of this book. In spite of the myths that have sometimes obscured its promise, the American Creed stands as a compelling vision that "all men are created equal, and [are] endowed with certain unalienable rights, that among these are life, liberty, and the pursuit of happiness." As such, the American Creed is a constant beacon of hope.

Conclusions

Much has changed since the late nineteenth century, to be sure. Unregulated laissez-faire capitalism as it was practiced in the late nineteenth century is a relic of the past. And while government often favors the rich at the expense of the poor, providing subsidies, welfare, and tax supports for giant corporations with relatively little relief for individual Americans who live at or below the poverty line, it is also true that over the past hundred years, government has put in place a variety of restrictions aimed at preventing the rich from exploiting the poor. Finally, since the civil rights movement of the 1950s and 1960s, black Americans and other minority citizens experience unprecedented economic opportunity. None of these facts can be denied.

At the same time, much remains the same. Americans made that alarming discovery in the aftermath of the corporate scandals that dominated the news in the summer of 2002, scandals about the manipulations that allowed CEOs to reap financial rewards that defied the imagination while their employees lost virtually everything. Even more important, many of the myths that surrounded American capitalism in the late nineteenth century remain in place today, providing "moral" justification for the behavior that led to those scandals.

The myth of Chosen People is a case in point. To be sure, few would argue that God has chosen some for wealth and others for poverty and deprivation, but this is only because the doctrine of "divine chosenness" has been largely secularized. In the place of God, nature reigns supreme in modern America, and most Americans would find little with which to quibble in either the so-called law of competition or the doctrine of the survival of the fittest.

Few today would agree with Russell Conwell that "the men who get rich may be the most honest men you find in the community." Americans have seen far too much corruption to subscribe to that proposition. But a great many privileged Americans would agree in principle with Henry Ward Beecher's dictum that "no man in this land suffers from poverty unless it be more than his fault—unless it be his sin." Those who remain on the bottom rungs of society, according to the common wisdom, should simply "pull themselves up by their bootstraps," and their failure to do so only demonstrates their moral turpitude. Many never consider that some Americans have neither boots nor bootstraps on which to pull.

Likewise, many Americans find axiomatic the proposition that the creation of free markets around the globe and the expanded production of wealth and material possessions will eventually launch a golden age that will bless the world. It is significant in this context that Americans commonly define the American dream, not in terms of inward peace and contentment but rather in terms of what one owns. Indeed, as Robert Bellah points out, Americans since the late nineteenth century have defined the very meaning of life in terms of monetary success and the accumulation of goods.[45]

It is little wonder, then, that upon entering America's universities, relatively few students ask the question of vocation ("What is my calling?") or the question of outreach ("How can I prepare academically for a life of service?"). Instead, most students enter the university with one question that towers above all other questions: "What can I choose for my major that will guarantee wealth, possessions, and economic security?" From this perspective, only a fool or a saint would major in religion, philosophy, history, or literary studies.

Because Americans imagine that the coming golden age hinges on increasing the production of wealth, most never question the notion that the health of the state depends on the expansion of the economy. After terrorists attacked the World Trade Center in New York and the Pentagon in Washington on September 11, 2001, government officials from the president down routinely told Americans that the most patriotic act they could perform was to "go spend money." That advice lends credence to Robert Bellah's judgment that "the economy is like a heroin addict; only another shot of the very profit narcotic that creates a recession will get us out of it." Indeed, Bellah suggests that "our economy could not survive a mass turn to voluntary poverty, however much our republican morality might be improved by such a turn."[46]

The fact that Americans are addicted to wealth as a narcotic and to material goods for the meaning of life poses significant problems for the future of the nation and even for the future of the world. What will this addiction mean for the *moral* health of the nation? What will this addiction mean for the world's environment on which all life finally depends? And since this addiction relies so heavily on radical individualism, what will it ultimately mean for human relationships and the possibility of forging meaningful community?

Cornell West has argued persuasively that this addiction has been particularly devastating for America's black community. For these people, West claims, "corporate market institutions" have both encouraged nihilism and undermined traditional morality. And how?

> Like all Americans, African Americans are influenced greatly by the images of comfort, convenience, machismo, femininity, violence, and sexual stimulation that bombard consumers. These seductive images contribute to the predominance of the market-inspired way of life over all others and thereby edge out nonmarket values—love, care, service to others—handed down by preceding generations. The predominance of this way of life among those living in poverty-ridden conditions, with a limited capacity to ward off self-contempt and self-hatred, results in the possible triumph of the nihilistic threat in black America.[47]

In the context of this book, however, the question that looms above all others is this: What will this addiction mean for our ability as Americans to implement the American Creed for *all the people,* not just for the privileged and the well-to-do?

So far, I have considered four of the myths that have helped define American self-understanding over the years—the myths of the Chosen Nation, Nature's Nation, the Christian Nation, and the Millennial Nation. And I have explored how both American capitalism and the doctrine of manifest destiny have drawn sustenance from each of these visions. Next I turn to the fifth and final myth—a myth that has exerted enormous power in American life, especially since World War II. That is the myth of America as the Innocent Nation.

Notes

1. Daniel Seely Gregory, *Christian Ethics,* 1875, cited in Ralph Henry Gabriel, *The Course of American Democratic Thought,* 2d ed. (New York: Ronald Press, 1956), 157; William Lawrence, "The Relation of Wealth to Morals," 1901, in *God's New Israel: Religious Interpretations of American Destiny,* rev. ed., ed. Conrad Cherry (Chapel Hill: University of North Carolina Press, 1998), 252; Charles Arthur Conant, *The United States in the Orient: The Nature of the Economic Problem* (Boston: Houghton Mifflin, 1900), 2.

2. William Lawrence, "The Relation of Wealth to Morals" (1901), in Cherry, *God's New Israel*, 250–52.

3. Russell Conwell, *Acres of Diamonds* (1890; New York: Harper and Row, 1905), 18.

4. Sidney E. Mead, *The Lively Experiment: The Shaping of Christianity in America* (New York: Harper and Row, 1963), 143.

5. Henry Ward Beecher, "The Tendencies of American Progress" (1870), in Cherry, *God's New Israel*, 237, 242, 245.

6. Quoted in Henry F. May, *Protestant Churches and Industrial America* (New York: Harper and Row, 1967), 69.

7. Sydney Ahlstrom, *A Religious History of the American People* (New Haven, Conn.: Yale University Press, 1972), 767.

8. Andrew Carnegie, "Wealth" (1889), in *The Role of Religion in American Life: An Interpretive Historical Anthology*, ed. Robert A. Mathisen (Dubuque, Iowa: Kendall/Hunt, 1994), 168, 173.

9. Josiah Strong, "Our Country" (1885), in *Nationalism and Religion in America: Concepts of American Identity and Mission*, ed. Winthrop Hudson (New York: Harper and Row, 1970), 115–16.

10. James Henderson Berry, *Congressional Record*, 55th Cong., 3d sess., vol. 32, pt. 2 (Washington, D.C.: Government Printing Office, 1899), 1299.

11. Beveridge cited in James Oliver Robertson, *American Myth, American Reality* (New York: Hill and Wang, 1980), 272; Kitchell cited in Emily S. Rosenberg, *Spreading the American Dream: American Economic and Cultural Expansion, 1890–1945* (New York: Hill and Wang, 1982), 22.

12. For an elaboration of this point, see Rosenberg, *Spreading the American Dream*, 38, 48–49, 230–31.

13. Conant cited in ibid., 50.

14. Ibid., 25.

15. Arthur M. Schlesinger Jr., *Orestes A. Brownson: A Pilgrim's Progress* (Boston: Little, Brown, 1939), 90.

16. Howard Zinn narrates these events in *A People's History of the United States* (New York: Harper Colophon, 1980), 263–65.

17. John R. Commons et al., *History of Labor in the United States* (New York: Macmillan, 1936), 2:373–74.

18. Speech of Jack White cited in Zinn, *People's History*, 325–26.

19. Walter Rauschenbusch, *Christianity and the Social Crisis* (1907; New York: Macmillan, 1913), 369–72.

20. Charles Sheldon, *In His Steps* (1897; Chicago: John C. Winston, 1957), 254–59.

21. Philip S. Foner and Robert James Branham, eds., *Lift Every Voice: African American Oratory, 1787–1900* (Tuscaloosa: University of Alabama Press, 1998), 655–56.

22. Lucy Parsons, "I Am an Anarchist" (1886), in Foner and Branham, *Lift Every Voice*, 657.

23. See the description of Fortune in Foner and Branham, *Lift Every Voice*, 642.

24. T. Thomas Fortune, "The Present Relations of Labor and Capital" (1886), in Foner and Branham, *Lift Every Voice*, 642–44.

25. Paul M. Gaston, *The New South Creed: A Study in Southern Mythmaking* (New York: Knopf, 1970), 17, 87–88. For the full text of Grady's speech, see Joel Chandler Harris, ed., *Life of Henry W. Grady, Including His Writings and Speeches* (New York: Cassell, 1890).

26. W. E. B. Du Bois, *The Souls of Black Folk* (1903), in *Three Negro Classics* (New York: Avon Books, 1965), 264.

27. Booker T. Washington, *Up From Slavery* (1901), in *Three Negro Classics*, 126–27.

28. Ibid., 131–32, 176, 190–91.

29. Ibid., 146–50.

30. Du Bois, *Souls of Black Folk,* 241.

31. Ibid., 321.

32. Ibid., 239.

33. Ibid., 350.

34. Frederick Douglass, "I Denounce the So-Called Emancipation As a Stupendous Fraud" (1888), in Foner and Branham, *Lift Every Voice,* 706, 698, 703.

35. D. P. Brown, "The State of the Country from a Black Man's Point of View" (1899), in Foner and Branham, *Lift Every Voice,* 893–94.

36. Gayraud Wilmore, *Black Religion and Black Radicalism: An Examination of the Black Experience in Religion* (New York: Doubleday, 1973), 190, 192.

37. Ida B. Wells, "Lynching, Our National Crime" (1909), in *Can I Get a Witness?: Prophetic Religious Voices of African American Women: An Anthology,* ed. Marcia Y. Riggs (Maryknoll, N.Y.: Orbis, 1997), 147–48.

38. Ibid., 147.

39. Ida B. Wells, "Lynch Law in All Its Phases" (1893), in *With Pen and Voice: A Critical Anthology of Nineteenth-Century African-American Women,* ed. Shirley Wilson Logan (Carbondale: Southern Illinois University Press, 1995), 92–93.

40. Ibid., 94.

41. Ibid., 99.

42. Ibid., 80.

43. Anna J. Cooper, "The Ethics of the Negro Question" (1902), in Riggs, *Can I Get a Witness?* 143.

44. Anna J. Cooper, "Womanhood a Vital Element in the Regeneration and Progress of a Race" (1886), in Logan, *With Pen and Voice,* 54.

45. Robert N. Bellah, *The Broken Covenant: American Civil Religion in Time of Trial,* 2d ed. (Chicago: University of Chicago Press, 1992), 73.

46. Ibid., 133 and 136.

47. Cornel West, *Race Matters* (Boston: Beacon Press, 1993), 16–17.

6 *The Myth of the Innocent Nation*

THE TWENTIETH CENTURY

In his splendid memoir that describes what it meant to grow up in the 1960s and 1970s, Lawrence Wright reflects on the innocence that characterized America during the period of World War II. "When my father went off to war," Wright recalls, "I understood that he was going to make the world safe for democracy and that that was what the world wanted. . . . [He had] matured in a magic age, the 1940s, when great evil and great good faced each other. In that splendid moment he knew which side he was on. He was an American farm boy doing what God and his country had designed for him. . . . Here he was, saving the world. I grew up expecting to inherit his certainty."[1]

The fact is, a profound sense of innocence characterized the American experience for much of the twentieth century, especially between World War I and the 1960s. Some periods were exceptions to that generalization, of course. The Great Depression, for example, generated enormous doubt and despair, not only among blacks and other minorities, but also among whites. Still, in the mainstream of American life, most had no doubt about the ultimate meaning of their nation: America stood for good against evil, right against wrong, democracy against tyranny, and virtue against vice. What can account for this extraordinary sense of innocence that many in later years would view as profoundly naïve?

The Arminian Worldview in the New Republic

Robert Bellah has suggested that at least one source for America's conviction of its own innocence was the Arminian worldview that accompanied the American revivals, especially the Second Great Awakening. Prior to the revivals, Calvinism dominated the religious climate in the colonies, and Calvinism taught that human beings are far from innocent. Instead, they are fundamentally sinful, through and through. God alone could transform a human being from a sinful state to a virtuous state, and such a transformation occurred only through a radical rebirth in Jesus Christ.

The revivalists of the nineteenth century turned the Calvinist vision upside down. If one sought virtue and innocence, they preached, one only had to will that change and make a determined effort to reform one's life. Jesus might cooperate in this transformation, but ultimately, the transformation was a matter of human initiative. Such was the Arminian vision that characterized much of the preaching of the Second Great Awakening.

In the Arminian vision, Bellah notes, "Both man and the world, at least in America, are essentially innocent. There are pitfalls and temptations to be avoided, but they are incidental rather than of the essence of the human condition."[2] There is no doubt that Bellah's analysis is correct, and that the Arminian worldview that controlled so much of American Protestantism in the nineteenth century provided a context in which a cult of innocence could flourish in American life in later years. Still, I would argue that if we seek to account for the radical sense of innocence that pervaded American life in the first half of the twentieth century, two other factors are even more critical. First, America really did face great evil in the twentieth century, especially during World War II. When one faces an enemy who is thoroughly evil, it is all too easy to imagine that one is thoroughly righteous and fundamentally innocent. This is precisely the posture that America assumed during and after World War II. Second, the myths already considered in this book contributed enormously to America's sense of innocence in the twentieth century.

The Ahistorical Dimensions of American Innocence

The myth of America as a Christian Nation is a case in point. By the early twentieth century fundamentalists worried that America had deserted its Christian moorings, although most Americans who claimed the Christian faith remained confident that America was a Christian civilization. That perception alone was enough to sustain a powerful sense of innocence.

In addition, the myth of the Chosen Nation was still a vibrant, dynamic theme in American life and culture. As Lawrence Wright notes in his memoir, "America had a mission—we thought it was a divine mission—to spread freedom, and freedom meant democracy, and democracy meant capitalism, and all that meant the American way of life."[3] Would God choose America for such a mission if America lacked the qualities of goodness, virtue, and innocence?

In my judgment, however, the two most important myths sustaining America's sense of innocence in the early twentieth century were the myths of Nature's Nation and the Millennial Nation. Important in this context is the way those myths converged to preclude any meaningful sense of history in the United States.

The notion of Nature's Nation pointed Americans to a mythic time when the world first began and all was good and right and true—the time of Eden before the fall. It was easy to imagine that the United States was a virtual re-creation of this golden age, an age that stood on the front end—and therefore outside the boundaries—of human history.

At the same time, the notion of the Millennial Nation pointed Americans to another golden age that would conclude the human saga. Because the millennium was also characterized by perfection, it, too, stood outside the boundaries of human history, this time on the back end. By restoring the virtues of the first perfect age, Americans imagined they would usher in the second perfect age and thereby bless the world.

By identifying itself so completely with these mythic periods of perfection, America lifted itself, as it were, above the plane of ordinary human history where evil, suffering, and death dominated the drama of human existence. America became, as the Great Seal of the United States so clearly states, a *novus ordo seclorum*, a new order of the ages. Other nations were mired in the bog of human history, but not the United States. Other nations had inherited the taint of human history, but not the United States. Other nations had been compromised by human history, but not the United States. In effect, then, America had removed itself from the power of human history with all the ambiguity that history inevitably bears. In this way, America emerged, as it were, as an innocent child among the nations of the world, without spot or wrinkle, unmarred and unblemished by the finite dimensions of human history.

President Ronald Reagan perhaps put it best when he said in his State of the Union address of 1987, "The calendar can't measure America because we were meant to be an endless experiment in freedom, with no limit to our reaches, no boundaries to what we can do, no end point to our hopes."[4]

Having rejected the bounds of finite human history, it is little wonder that when America launched a war against Islamic terrorists in retaliation for the September 11, 2001, bombings, U.S. military strategists initially called the war "Operation Infinite Justice." They finally scuttled that phrase when people of religious faith—Muslims, Christians, and Jews—pointed out that only God can dispense "infinite justice."

Indeed, the starting point for the American illusion of innocence lies in the way Americans typically deal with history and its contents. Henry Ford perhaps put it best when he said flatly "History is bunk." If Americans wish to say that someone is irrelevant to a particular situation, we often say to that person, "You're history." American students typically avoid history, believing that history itself is irrelevant. We bulldoze buildings of any age at all in order to create something that is bright, shining, and new. These are just some of the ways that Americans routinely reject the reality of history. The truth is that many Americans live their lives in the eternal present, a present informed and shaped not by history but by those two golden epochs that bracket human time.

Because many Americans so often reject history, they also reject the most fundamental contents of history, especially finitude, suffering, and death. In 1963 Jessica Mitford published an important book called *The American Way of Death*. While many cultures cope with death by embracing it—by handling the corpse, for example—Americans, Mitford noted, have adopted funeral practices that effectively mask the reality of death so that it never intrudes on the perfect world they seek to create.[5]

Americans often deal with suffering in the very same way, as the patterns of our neighborhoods abundantly attest. Indeed, one could easily argue that racial segregation has always had more to do with economics than with color. In this scenario, black people were despised because black skin became in the United States a powerful symbol of the grinding poverty that no one wanted and with which no one wished to come into contact. And so we segregate poor people into neighborhoods far removed from the manicured lawns and the beautiful homes of the privileged. In effect, then, many Americans often deny—or at least seek to deny—those profoundly human activities we call suffering and death.

Our national wealth has allowed us to perpetuate these illusions. Our health care system, for example, is the best in the world, and for that, Americans can be profoundly grateful. Who would wish it otherwise? At the same time, the marvels of modern medicine enable many Americans to banish suffering and death so that they seldom impinge on what we like to call the "American way of life."

Our prison system performs much the same function. Obviously, any society requires prisons. The necessity of prisons, however, does not negate the fact that prisons effectively remove from our presence those who remind us of evil and of lives gone bad. Our concern to remove this kind of people from the perfect world we seek to create is particularly evident in our resistance to prevention and our commitment to punishment. In other words, we would far prefer locking people up to providing the kinds of programs that might prevent crime in the first place or that might rehabilitate offenders. As a result, we find we cannot build prisons quickly enough to cope with the vast population that we seek to place behind bars.

The point I seek to make through all these examples should be clear: Americans are committed to creating for themselves a perfect world in a golden age that has little to do with the messy contents of human history with which so many people in so many other parts of the world must deal every day, especially the realities of tragedy, suffering, and death. In this context, historian Edward T. Linenthal, describing the April 19, 1995, bombing of the Alfred P. Murrah Federal Building in Oklahoma City, wrote, "There was, seemingly, nowhere in the storehouse of American meaning to place the bombing, to make sense of it. It was, quite literally, 'out of place.'" It was out of place, Linenthal wrote, because it "activated enduring convictions that Americans were peaceable citizens of an innocent and vulnerable nation in a largely wicked world. Thus the evocative power of headlines: 'Myth of Midwest safety shattered' . . . [and] 'American innocence buried in Oklahoma.'"[6]

Similarly, Mark Slouka suggested that Americans found the September 11, 2001, attack on the Pentagon and the World Trade Center particularly traumatic because

> it simultaneously exposed and challenged the myth of our own uniqueness. A myth most visible, perhaps, in our age-old denial of death.
>
> Consider it. Here in the New Canaan, in the land of perpetual beginnings and second chances, where identity could be sloughed and sloughed again and history was someone else's problem, death had never been welcome. Death was a foreigner—radical, disturbing, smelling of musty books and brimstone. We wanted no part of him.
>
> And now death had come calling. That troubled brother, so long forgotten, so successfully erased, was standing on our porch in his steel-toed boots, grinning. He'd made it across the ocean, passed like a ghost through the gates of our chosen community. We had denied him his due

and his graveyards, watered down his deeds, buried him with things. Yet here he was. He reminded us of something unpleasant.

Slouka concluded, "This was not just a terrorist attack. This was an act of metaphysical trespass."[7]

I am convinced that the American predisposition to create such an idyllic world has its deepest roots in the two great myths that gripped the imagination of the American people when the nation was young—the myth of Nature's Nation and the myth of the Millennial Nation. Because these two myths effectively sidestepped human history, they allowed the American people to nurture illusions of a perfect world, just as they allowed Americans to nurture illusions of innocence.[8]

The Paradox of the Myth of Innocence

Any exploration of the history of the myth of innocence almost invariably reveals that it finally transforms itself into its opposite. Indeed, it typically encourages those who march under its banner to repress those they regard as corrupted or defiled. Paradoxically, then, the innocent become guilty along with the rest of the human race, though the myths they have embraced prevent them from discerning their guilt. This is the point Reinhold Niebuhr made when he observed "the ironic tendency of virtues to turn into vices when too complacently relied upon."[9]

The dynamics of this paradox are illumined by two new religious traditions that emerged in the early nineteenth century when the country still was young and when the myths of Nature's Nation and the Millennial Nation had gripped the American imagination. Those two traditions are the Latter-day Saints (Mormons) and the movement variously known as Disciples of Christ, Christian Churches, and Churches of Christ, which I will refer to hereafter as Disciples/Churches of Christ.

While historians have paid substantial attention to the Latter-day Saints over the years, they have seldom explored the history and meaning of the Disciples/Churches of Christ in the context of American culture. That is a shame, since these two traditions stand at the very heart of America's mythic past. Indeed, it would be difficult to find a single religious tradition in American life that embodies and reflects more fully than these the inner dynamics of the two myths that frame this discussion— Nature's Nation and the Millennial Nation.

Though very different from one another in significant ways, Mormons and Disciples/Churches of Christ had one thing in common: Both built their core identities around the effort to restore a golden age of the past as the means to introduce the golden age of the future. In the first place, both defined themselves as "restoration movements." By using the term *restoration,* they meant to suggest that the church had fallen from its original purity. In the early nineteenth century, therefore, both Mormons and Disciples/Churches of Christ leapfrogged over 1,800 years of Christian history in order to restore the purity that characterized the earliest Christians. It must be obvious that this commitment implicitly suggested that no one in Christian history, from the close of the founding age to the dawn of the nineteenth century, had maintained the purity of the faith. To one degree or another, then, the entire history of the Christian church was a history of apostasy and corruption. Here one finds a rejection of history fully as pronounced as the rejection of history that characterized the larger nation.

MORMONS

While Mormons and Disciples/Churches of Christ shared a common commitment to the goal of restoration, they differed significantly in what they hoped to restore. Mormons sought to restore a golden age when God communicated directly with humankind, just as he had with Adam, Moses, and Jesus. For 1,800 years, they argued, Christians had made a terrible mistake when they claimed that, since the earliest days of the faith, God had spoken to humankind only through a book—the Bible. Accordingly, Mormons taught that God had spoken directly to their prophet, Joseph Smith, who now had the mandate and the blueprint for restoring the ancient church in these latter days.

For Mormons, the restoration of the ancient church meant the restoration of all sorts of ceremonies and practices that one finds in both Old and New Testaments, especially the baptism of adults for the remission of sins, polygamy, baptism for the dead, latter-day miracles, and the rebuilding of Solomon's temple in middle America. When this restoration was complete, Mormons argued, and especially when the temple had been restored, Jesus himself would return to the earth and rule for a thousand years. Here emerges the significance of the name the Mormons took for themselves: Church of Jesus Christ (i.e., the true, restored church of Christ) of Latter-day Saints (those saints who are ushering in the final, golden age).[10]

In these ways, like the American nation that was their home, the Latter-day Saints sidestepped human history and grounded their movement in a golden age of the past and a golden age yet to come. They therefore imagined that they had achieved a level of purity and innocence denied to those earthlings still rooted in the messy ambiguities of human history.[11]

Though defending their innocence all the while, it was therefore not uncommon for early Mormons to threaten other Christians with divine retribution. Parley Pratt, for example, was an early Mormon missionary, highly regarded in the church. Mormon scholars have argued that his book *A Voice of Warning* was "the most important of all non-canonical Mormon books" and "the most important missionary pamphlet in the early history of the church."[12] Pratt argued in that book in 1837 that the Mormon faith "is the gospel which God has commanded us to preach. . . . And no other system of religion . . . is of any use; every thing different from this, is a perverted gospel, bringing a curse upon them that preach it, and upon them that hear it." In fact, all who resisted the Mormon message "shall alike feel the hand of the almighty, by pestilence, famine, earthquake, and the sword: yea, ye shall be drunken with your own blood . . . until your cities are desolate . . . until all lyings, priestcrafts, and all manner of abomination, shall be done away."[13]

Mormons freely admitted that non-Mormons would inherit a degree of glory in the final, millennial age. Still, they contended that God had reserved for Mormons themselves the highest levels in that kingdom, with honorable men inheriting a lesser, "terrestrial glory" and non-Christians inheriting a still lesser "telestial glory."[14] Parley Pratt admitted that even "the heathen nations . . . will . . . be redeemed." However, they "will be exalted to the privilege of serving the saints of the Most High. They will be the ploughmen, the vinedressers, the gardeners, builders, etc. But the saints will be the owners of the soil, the proprietors of all real estate and other precious things, and the kings, governors, and judges of the earth."[15]

Here one finds a vision remarkably similar to the doctrine of manifest destiny that governed the larger nation. Because Mormons had restored the perfect, golden age of the past, it was their "manifest destiny" to rule the earth in the final age of the future. Others would either serve the Saints or suffer from "pestilence, famine, earthquake, and the sword"—a vision not unlike that articulated by General James Carleton when he said of the Navajos, as I noted earlier in this text, "When at length, they found it was their destiny, too, as it had been that of their brethren, tribe after tribe, away back toward the rising of the sun, to give way to the insatiable progress of our race, they threw down their arms, and, as brave men entitled to our admiration and respect, have come to us with confidence in our magnanimity."[16]

Clearly, in the case of early nineteenth century Mormons, the innocent were not so innocent after all. Few Mormons, however, could understand this point since, by definition, they had identified themselves with those two great times of perfection that bracket human history and transcend the guilt that history always bears.

DISCIPLES/CHURCHES OF CHRIST

The story of the Disciples/Churches of Christ of the nineteenth century differs only in details, but not in substance. Alexander Campbell led a significant wing of this religious movement from his home in Bethany, Virginia (later West Virginia) for some forty years, beginning in roughly 1820. By 1860 the movement had become the fourth-largest Christian denomination in the country, trailing only Baptists, Methodists, and Presbyterians. After a series of divisions and subdivisions, the church is represented today by three major American denominations: the Disciples of Christ, the Churches of Christ, and the Independent Christian Churches.

Like the Mormons, Disciples/Churches of Christ built their core identity by seeking to restore the golden age of the past (primitive church) as a means to usher in the golden age of the future (the millennium). As Campbell proclaimed in 1825, "just in so far as the ancient order of things, or the religion of the New Testament, is restored, just so far has the Millennium commenced."[17] So enchanted was Campbell with his vision that for a third of a century, beginning in 1830, he edited a journal that he called the *Millennial Harbinger.*

Campbell and his followers, however, completely rejected the Mormons' contention that God might speak to humankind in the modern world apart from the biblical text. Accordingly, Disciples/Churches of Christ sought to restore the ancient church as they found the outlines for that church clearly spelled out in the Bible.

It is important to understand that in spite of the rejection of history that his theology inevitably fostered, Campbell nurtured in himself a profoundly ecumenical spirit. It was perhaps inevitable, however, that among his followers, attitudes toward other Christians would not be so amiable. In fact, some of Campbell's followers rather quickly concluded that they and they alone had restored the ancient church. It followed, then, that other so-called Christians were simply beyond the pale. In 1843, for example, John R. Howard warned "sectarians," as he called them, that "the coming of the Lord, in vengeance to destroy his enemies, cannot . . . be very far off. . . . And should *you* not be found among his true people—his genuine disciples—but arrayed in opposition against them, he will 'destroy' you 'with the *breath* of his *mouth*, and with the *brightness* of his *coming.*'"[18]

By the early twentieth century, the Churches of Christ—the southern wing of the movement—had come to a parting of the ways with the larger Campbell tradition. Though they would never exhibit much interest in millennial themes after that division, the Churches of Christ nonetheless committed themselves to the restoration of the primitive church and made that commitment central to their identity and self-understanding.

Because they were so preoccupied with the ancient church, they rejected Christian history almost entirely, claiming that they owed no debt to the past except to the earliest Christian communities, which, they imagined, they had faithfully replicated. Augustine, for them, was of no consequence. Neither was Martin Luther or Jean Calvin or Ulrich Zwingli or John Wesley or any other significant figure in Christian history. In fact, Churches of Christ often rejected their *own* history, claiming that if they acknowledged a human history with human leaders, they would thereby become a denomination among other denominations and fall into the guilt of history along with everyone else. So, for most of the twentieth century, they steadfastly identified themselves only with the ancient church of the apostolic age. In this way, they could preserve their innocence.

It goes without saying that by separating themselves from the common lot of humankind on the grounds that they and they alone had restored the ancient Christian faith, Churches of Christ maintained a strongly heteronymous stance not only toward other religions but also toward other Christians. In fact, they commonly taught that they were the only legitimate Christians. Others who claimed to follow Christ were only pretenders.

Like the Mormons, members of Churches of Christ claimed innocence on the grounds that they had fully replicated the perfections of the first age. As it turned out, however, those who claimed innocence on these grounds fell into the guilt of history in spite of themselves. The innocence they presumed prompted an arrogance they could not admit, for the myth of innocence shielded them from their sins. So they persisted in their claims to perfection, even as they broke community and ruptured relations with their brothers and sisters in other communities of the Christian faith.

THE DYNAMICS OF INNOCENCE IN THE NATION AT LARGE

By the close of the twentieth century, those sorts of attitudes were rapidly fading. Churches of Christ were taking their own history with greater seriousness and were more and more open to ecumenical relations with other Christians.[19]

But the point remains. In the early nineteenth century, Churches of Christ, like the Mormons, presented in microcosm the dynamics at work in the myth of innocence, even as that myth played itself out in the larger republic. Both these traditions emerged and grew up when the nation was young and borrowed from the larger culture the mythic themes that defined them. For this reason, when we explore the mythic dimensions of these two traditions, we can learn much about the mythic dimensions of the nation at large. Like the Mormons and Churches of Christ, the larger nation grounded its sense of innocence in the way it identified with the golden age of the past (the time of creation) and the golden age of the future (the millennium). Since America refused to admit its debt to human history and imagined itself a "new order of the ages," it also imagined it could lead the world into a golden age of "liberty and justice for all."

The problems emerged when other nations resisted the American version of "liberty and justice for all" or when America failed—as it did from time to time—to separate its vision of "liberty and justice for all" from its own political, economic, and military interests. In this way, while proclaiming its innocence and the purity of its motives, America—like the other nations of the world—also fell into the guilt of history. This is the point, however, that Americans seldom see, since the myth of the Innocent Nation shields them from the realities that are so apparent to so many others around the world.

America: The Innocent Nation

The myth of the Innocent Nation is an enduring theme in American history but was especially apparent in American life from World War I to the Vietnam War.

WORLD WAR I

The way America defined its role in World War I established the essential pattern to which the myth of innocence would conform itself for the rest of the twentieth century. No one did more to define that pattern than President Woodrow Wilson. Earlier in this chapter, I observed that when we face a foe that we regard as unalterably evil, it is much easier to regard our own cause as righteous and ourselves as completely innocent of any motives except the most altruistic. That observation surely characterized the convictions of Woodrow Wilson. In a message to the Congress on April 2, 1917, Wilson described the Imperial German government as one "which has thrown aside all considerations of humanity and of right and is running amuck."[20] When the war was over and Wilson presented the treaty for ratification, he reflected once again on what he regarded as the demonic character of the Imperial German government. America entered this war, he said, "because we saw the supremacy, and even the validity, of right everywhere put in jeopardy and free government likely to be everywhere imperiled by the intolerable aggression of a power which respected neither right nor obligation and whose every system of government flouted the rights of the citizen as against the autocratic authority of his governors."[21]

At the same time, Wilson presented the American cause as righteous, innocent, and free of self-interest. Shortly after America entered the war in 1917, Wilson explained to the American people that "there is not a single selfish element so far as I can see, in the cause we are fighting for. We are fighting for what we believe and wish to be the rights of mankind and for the future peace and security of the world."[22]

Two weeks earlier, he presented a similar case to the U.S. Congress: "We have no selfish ends to serve. We desire no conquest, no dominion. We seek no indemnities for ourselves, no material compensation for the sacrifices we shall freely make. We are but one of the champions of the rights of mankind."[23]

When the war was over, he confirmed that judgment. "The United States entered the war upon a different footing from every other nation except our associates on this side of the sea," he said. "We entered it, not because our material interests were directly threatened or because any special treaty obligations to which we were parties had been violated." Rather, America entered the war "only as the champion of rights which she was glad to share with free men and lovers of justice everywhere. . . . We were welcomed as disinterested friends. . . . We were generously accepted as the unaffected champions of what was right."[24]

Wilson could make these claims because he so completely grounded the American mission in the golden age of the past, that is, in the principles built into the natural order from the time of creation. Because American principles were grounded in that natural order of things, Wilson believed they were the universal principles of all humankind. Accordingly, in a speech to the Senate on January 22, 1917, he stated flatly, "American principles [and] American policies . . . are the principles of mankind, and must prevail."[25]

Wilson also believed that American principles and policies would usher in a final golden age for all humanity. America soldiers fought, he said, not for a penultimate or short-term peace, but for "the ultimate peace of the world." Because Wilson aimed at "ultimate peace," he hoped, like the British politician David Lloyd George, that this conflict would be the war to end war. Further, through the implementation of American principles and policies, he hoped to make the world "safe for democracy."[26] Clearly, Wilson aimed for nothing less than a golden age of liberty, democracy, and justice for all humankind. Because this was the goal, Wilson believed that American involvement in the war was innocent of self-serving motivations.

Several statements and events belied Wilson's claims of American innocence and of a completely disinterested American mission in the war. First, only twenty years prior to America's entry into World War I, leading Americans had spoken of America's manifest destiny to dominate the commerce of the world. An example was Senator Albert Beveridge's proclamation that "we are enlisted in the cause of American supremacy, which will never end until American commerce has made the conquest of the world."[27] One might also recall Senator James Henderson Berry's contention that America fought the Spanish-American War "on the pretense, it may be, of humanity and Christianity, but behind it all . . . is the desire for trade and commerce."[28] In addition, as I have noted, during the early years of the twentieth century American business established numerous plants and factories around the world, especially in Europe, and that from 1897 to 1914—the year World War I began—American overseas investments soared from $634 million to $2.6 billion. I reviewed all these facts in chapter 5.

America entered the war in response to German submarine attacks on American ships. As Wilson noted in a message to the U.S. Congress, "even hospital-ships and ships carrying relief to the sorely bereaved and stricken people of Belgium" had been sunk by German submarine warfare.[29] In the context of the manifest destiny of American business, the American dream of economic "conquest of the world," and the quadrupling of American commercial investments abroad between 1897 and 1914, Wilson's comments on commerce become particularly significant. Wilson described how the German attacks had produced a "very serious congestion of our commerce . . . which is growing rapidly more and more serious every day." Indeed, he noted, American commerce suffered not only from direct attack, but because so many commercial vessels were sitting idle in port "because of the unwillingness of our ship-owners to risk their vessels at sea without insurance or adequate protection."[30]

When the war was over, Edward N. Hurley, head of the U.S. Shipping Board, confirmed the way Americans at that time often confused the dream of universal peace and justice with the dream of the economic conquest of the world. In a memo to Bernard Baruch, head of the War

Industries Board, Hurley wrote, "If America would invest substantially in the essential raw materials of all foreign countries . . . America would then be in a position to say to the rest of the world, that these commodities would be sold at a fair price. . . . In what better way could we be of real service than by the use of our financial strength to control the raw materials for the benefit of humanity?"[31]

Nonetheless, Wilson obscured the commercial motivation for American involvement in the war when he told the Congress "I have spoken of our commerce and of the legitimate errands of our people on the seas, but you will not be misled as to my main thought. . . . I am thinking not only of the rights of Americans to go and come about their proper business by way of the sea, but also of something much deeper, much more fundamental than that. I am thinking of those rights of humanity without which there is no civilization."[32]

There is no reason to doubt Wilson's sincerity when he claimed that his foremost consideration was the "rights of humanity without which there is no civilization," but why did he obscure the commercial motivation for American involvement in the war? It is safe to say that Wilson—along with many other Americans—did not and could not discern the dimensions of self-interest inherent in American commerce. After all, Americans had for many years understood capitalism and commercial activity as fundamental "American principles and policies" that were also "the principles of mankind." Accordingly, Wilson simply spoke of "the rights of Americans to go and come about their proper business by way of the sea."

One other event belied American claims during World War I that it was an innocent participant, altogether free of self-interested motivation. When the government took extraordinary steps to punish dissenters and to convince the American people to support the war, one can only conclude that the official rationale—to secure the rights of all humankind—was not all that self-evident, and that many Americans detected a dimension of self-interest that the government refused to admit.

Indeed, the Committee on Public Information (CPI), directed by Denver newsman George Creel, aimed a vigorous propaganda campaign directly at the American people. Employing artists, musicians, journalists, historians, and a host of other creative professionals, the CPI produced patriotic posters, books like *German War Practices*, and films like *The Beast of Berlin*, all designed to demonize the enemy and portray the American cause as both innocent and righteous. Strikingly, Creel never admitted that CPI productions were propagandistic in any sense at all. Rather, they simply presented "value-free" facts that were self-evident to any reasonable observer—a conclusion completely in harmony with the notion that America was an "innocent nation," standing for "the principles of mankind."[33]

By and large, the American public responded positively to the campaign, demonizing all things German and equating German people, German language, and German culture with disloyalty to American principles and the American mission. Schools throughout the country, for example, dropped the study of the German language, and while Americans continued to eat sauerkraut, they renamed it "liberty cabbage."

Still, there were dissenters. Consequently, the CPI censored materials that disagreed with its own propaganda and sought to squelch those who dared to question the dominant ideology. The Espionage and Sedition Acts, in fact, essentially made criticism of the government and its war policies illegal. Passed on June 15, 1917, the Espionage Act made it possible to fine dissenters up to $10,000 and imprison them for up to twenty years. Possible offenses included disloyalty, statements that might interfere with the war effort, giving aid to the enemy, refusing duty in the armed services, or inciting insubordination in the armed services. Passed almost a year later, on May 16, 1918, the Sedition Act extended these penalties to anyone who spoke, wrote, or printed anything that might be considered "disloyal, profane, scurrilous, or abusive" about the government, the Constitution, or the armed services.

The irony, of course, lies in the fact that while America sought, through participating in World War I, to secure the rights of all humankind and to make "the world safe for democracy," it abridged the rights of American citizens and undermined the democratic process in the homeland. In this way, the myth of innocence turned in upon itself. When all was said and done, America participated in the guilt that inevitably belongs to participants in human history in spite of every effort to avoid it. Most Americans, however, could scarcely discern that guilt, so strong was the myth of America as the Innocent Nation.

Finally, it is important to observe that World War I helped to breathe new life into the myth of America as a Christian Nation. I noted in chapter 4 that prior to World War I, the rise of virulent modernism prompted fundamentalists to worry that America had deserted its Christian calling. Up to 1918, many fundamentalists were so discouraged by the modernistic aspects of American culture that they essentially dropped out of political activity and took refuge in the hope that the second coming of Christ might occur soon. Accordingly, they took little interest in the war.

By 1918, however, most fundamentalists had changed their minds. They had embraced the government's line on the demonic character of

Imperial Germany but took it one step further. Imperial Germany, they concluded, was the ultimate source of the modernist ideology threatening the United States. From that perspective, there was hope for America, but only if Christians did what they could to save the country from German modernism. Almost overnight, therefore, fundamentalists embraced America as a Christian nation waging a Christian crusade against a demonic foe. One of the standard fundamentalist journals of that time made the point crystal clear: "The Kaiser boldly threw down the gage of battle—infidel Germany against the believing world—Kultur against Christianity—the Gospel of Hate against the Gospel of Love. Thus is Satan personified—'Myself and God.' . . . Never did Crusader lift battle-ax in holier war against the Saracen than is waged by our soldiers of the cross against the Germans."[34] In the aftermath of the Scopes "Monkey Trial" of 1925, however, fundamentalists disappeared from the stage of American political life just as abruptly as they had entered that stage in 1918, though that is a story whose thread I will pick up shortly.

For now, the point to grasp is this: The American experience in World War I prepared the country to imagine itself an innocent, disinterested participant in the conflicts of the world. Grounded in the laws of "Nature and Nature's God" and defined by Christian virtues, America stood poised to lead the world into a golden age of liberty and justice for all.

WORLD WAR II

American involvement in World War II only confirmed the validity of these myths in the minds of the American people. In part, this was because in that particular war, the face of evil was so thoroughly apparent. America entered World War II only after the Japanese attacked Pearl Harbor on December 7, 1941. Conrad Cherry is correct to note that the war brought "much less talk of a holy crusade aimed at the final destruction of evil" than had been the case in World War I.[35] Yet it is undeniably clear that Americans viewed the war as a battle between a righteous, Innocent Nation and the forces of iniquity.

President Franklin D. Roosevelt framed the issues in his message to the Congress on January 6, 1942, only a month after the Japanese attacked Pearl Harbor. Above all else, Roosevelt sought to portray the Axis forces as fundamentally demonic and America as fundamentally good. Here, then, was a classic war of good versus evil.

> Our enemies are guided by brutal cynicism, by unholy contempt for the human race. We are inspired by a faith which goes back through all the years to the first chapter of the Book of Genesis: "God created man in

His own image." We on our side are striving to be true to that divine heritage. We are fighting, as our fathers have fought, to uphold the doctrine that all men are equal in the sight of God. Those on the other side are striving to destroy this deep belief and to create a world in their own image—a world of tyranny and cruelty and serfdom. . . . There never has been—there never can be—successful compromise between good and evil. Only total victory can reward the champions of tolerance and decency, and freedom, and faith.[36]

In this way, Roosevelt kept alive the theme of American innocence that had been articulated so well by Woodrow Wilson a quarter of a century earlier.

In addition, Roosevelt grounded the theme of American innocence in the very same myths to which Wilson had appealed. He invoked the myth of Nature's Nation when he declared the American cause a universal cause. Americans were fighting, he said, "not only for ourselves, but for all men, not only for one generation, but for all generations."[37] And he invoked the venerable myth of the Millennial Nation when he declared the American intention "to cleanse the world of ancient evils, ancient ills" and "to make very certain that the world will never suffer again."[38] Here, once again, is the old, familiar pattern: The anticipated golden age of liberty and justice for all is grounded in the golden age of creation. By identifying with these mythic times that bracketed the history of humankind, America emerged as God's agent for good in a sinful world. Perhaps most striking, one of the myths to which Roosevelt appealed was the myth of the Christian Nation: "The world is too small to provide adequate 'living room' for both Hitler and God. In proof of that[, the] Nazis have now announced their plan for enforcing their new German, pagan religion throughout the world—the plan by which the Holy Bible and the Cross of Mercy would be displaced by 'Mein Kampf' and the swastika and the naked sword."[39]

This sort of rhetoric—and the realities to which it pointed—seemed almost tailor-made for a resurgence of American fundamentalism. As I have remarked more than once, after the fundamentalists suffered national humiliation at the Scopes "Monkey Trial" of 1925, they went underground, deserted national politics, and took refuge in their local churches.

World War II, defined as it was in terms of good versus evil, summoned fundamentalists back onto the political playing field. The wartime climate of opinion seemed to beg for someone to interpret the conflict in terms of Christ versus Satan. World War II, therefore, provided the fundamentalists with a critical opportunity to resurrect the Christian America myth with great power. Through a series of postwar revivals, and especially through the work of Billy Graham, fundamentalists set about the task of reclaiming America for the Christian faith.[40] From that time on, the myth of Christian America, while not the exclusive domain of fundamentalist Christians, became more and more confined to that segment of the American population.

Nevertheless, during the 1950s, it is undeniably true that America turned more and more, if not to historic Christianity, at least to a broad religious sentiment that William Lee Miller described as "religion-in-general,"[41] a religion promoted not by Christians alone but by all the religious traditions represented in the United States. Who is the God who was the object of this revival? Martin E. Marty tells us, "There is little to say about this God," since this revival essentially promoted "faith in faith."[42] The undisputed apostle of this "faith in faith" was Norman Vincent Peale, whose book *The Power of Positive Thinking* took the country by storm when it was published in 1952.

Will Herberg helps us understand the contours of this religion in general when he explains that from 1949 to 1953, Bible distribution in America increased by 140 percent. Four-fifths of adult Americans polled on the question claimed the Bible to be the "revealed word of God," not simply "a great piece of literature." When asked to name "the first four books of the New Testament," however, 53 percent of those same Americans could not name one. Writing in 1955, Herberg observed that "This is at least part of the picture presented by religion in contemporary America: Christians flocking to church, yet forgetting all about Christ when it comes to naming the most significant events in history; men and women valuing the Bible as revelation, purchasing and distributing it by the millions, yet apparently seldom reading it themselves." Herberg concluded, "America seems to be at once the most religious and the most secular of nations."[43]

This revival of religion in general is a part of our story for two reasons. First, in these developments an important transformation of America as a Christian Nation was in process. On the one hand, fundamentalists continued their efforts to Christianize the United States, but they defined the Christian faith with reference to such highly particular issues—evolution and biblical criticism, for example—that they failed to speak to the vast majority of the American people.

At the same time, a new breed of fundamentalists who called themselves "evangelicals"—perhaps best represented by Billy Graham—preached a kinder, gentler version of the old-time religion and a version more in keeping with the historic Christian faith. Judaism also experienced a significant revival. Through it all, the vast majority of the American people, as Will Herberg amply illustrates, had turned to religion in general and faith in faith—sentiments that many Americans mistakenly identified as Christianity. In this way, the myth of America as a Christian Nation continued into the 1950s with a vengeance, though it bore little resemblance to the kind of Christian nation the revivalists sought to build during the Second Great Awakening.

The second reason the revival of religion in general is a part of our story is the fact that it connected so powerfully to American politics and to American self-understanding. President Dwight D. Eisenhower essentially claimed this generalized religion as America's national faith when he made statements like these: "A democracy cannot exist without a religious base" or "Free government is the expression of a deeply felt religious faith."[44] Eisenhower put it best when he said in 1954 "Our government makes no sense unless it is founded on a deeply felt religious faith—and I don't care what it is."[45]

William Lee Miller, the leading commentator on political religion in the 1950s, observed in 1964 that Eisenhower's oft-used phrase "a deeply felt religious faith" was all too revealing. "Depth of feeling is the important thing," Miller wrote, "rather than any objective meaning. One might say that President Eisenhower, like many Americans, is a very fervent believer in a very vague religion."

Eisenhower coupled this "deeply felt religious faith" with an insistence on "spiritual and moral values," but that phrase, too, was vague and amorphous. As Miller wrote, "The values that spring from this commitment to religion in general are values in general. Once he [Eisenhower] named some of them this way, 'Honesty, decency, fairness, service—all that sort of thing.'"[46]

Eisenhower implemented the revival of religion in general in a variety of ways. He hosted regular prayer breakfasts at the White House. He spearheaded the effort to add "under God" to the pledge of allegiance. During his administration, a new postage stamp appeared bearing the motto "In God We Trust." All these developments must be seen against the backdrop of America's struggle against international communism. In that context, Eisenhower symbolized for Americans the "deeply felt religious faith" that he so fervently espoused, and because Americans had rallied to this "deeply felt religious faith," many assumed that America was still a Christian nation.

The important point to grasp, in the context of this book, is the way President Eisenhower—and Americans at large—identified the religious revival with patriotism, Americanism, and a strident anticommunism and thereby promoted a profound sense of American virtue and innocence.

THE COMMUNIST THREAT

I have observed several times in this chapter that it is far easier to think of one's self as righteous and pure if one confronts an enemy who can be characterized as utterly evil. Germany became that enemy during World War I, and Germany, Japan, and Italy all presented Americans with the face of evil during World War II. After those wars were over, and the enemy had disappeared, communism—symbolized best by the Soviet Union—emerged during the 1950s to fill the void. In order to counteract the Soviet threat, Americans routinely juxtaposed their religion in general and their "deeply felt religious faith" against "godless" and "atheistic" communism. The juxtaposition led William Lee Miller to comment that the revival of the 1950s typically employed two themes: "religion and Americanism, God and country, cross and flag."[47] While many Americans confused religion in general with the Christian faith and therefore imagined that America was still a Christian nation, one American quite explicitly summoned America to "faith in Jesus Christ" as the best and surest defense against "godless" communism. That American was Billy Graham.

Graham came to national prominence in 1949 when he held a revival in Los Angeles and told the crowd, "Do you know that the Fifth Columnists, called Communists, are more rampant in Los Angeles than any other city in America?" Graham saw a solution, a solution rooted deeply in William Tyndale's notion of the national covenant (see chapter 1). "If we repent, if we believe, if we turn to Christ in faith and hope, the judgment of God can be stopped."[48]

Graham's appeal to the nation to turn to Christ as the way to fulfill the requirements of the national covenant and thereby defeat godless communism became a feature of Graham's preaching for many years. In sermon after sermon, he appealed to the covenant theme. On another occasion, he counseled his audience, "Until this nation humbles itself and prays and . . . receives Christ as Savior, there is no hope for preserving the American way of life." On another occasion, he flatly stated, "Only as millions of Americans turn to Jesus Christ at this hour and accept him as their Savior, can this nation possibly be spared the onslaught of a demon-possessed communism."[49] William G. McLoughlin Jr., a historian of American religion at Brown University, observed in 1960 that "scarcely one of his Sunday afternoon sermons over a nine-year period has failed to touch on communism."[50]

In this way, Graham perhaps did as much as any other American in the 1950s to divide the world into good versus evil. "Christian America" embodied good while communism and the Soviet Union embodied evil. "America," he said in 1952, "is the last bulwark of Christian civilization." On the other hand, "Communism is . . . master-minded by Satan," and the two were engaged in a life-and-death struggle. In this way, Graham reaffirmed the myth of American innocence.

Little wonder that Graham rejoiced when Dwight Eisenhower was elected president in 1952. After Eisenhower prayed at his own inauguration, Graham exulted, "The overwhelming majority of the American people felt a little more secure realizing that we have a man who believes in prayer at the helm of our government at this critical hour." After he attended a prayer meeting with Eisenhower in 1953, Graham affirmed that "God is giving us a respite, a new chance. . . . We are no longer going to be pushed around" by the Communists.[51]

By 1955 the innocence that Americans believed was their birthright seemed to have been realized. As William Lee Miller put it, "Ike [Eisenhower] was in his White House and all was right with the world."[52] By then Americans had inherited the entire mythic history of the Republic. They understood themselves as an Innocent Nation, standing with one foot in the golden age of the past (Nature's Nation) and the other in the golden age of the future (the Millennial Nation). They had been chosen by Almighty God to enlighten the world with liberty and justice for all. And if America was not altogether a Christian nation, at least it was infused with the virtues taught by the Christian faith.

An African American Critique of the Myth of American Innocence

Suddenly, almost without warning, a bombshell dropped into the idyllic American garden of the 1950s. We call that bombshell the 1960s. When we use the phrase *the 1960s*, we don't mean a decade that ran from 1960 to 1969. Rather, we mean a period of American history defined by intense social unrest that focused especially on racial discrimination and civil rights, on the one hand, and the Vietnam War, on the other. In a very real sense, that period began in Montgomery, Alabama, in 1955, when Rosa Parks refused to give up her seat on a city bus to a white man. It is difficult to determine precisely when that period ended, but one convenient date is March 29, 1973, when the last American combat troops left Vietnam.

One of the most striking features of the period is the fact that it followed so closely on the heels of the 1950s—a period when Americans were utterly convinced of their rectitude and innocence. This remarkable transition demonstrates the tendency of the myth of innocence to devour itself. Those who think themselves innocent almost invariably repress those whom they judge to be defiled. If white Americans were too taken with their own sense of innocence to discern this fact, black Americans were not. After all, black Americans for many, many years had been the objects of white brutality and oppression.

Richard Wright, for example, recalled what it was like to grow up black in Mississippi and later in Memphis, Tennessee. "I had . . . read my Horatio Alger stories," he recalled, "and I knew my Get-Rich-Quick Wallingford series from cover to cover, though I had sense enough not to hope to get rich; even to my naive imagination that possibility was too remote. I knew that I lived in a country in which the aspirations of black people were limited, marked off."[53]

Years later Martin Luther King described in even more graphic terms the same realities. He explained how blacks "take a cross-country drive and find it necessary to sleep night after night in the uncomfortable corners of your car because no motel will accept you"; how blacks "are humiliated day in and day out by nagging signs reading 'white' and 'colored'"; how, if you are black, "your first name becomes 'nigger,' your middle name becomes 'boy' (however old you are) and your last name becomes 'John,' and your wife and mother are never given the respected title 'Mrs.'"; how blacks "are harried by day and haunted by night by the fact that you are a Negro, living constantly at tiptoe stance, never quite knowing what to expect next, and are plagued with inner fears and outer resentments"; and how blacks "are forever fighting a degenerating sense of 'nobodiness.'"[54]

For all these reasons, it is hardly surprising that black Americans emerged in the 1960s as some of the nation's most insightful social critics. Four black voices stand out: those of Martin Luther King Jr., Angela Davis, Eldridge Cleaver, and Malcolm X. The stories of the two most important events in this period—the civil rights movement and the war in Vietnam—frame their critiques of the myth of American innocence.

In December 1955 the social realities Wright and King described began to penetrate the consciousness of white Americans whose myths had protected them from discerning these realities for a very long time. In that year, Rosa Parks, a black woman in Montgomery, Alabama, refused to abandon her seat on a city bus for a white man. For this infraction of the southern code, she was arrested.

MARTIN LUTHER KING JR.

The black community in Montgomery, under the leadership of Martin Luther King Jr., a young minister for the Dexter Avenue Baptist Church, responded with a massive nonviolent bus boycott that crippled downtown businesses and eventually won bus desegregation. Similar protests, organized and executed by blacks, soon erupted in other parts of the South.

Inspired by King's nonviolent philosophy, blacks protested the segregation of southern restaurants in a series of lunch-counter sit-ins, staged in numerous southern cities, beginning in 1960. The following year, they protested the segregation of interstate buses in the South that continued despite a 1946 U.S. Supreme Court ruling (*Morgan* v. *Virginia*) and an Interstate Commerce Commission order in 1955, both of which had made segregation on interstate travel facilities illegal. The Congress of Racial Equality (CORE), therefore, commissioned "freedom rides," buses that carried blacks and whites together through many sections of the American South, testing whether the federal government would sustain its own laws. Though nonviolent themselves, protesters in almost all these efforts met with violence, instigated by whites.

Because the Montgomery Bus Boycott catapulted Martin Luther King into national leadership of the civil rights movement, it is important to come to terms with his character and his commitments. First, it is impossible to understand King apart from his allegiance both to the American nation and to the American Creed. At the same time, he was convinced that, through years of segregation and racial discrimination, the nation had sold its soul and abandoned its founding aspirations. In his view, most white Americans had no clear sense of the nation's meaning or, if they did, they paid it no serious heed. He therefore determined to call the nation back to its own noblest ideals.

Perhaps nowhere did King make that case more effectively than in his "I Have a Dream" speech, delivered to the throngs of people who had assembled for a massive March on Washington in 1963. At one point in that speech he told the crowd, "When the architects of our republic wrote the magnificent words of the Constitution and the Declaration of Independence, they were signing a promissory note to which every American was to fall heir." That note, King believed, promised "that all men, yes, black men as well as white men, would be guaranteed the unalienable rights of life, liberty, and the pursuit of happiness." Nevertheless, he noted,

> It is obvious today that America has defaulted on this promissory note in so far as her citizens of color are concerned. Instead of honoring this sacred obligation, America has given the Negro people a bad check; a check which has come back marked "insufficient funds." We refuse to believe that there are insufficient funds in the great vaults of opportuni-

ty of this nation. And so we've come to cash this check, a check that will give us upon demand the riches of freedom and the security of justice.

King explained that this dream was "a dream deeply rooted in the American dream that one day this nation will rise up and live out the true meaning of its creed—we hold these truths to be self-evident, that all men are created equal."[55] For King, the true meaning of the American Creed demanded racial integration at every significant level of American life.

Nor can one understand King apart from his Christian heritage. A Baptist minister himself, and the son and the grandson of Baptist ministers, King understood the message of Jesus on the value of every human being. In addition, the works of Reinhold Niebuhr—especially his book *Moral Man and Immoral Society*—had convinced King that dispossessed peoples must challenge their oppressors through "direct action"—behavior that would inconvenience the oppressor in some significant way. Finally, inspired both by Jesus and by India's Mahatma Gandhi, King preached a message of nonviolent resistance against the policies of segregation and discrimination. King argued that only a nonviolent approach to these issues would preserve the integrity of the protesters while revealing the racist dimensions of American life for all to see.

That strategy paid especially rich dividends in 1963 when King led a protest march through the streets of Birmingham, Alabama. Television cameras were rolling when Sheriff Eugene "Bull" Connor's men turned police dogs and high-powered fire hoses on the nonviolent demonstrators, most of them children. The next day, pictures of police hosing demonstrators and clubbing young black girls appeared in newspapers and magazines throughout the United States and the world. These events captured the imaginations of many young whites throughout the nation. The issues for them were clear: Blacks were demanding only what the American Creed had promised them, but their parents' generation had refused to make that promise good.

Lawrence Wright was a case in point. "In Dallas," he recalled,

we didn't know what to make of the Freedom Riders. When the first busload . . . approached Anniston, Alabama, in 1961, a mob punctured the bus's tires and set it on fire. The next bus made it to Birmingham, where the police stood aside and let the white mob beat the riders nearly to death. . . . I didn't clearly understand that the Freedom Riders were not fighting back. Nonviolence was such a foreign idea to me that I assumed the blacks and several whites on the buses had provoked the mob and got what was coming to them. I didn't grasp the philosophy of nonresistance—but then nothing in my years of churchgoing had prepared me to understand the power of suffering, or redemptive love.

Wright found it "unsettling to hear Martin Luther King . . . talking about Jesus." He recalled King's words at the 1960 lunch-counter sit-ins in Durham, North Carolina: "I am still convinced that Jesus was right. . . . I can hear Him saying, 'He who lives by the sword will perish by the sword.' I can hear him crying out, 'Love thy enemies.'"

King's rhetoric, coupled with black-led struggles for equal opportunity, caused Larry Wright—as it caused a whole generation of white youth—to raise serious questions about the meaning of the American experiment. King's injunctions to "love thy enemies" were themes, Wright recalled, that "I also heard nearly every Sunday, but didn't we, as a nation, live by the sword? . . . Our doctrine was brotherly love. And yet no one ever proposed that Jesus might return as a Negro."[56]

If Martin Luther King Jr. and the nonviolent, southern phase of the civil rights movement called on America to "live out the true meaning of its creed," other blacks wondered whether the American Creed had been so badly betrayed that there was little left to retrieve. As a result, many of these blacks turned their backs on nonviolence as a workable strategy for change and embraced black power instead. Some in this group advocated socialism and the overthrow of capitalism. James Forman, for example, wrote, "Our fight is against racism, capitalism and imperialism, and we are dedicated to building a socialist society inside the United States."[57]

Who were these radicals, many of whom had lost faith both in America and in the American Creed?

ANGELA DAVIS

One was a woman named Angela Davis. Born in 1944, Davis grew up in Birmingham, Alabama, where whites rigidly maintained segregation by force and the threat of force. She recalled in her autobiography what life was like for her as a child.

Near my father's service station downtown was a movie house called The Alabama. . . . A luxurious red carpet extended all the way to the sidewalk. On Saturdays and Sundays, the marquee always bore the titles of the latest children's movies. . . . We weren't allowed in The Alabama—our theaters were the Carver and the Eighth Avenue, and the best we could expect in their roach-infested auditoriums was reruns of Tarzan. . . . Downtown . . ., if we were hungry, we had to wait until we retreated back into a Black neighborhood, because the restaurants and food stands were reserved for whites only. . . . If we needed to go to the toilet or wanted a drink of water, we had to seek out a sign bearing the inscription "Colored." Most Southern Black children of my generation learned how to read the words "Colored" and "White" long before they learned "Look, Dick, look."[58]

She learned as a child "the prevailing myth . . . that poverty is a punishment for idleness and indolence. If you had nothing to show for yourself, it meant that you hadn't worked hard enough." Further, at Carrie A. Tuggle Elementary School, many of her teachers "tended to inculcate in us the official, racist explanation for our misery" and explained to the children that if they would only work hard, "[we could] lift ourselves singly and separately out of the muck and slime of poverty by 'our own bootstraps.'"

These explanations made less and less sense to Davis. She knew how hard her parents had worked, and "it didn't make sense to me that all those who had not 'made it' were suffering for their lack of desire and the defectiveness of their will to achieve a better life for themselves. If this were true, then, great numbers of our people—perhaps the majority—had really been lazy and shiftless, as white people were always saying."[59]

At the age of fourteen, Davis left Birmingham to participate in a program in New York City that brought black students from the South to integrated schools in the North. There she first read the *Communist Manifesto* and there she first encountered a circle of blacks devoted to Marxist ideals. She later recalled that "the *Communist Manifesto* hit me like a bolt of lightning."[60]

In 1963 Angela Davis was studying in France when she happened to read in an English language newspaper a story about some murders in her own hometown of Birmingham: "I saw a headline about four girls and a church bombing. At first I was only vaguely aware of the words. Then it hit me! It came crashing down all around me. Birmingham. 16th Street Baptist Church. The names. I closed my eyes, squeezing my lids into wrinkles as if I could squeeze what I had just read out of my head. . . . I kept staring at the names. Carole Robertson. Cynthia Wesley. Addie Mae Collins. Denise McNair."

Davis had known each of these girls and known them well. "When the lives of these four girls were so ruthlessly wiped out," she wrote, "my pain was deeply personal." In time she began to think clearly about the meaning of these murders. "This act was not an aberration," she wrote. "On the contrary, it was logical, inevitable. The people who planted the bomb in the girls' restroom in the basement of 16th Street Baptist Church were not pathological, but rather the normal products of their surroundings." Whoever committed this act, she believed, "wanted to terrorize Birmingham's Black population," regardless of who might be killed. "The broken bodies of Cynthia, Carole, Addie Mae and Denise were incidental to the main thing—which was precisely why the murders were even more abominable than if they had been deliberately planned."[61]

In 1968 Angela Davis joined the Communist party.[62] In 1970 Governor Ronald Reagan fired her from her position as professor of philosophy at UCLA on the grounds that "the board will not tolerate any Communist activities at any state institution." In that same year, she found herself on the FBI's "Ten Most Wanted" list. The bureau charged her with planning the rescue of three San Quentin prisoners and supplying the gun that killed four people during the rescue attempt. In 1972, thanks to a massive international campaign, she was acquitted.

The year before her acquittal, Davis wrote from her cell in the Marin County, California, jail of the system she had come to reject. She wrote of "unjust laws, bolstering the oppression of Black people." She wrote of the "racist oppression [that] invades the lives of Black people on an infinite variety of levels." And she wrote of the police who, she said, were "the oppressor's emissaries, charged with the task of containing us within the boundaries of our oppression."[63] Quite clearly, for Angela Davis, the notion that America was an Innocent Nation was a myth completely lacking in legitimacy or justification.

The story of Angela Davis helps us understand in considerable depth how and why the meaning of America was unraveling in the 1960s and early 1970s, at least within the black community. Indeed, Davis viewed her story as the story of a much larger cause. "The forces that have made my life what it is are the very same forces that have shaped and misshaped the lives of millions of my people," she wrote.[64] This is why her story demands thoughtful consideration.

ELDRIDGE CLEAVER

Eldridge Cleaver, minister of information of the Black Panther party, offered a striking critique of several American myths in *Soul on Ice*, a book that he wrote from his cell at Folsom Prison. In that book Cleaver rejoiced that "the white youth of today are coming to see" what many blacks had felt for a very long time, namely, that these young people

> must face and admit the moral truth concerning the works of their fathers. That such venerated figures as George Washington and Thomas Jefferson owned hundreds of black slaves, that all of the Presidents up to Lincoln presided over a slave state, and that every President since Lincoln connived politically and cynically with the issues affecting the human rights and general welfare of the broad masses of the American people—these facts weigh heavily upon the hearts of these young people.[65]

For Cleaver, however, the problem was not just America. It was the entire white race "whose heroes have been revealed as villains and its greatest heroes as the arch-villains; . . . heroes whose careers rested on a system of foreign and domestic exploitation, rooted in the myth of white supremacy and the manifest destiny of the white race."[66] For many years white Americans could not discern these realities, protected as they were by the myths presented in this book. As Cleaver noted, "Even when confronted with overwhelming evidence to the contrary, most white Americans have found it possible, after steadying their rattled nerves, to settle comfortably back into their vaunted belief that America is dedicated to the proposition that all men are created equal and endowed by their Creator with certain inalienable rights—life, liberty and the pursuit of happiness." Indeed, Cleaver observed, "It is remarkable how the system worked for so many years, how the majority of whites remained effectively unaware of any contradiction between their view of the world and that world itself."[67]

One can respond to Cleaver in a number of ways. But however one might regard him, his words can help us understand the dynamics that accompanied the erosion of America's myths in the 1960s and 1970s, especially the myth of America as an Innocent Nation.

MALCOLM X

Typically, blacks who argued as Cleaver did were northern and urban, or perhaps western and urban like Cleaver himself, but generally not southern or rural. In their view, King's nonviolent strategies might work well in the South but were unsuited to major urban centers outside the South like New York, Boston, Los Angeles, and Chicago. They also differed with King's support for racial *integration*. Often more militant than King, these blacks rejected the ideal of integration, insisting on racial *separation* instead. They increasingly abandoned the banner of civil rights, defined by Martin Luther King, and embraced instead the banner of black power.

No one typified this more militant tradition better than Malcolm X. Malcolm spent his early years in Michigan, and he experienced there the same intense level of discrimination that so many Americans today associate only with the historic American South. His eighth-grade teacher in Mason, Michigan, one day told him, "Malcolm, you ought to be thinking about a career. Have you been giving it thought?" When Malcolm explained, "I've been thinking I might want to be a lawyer," his teacher

> leaned back in his chair and clasped his hands behind his head. He kind
> of half-smiled and said, "Malcolm, one of life's first needs is for us to be

realistic. Don't misunderstand me, now. We all here like you, you know that. But you've got to be realistic about being a nigger. A lawyer—that's no realistic goal for a nigger. You need to think about something you *can* be. You're good with your hands—making things. Everybody admires your carpentry shop work. Why don't you plan on carpentry? People like you as a person—you'd get all kinds of work."[68]

Later, in Boston's Roxbury district, Malcolm found that jobs of all kinds were closed to blacks. After a short career of thieving, hustling, and pimping, he landed in prison, where he encountered a new religion, the Nation of Islam, popularly styled the Black Muslim tradition. He embraced that faith and soon became its most prominent spokesperson. His new faith taught him that "the only way the black people caught up in this society can be saved is not to *integrate* into this corrupt society, but to *separate* from it, to a land of our *own*, where we can reform ourselves, lift up our moral standards, and try to be godly."

Malcolm carefully distinguished, however, between *separation* and *segregation*. "We reject *segregation* even more militantly than you say you do," Malcolm told more moderate black leaders. "Segregation is that which is forced upon inferiors by superiors. But *separation* is that which is done voluntarily, by two equals—for the good of both!" Separation, he said, was important, since "as long as our people here in America are dependent upon the white man, we will always be begging him for jobs, food, clothing, and housing. And he will always control our lives, regulate our lives, and have the power to segregate us."[69]

Especially in his early years, Malcolm strongly criticized Martin Luther King on this issue. "I knew," he wrote, "that the great lack of most of the big-name 'Negro leaders' was their lack of any true rapport with the ghetto Negroes. How could they have rapport when they spent most of their time 'integrating' with white people?"[70] Malcolm therefore argued for a strategy he called "black nationalism."[71] He meant by this term that blacks should strive for total independence from whites. He meant that blacks should run their own farms, their own businesses, and their own banks. He meant that blacks should cultivate their own traditions and value their own heritage and culture. Malcolm took a major step in that direction when he embraced the Nation of Islam. That decision symbolized his deepest misgivings both about America and about the Christian faith. In his judgment, western society in general and America in particular had "become overrun with immorality, and God is going to judge it, and destroy it."[72]

Nor would Christianity lag far behind. With the collapse of western colonialism, Malcolm noted that nonwhite peoples around the globe were "returning in a rush to their original religions which had been labeled 'pagan' by the conquering white man." He argued that "the 'Christian' civilization of America—which is propping up the white race around the world—is Christianity's remaining strongest bastion." For this reason, "no one in his right mind should need any much greater proof that very close at hand is the *end* of Christianity."

Sounding remarkably like Frederick Douglass a century before, Malcolm prophetically asked, "And what is the greatest single reason for this Christian church's failure? It is its failure to combat racism. It is the old 'You sow, you reap' story. The Christian church sowed racism—blasphemously; now it reaps racism."[73] For all these reasons, Malcolm rejected his Anglo and Christian surname, "Little," and adopted instead the name "X." The X, he said, symbolized his African name, long since sacrificed to the racism that dominated Anglo-American culture.

Malcolm differed profoundly from Martin Luther King on the issue of violence. "I'm not for wanton violence," he said. "I'm for justice." This meant for Malcolm, however, that violence might sometimes be appropriate: "I believe it's a crime for anyone who is being brutalized to continue to accept that brutality without doing something to defend himself. If that's how 'Christian' philosophy is interpreted, if that's what Gandhian philosophy teaches, well, then, I will call them criminal philosophies."[74] In 1964 Malcolm made his position unmistakably clear: "We should be peaceful, law-abiding—but the time has come for the American Negro to fight back in self-defense whenever and wherever he is being unjustly and unlawfully attacked."[75]

Malcolm and his message grew immensely popular with American blacks, especially the younger generation of blacks who lived in northern cities. Typified by second-wave leaders of the civil rights movement like H. Rap Brown and Stokely Carmichael, those blacks modeled their protest on Malcolm's strategies and essentially rejected King's nonviolent tactics along with his dream of racial integration.

By the 1990s, Malcolm's vision remained the model for thousands of blacks throughout America. In 1991, for example, Sam Fulwood, a black professional, explained how "my generation . . . is so disillusioned by the persistent racism that continues to define and limit us that we are abandoning efforts to assimilate into the mainstream of society." Although they were the "sons and daughters of those who faced the dogs, water hoses and brutal cops" for the sake of integration, thousands of black professionals, Fulwood reported, were "turning away from our parents' great expectations of an integrated America." He told how "many middle-class black executives are moving out of their corporate roles to create fulfilling jobs that serve black customers. Black colleges are experiencing a renaissance. Black organizations—churches, fraternities, sororities and professional groups—are attracting legions of new members. And, most surprising to me, upscale blacks are moving to neighborhoods that insulate them from the slings and arrows of the larger society." And why? "Trying to explain my life to white people, who just don't care to understand," Fulwood explained, "is taxing and, ultimately, not worth the trouble. Sort of like singing 'Swing Low, Sweet Chariot' *en français.* Why bother? Once translated, it's just not the same song."[76]

What, then, should we make of the Black Revolution and its two most prominent first-generation leaders, Martin Luther King and Malcolm X? Simply put, both men articulated what every African American had always known, that powerful American myths had long defined the American Creed, subverted its true meaning, and crippled its ability to fulfill its promise for all human beings. As a result, blacks formed the vanguard of the counterculture of the 1960s. Some, like Martin Luther King, called on Americans "to live out the true meaning of the American creed." Others, like Malcolm X, argued that if blacks were to find any meaning in the American experience, they would have to find that meaning in themselves.[77]

The Vietnam War

American involvement in Vietnam grew from small beginnings. In the aftermath of World War II, numerous Third World countries declared their independence from European colonial domination. Among these was the Democratic Republic of Vietnam, led by Ho Chi Minh, who in 1945 declared his country's independence in words borrowed from Thomas Jefferson: "We hold these truths to be self-evident, That all men are created equal."

When the French, dominant in that region since the nineteenth century, refused to abandon Vietnam and sought to establish a new colonial outpost in the southern provinces, the First Indochina War erupted in 1946. Ho Chi Minh increasingly turned to Red China for support, while the French turned to America and Great Britain.

The government of the United States sympathized with Ho Chi Minh and his declarations of independence for his nation. At the same time, America feared the expansion of communism in Southeast Asia and increasingly provided support for French control of that region. That support began under the Harry Truman administration but accelerated under President Eisenhower. In 1953 the United States paid $1 billion to achieve its objective—two-thirds of the cost of the French occupation. In 1954 President Dwight D. Eisenhower articulated the infamous "domino theory": "You have a row of dominoes set up, you knock over the first one, and what will happen to the last one is the certainty that it will go over very quickly." For years to come, that theory would govern the American response to Vietnam.

When the French first enlisted American support in their ongoing struggle with Ho Chi Minh, the U.S. government sent "advisers" into the region. By 1963 the number of "advisers" had escalated to 16,000. In 1964 President Lyndon Johnson ordered bombings of North Vietnam, and in 1965 America committed combat troops to defend the South against Communist aggression from the North.

Public support for American involvement in that war soon began to erode for one fundamental reason. The administration feared that an American commitment to total victory might risk a military engagement with the Chinese and the Soviets. As a result, America settled for a more limited objective: to prevent the Communists from winning.

In the meantime, the number of American ground troops committed to the war escalated dramatically, reaching 385,000 in 1966 and 542,000 in 1969. American casualties escalated as well. Each night, the American public learned the official body count for the day on the evening news, and when the war finally concluded in 1973, 51,000 Americans had died. By the mid-1960s, when it became apparent that the government had no strategy to end the war, the mood of a very large segment of the public turned sour.

While America's failure to win the war fueled a broad, general dissatisfaction with the military venture in Vietnam, moral issues related to the war inflamed the counterculture. In the first place, the government of South Vietnam, which the United States supported, seemed as brutal and oppressive as the Communist government of the North. Many wondered how America could possibly support such a regime without betraying its noblest ideals. Beyond that consideration, many placed the war squarely in the context of the struggle for equal rights for blacks and other minorities in the United States. Inescapably, the war wrought devastation on the homes, lands, and lives of people of color. Many therefore saw the war as yet another manifestation of American racism and western imperialism.

On April 4, 1967, Martin Luther King Jr. addressed many of these issues at a meeting of Clergy and Laity Concerned at the Riverside Church in New York City. Early in that speech, he anticipated the inevitable question, "Why are *you* speaking about war, Dr. King? Why are *you* joining the voices of dissent?" To this question, King affirmed that he was a minister of Jesus Christ, and for that reason, "the path from Dexter Avenue Baptist Church—the church in Montgomery, Alabama, where I began my pastorate—leads clearly to this sanctuary tonight." Because of his Christian convictions, he had to speak.

King argued that the war worked hand in hand with domestic racism to destroy the lives of poor black people. The war, he pointed out, sent the poor "to fight and to die in extraordinarily high proportions to the rest of the population." It took "black young men who had been crippled by our society" and sent "them eight thousand miles away to guarantee liberties in Southeast Asia which they had not found in southwest Georgia and East Harlem." He also lamented the fact that the war diverted money, energy, and attention from the domestic war for civil rights. He recalled that "a few years ago there was a shining moment in [the] struggle [for equal rights]. . . . Then came the buildup in Vietnam and I watched the program broken and eviscerated as if it were some idle political plaything of a society gone mad on war."

For King, the most fundamental issue by far was the massive level of destruction that America had rained on Vietnam. Because of that destruction, King concurred with a man he called "one of the great Buddhist leaders of Vietnam": "The image of America will never again be the image of revolution, freedom and democracy, but the image of violence and militarism." In that context, King spoke of the violence in America's ghettos. When he tried to counsel young blacks to embrace nonviolent protest, they inevitably asked, "What about Vietnam?" "They asked if our own nation wasn't using massive doses of violence to solve its problems, to bring about the changes it wanted. Their questions hit home, and I knew that I could never again raise my voice against the violence of the oppressed in the ghettos without having first spoken clearly to the greatest purveyor of violence in the world today—my own government."

King spoke to these issues, he said, because of his "commitment to the ministry of Jesus Christ." Because of that commitment, he felt "called to speak for the weak, for the voiceless, for victims of our nation and for those it calls enemy, for no document from human hands can make these humans any less our brothers."

The audience at the Riverside Church that night was a sympathetic audience. When King's remarks hit the newspapers the following morning, though, many Americans were puzzled, perplexed, and angry. It was fine to speak on behalf of the weak, the voiceless, and the poor. But to speak on behalf of the nation's enemies? That was going too far. King knew his remarks would prompt that reaction. Perhaps that is why, at one point in his speech, he explained what he called "the true meaning and value of compassion and nonviolence": "It helps us to see the enemy's point of view, to hear his questions, to know his assessment of ourselves. For from his view we may indeed see the basic weaknesses of our own condition, and if we are mature, we may learn and grow and profit from the wisdom of the brothers who are called the opposition."[78]

Conclusions

In the beginning of this chapter, I noted how Lawrence Wright envied his father. "He matured in a magic age, the 1940s," Wright recalled, "when great evil and great good faced each other." And Wright "grew up expecting to inherit his [father's] certainty."

As a child of the 1960s, he found himself part of a disillusioned generation, entertaining the deepest doubts regarding the meaning of the United States. "It is easy to understand my anger, and the anger of my generation when we realized that our country had taken a wrong turn," Wright wrote. "Eisenhower was right: we had forfeited our moral position. We had surrendered our anticolonial past. Now that we were compromised, the world did not divide so neatly between good and evil."[79]

This chapter—indeed, this entire book—has argued, in effect, that Lawrence Wright finally came to the realization of a significant truth—that the world does not, in fact, divide as neatly between good and evil as the myth of America as the Innocent Nation might suggest. Just how difficult it is for Americans to realize this truth became apparent in the days after the terrorist attacks of September 11, 2001, as Americans once again divided the world into rigid categories of good and evil, with America standing clearly and unambiguously on the side of the right, and as the president of the United States identified three nations—North Korea, Iran, and Iraq—as "an axis of evil, arming to threaten the peace of the world."[80]

Notes

1. Lawrence Wright, *In the New World: Growing Up with America, 1960–1984* (New York: Alfred A. Knopf, 1988), 109–10.

2. Robert N. Bellah, *The Broken Covenant: American Civil Religion in Time of Trial*, 2d ed. (Chicago: University of Chicago Press, 1992), 75–76.

3. Wright, *In the New World*, 109.

4. Ronald Reagan, "Address before a Joint Session of Congress on the State of the Union," January 27, 1987, in *Public Papers of the Presidents of the United States:*

Ronald Reagan: 1987, vol. 1: *January 1 to July 3, 1987* (Washington: Government Printing Office, 1989), 59–60.

5. Jessica Mitford, *The American Way of Death* (New York: Simon and Schuster, 1963), 13–17.

6. Edward T. Linenthal, *The Unfinished Bombing: Oklahoma City in American Memory* (Oxford, Eng.: Oxford University Press, 2001), 16.

7. Mark Slouka, "A Year Later: Notes on America's Intimations of Mortality," *Harper's Magazine*, Sept. 2002, 36.

8. For a far more expanded discussion of the illusions of innocence in American life, and the way those illusions grow from the attempt to sidestep human history, see Richard T. Hughes and C. Leonard Allen, *Illusions of Innocence: Protestant Primitivism in America, 1630–1875* (Chicago: University of Chicago Press, 1988). In addition, Robert Jewett and John Shelton Lawrence have written perceptively on the myth of American innocence in a variety of texts, though their focus is somewhat different from my own. See, for example, Jewett's *Captain America Complex*, rev. ed. (Santa Fe, N. Mex.: Bear, 1984); Jewett and Lawrence, *The American Monomyth* (Garden City, N.J.: Doubleday, 1977); and most recently, Jewett and Lawrence, *The Myth of the American Superhero* (Grand Rapids, Mich.: Eerdmans, 2002).

9. Reinhold Niebuhr, *The Irony of American History* (New York: Scribner's, 1962), 133.

10. On Mormon millennialism, see Grant Underwood, *The Millenarian World of Early Mormonism* (Urbana: University of Illinois Press, 1993).

11. On this point, see Richard T. Hughes, "Soaring with the Gods: Early Mormons and the Eclipse of Religious Pluralism," in *Mormons and Mormonism: An Introduction to an American World Religion*, ed. Eric A. Eliason (Urbana: University of Illinois Press, 2001), 23–46.

12. Peter Crawley, "The Passage of Mormon Primitivism," *Dialogue* 13 (Winter 1980): 33, and Introduction to *Key to the Science of Theology/A Voice of Warning* (Salt Lake City: Deseret, 1978), i–ii.

13. Parley P. Pratt, *A Voice of Warning and Instruction to All People, Containing a Declaration of the Faith and Doctrine of the Church of the Latter Day Saints, Commonly Called Mormons* (New York: W. Sanford, 1837), 140–42. This chapter, which is the pivotal "warning" section of *Voice of Warning*, has been deleted from the modern 1978 edition.

14. Doctrine and Covenants, 76.

15. Pratt, *Key to the Science of Theology* (Liverpool, Eng., 1855), 134.

16. Cited in Dee Brown, *Bury My Heart at Wounded Knee: An Indian History of the American West* (New York: Bantam, 1972), 31.

17. Alexander Campbell, "A Restoration of the Ancient Order of Things: No. 1," *Christian Baptist* 2 (Feb. 7, 1825): 136.

18. John R. Howard, "A Warning to the Religious Sects and Parties in Christendom," *Bible Advocate* 1 (Jan. 1843): 82. The Scripture citation is 2 Thessalonians 2:8.

19. On the history of the Churches of Christ, see Richard T. Hughes, *Reviving the Ancient Faith: The Story of Churches of Christ in America* (Grand Rapids, Mich.: Eerdmans, 1996).

20. Woodrow Wilson, "We Must Accept War" (Apr. 2, 1917), in Woodrow Wilson, *Why We Are at War: Messages to the Congress, January to April, 1917* (New York: Harper and Brothers, 1917), 57.

21. Woodrow Wilson, "Presenting the Treaty for Ratification," in *God's New Israel: Religious Interpretations of American Destiny*, ed. Conrad Cherry (Chapel Hill: University of North Carolina Press, 1998), 280.

22. Woodrow Wilson, "Speak, Act and Serve Together" (Apr. 15, 1917), in Wilson, *Why We Are at War*, 71.

23. Wilson, "We Must Accept War," 55.

24. Wilson, "Presenting the Treaty for Ratification," 280, 287.

25. Woodrow Wilson, "A World League for Peace" (Jan. 22, 1917), in Wilson, *Why We Are at War*, 16.

26. Wilson, "We Must Accept War," 55.

27. Beveridge cited in James Oliver Robertson, *American Myth, American Reality* (New York: Hill and Wang, 1980), 272.

28. *Congressional Record*, 55th cong., 3d sess., 1899, 32, pt. 2:1299.

29. Wilson, "We Must Accept War," 42–43.

30. Woodrow Wilson, "Request for a Grant of Power" (Feb. 26, 1917), in Wilson, *Why We Are at War*, 31.

31. Cited in Emily S. Rosenberg, *Spreading the American Dream: American Economic and Cultural Expansion, 1890–1945* (New York: Hill and Wang, 1982), 74.

32. Wilson, "Request for a Grant of Power," 36–37.

33. Emily Rosenberg explores the "self-evident" qualities of CPI propaganda in *Spreading the American Dream*, 86.

34. *King's Business* 9 (May 1918): 365–66, cited in George Marsden, *Fundamentalism and American Culture: The Shaping of Twentieth-Century Evangelicalism, 1870–1925* (New York: Oxford University Press, 1980), 150–51.

35. Cherry, *God's New Israel*, 270.

36. Franklin D. Roosevelt, "Annual Message to Congress" (Jan. 6, 1942), in Cherry, *God's New Israel*, 295.

37. Ibid.

38. Ibid., 290, 295.

39. Ibid., 291.

40. Joel A. Carpenter tells this story especially well in *Revive Us Again: The Reawakening of American Fundamentalism* (New York: Oxford University Press, 1997); see esp. 110–23, 187–232.

41. William Lee Miller, *Piety along the Potomac: Notes on Politics and Morals in the Fifties* (Boston: Houghton Mifflin, 1964), 128.

42. Martin E. Marty, *The New Shape of American Religion* (New York: Harper and Row, 1958), 31.

43. Will Herberg, *Protestant—Catholic—Jew* (New York: Doubleday, 1955), 2–3.

44. Marty, *New Shape of American Religion*, 83.

45. *Christian Century* 71 (1954), cited in Sydney E. Ahlstrom, *A Religious History of the American People* (New Haven, Conn.: Yale University Press, 1972), 954.

46. Miller, *Piety along the Potomac*, 34.

47. Ibid., 129.

48. Cited in William G. McLoughlin Jr., *Billy Graham: Revivalist in a Secular Age* (New York: Ronald Press, 1960), 48.

49. All quotations from McLoughlin, *Billy Graham*, 139, 142–43.

50. Ibid., 138–39.

51. All quotations from ibid., 117.

52. Miller, *Piety along the Potomac*, 28.

53. Richard Wright, *Black Boy* (1937; New York: Harper and Row, 1966), 186.

54. Martin Luther King Jr., "Letter from Birmingham City Jail," in *A Testament of Hope: The Essential Speeches and Writings of Martin Luther King Jr.*, ed. James M. Washington (San Francisco: HarperSanFrancisco, 1986), 293.

55. Martin Luther King Jr., "I Have a Dream," in *Testament of Hope*, 217, 219.

56. Wright, *In the New World*, 137.

57. James Forman, "The Black Manifesto," in *To Redeem a Nation: A History and Anthology of the Civil Rights Movement*, ed. Thomas R. West and James W. Mooney (St. James, N.Y.: Brandywine Press, 1993), 251.

58. Angela Davis, *Angela Davis: An Autobiography* (New York: Random House, 1974), 83.

59. Ibid., 89–90, 92–93.

60. Ibid., 109.

61. Ibid., 128–31. One of the suspects in the crime died in 1994 without being charged. Three others were convicted, one in 1977, one in 2001, and one in May 2002, almost forty years after the bomb exploded and the girls were killed.

62. Ibid., 189.

63. Angela Davis, *If They Come in the Morning: Voices of Resistance* (New York: Third Press, 1971), 20, 31, 32.

64. Davis, *Autobiography*, ix.

65. Eldridge Cleaver, *Soul on Ice* (New York: Dell, 1968), 70.

66. Ibid., 68.

67. Ibid., 76–78.

68. Malcolm X as told to Alex Haley, *The Autobiography of Malcolm X* (1964; reprint, New York: Ballantine Books, 1992), 36.

69. Ibid., 246.

70. Ibid., 310.

71. Ibid., 374.

72. Ibid., 246.

73. Ibid., 369.

74. Ibid., 366–67.

75. Malcolm X, "A Declaration of Independence" (Mar. 12, 1964), in *Malcolm X Speaks: Selected Speeches and Statements*, ed. George Breitman (New York: Grove Weidenfeld, 1965), 22.

76. Sam Fulwood, "The Rage of the Black Middle Class," *Los Angeles Times Magazine*, Nov. 5, 1991. See also "White and Black Lies," *Newsweek*, Nov. 15, 1993, 52–54.

77. See James H. Cone, *Martin and Malcolm and America: A Dream or a Nightmare* (Maryknoll, N.Y.: Orbis Books, 1991).

78. All citations are from Martin Luther King Jr., "A Time to Break Silence" (Apr. 4, 1967), in *A Testament of Hope*, 231–43.

79. Wright, *In the New World*, 110–11.

80. George W. Bush, "State of the Union Address," Jan. 29, 2002.

Conclusion

Most of the myths explored in this book hold great potential for good. Indeed, most can complement and sustain the promise of the American Creed.

The myth of the Chosen Nation, in its best and highest form, always embraced the doctrine of the national covenant and pointed not so much to privileges and rights as to duties and responsibilities, not only to God but also to other human beings.

The myth of Nature's Nation was simply a way of reaffirming the American Creed itself. Far from suggesting that certain folkways are grounded in nature while other folkways are not, the myth of Nature's Nation underscored the conviction that "all men are created equal, that they are endowed by their Creator with certain unalienable rights, that among these are Life, Liberty, and the pursuit of Happiness." Because the myth of Nature's Nation grounded these convictions in "Nature and Nature's God," it therefore proclaimed them as self-evident truths.

The myth of the Christian Nation, in its noblest form, called on the nation to live out the values of the two great religious traditions that, in so many ways, inspired the creation of the republic: Judaism and Christianity.

The myth of the Millennial Nation suggested that the United States, devoted as it was to covenant duties and responsibilities, to equality and liberty for all human beings, and to the noblest principles of Christianity and Judaism, would extend the blessings of liberty and equality to all humankind, but only if it remained faithful to those principles.

Manifest destiny was a myth to be sure, but because it served a particular purpose in a particular time—the late nineteenth century—it was not a myth that served the nation's self-understanding over the long term. Moreover, because the architects of manifest destiny constructed it on absolutized versions of all the other myths considered in this book, it emerged as a particularly demonic transformation of values, encouraging Americans of that period to call the good evil and the evil good.

As an economic system, capitalism was also a myth in the sense that it told a story that helped define a nation. Capitalism promised substantial good, in part because it emphasized hard work and individual responsibility. In the late nineteenth century, however, capitalism—like the doctrine of manifest destiny—took refuge in the absolutized and corrupted versions of the great American myths. Those who promoted this version of capitalism abandoned the covenant duties of the Chosen People, the commitment to freedom and equality that lay at the heart of Nature's Nation, and the altruistic teachings of the Christian faith. Instead they promoted naked aggression, self-interest, and greed and, ironically, justified these vices by appealing to the virtues that stood at the core of the dominant American myths.

The fifth of our foundational myths is the myth of America as the Innocent Nation. This myth offered no redeeming qualities, since it was so completely grounded in self-delusion. At its very best, the myth reminded the American people of the virtues on which the republic had been built. Therein, however, lay the irony that stood at the heart of the myth. For a preoccupation with national virtues would inevitably crowd out any serious consideration of the nation's shortcomings. In due time, that shortsighted vision would prompt some Americans to imagine the United States as the very embodiment of good and its enemies as the embodiment of evil.

The fact that Americans have so often transformed their national myths into their moral opposite prompts us to recall one of the important points with which this book began: "the ironic tendency of virtues to turn into vices when too complacently relied upon," as Reinhold Niebuhr put it. In addition, I should note that those who absolutized America's national myths were often the powerful and the privileged and, as I noted at the outset, "it is precisely when powerful people absolutize their virtues that the interests of the poor and marginalized are most at risk." Indeed, I have tried to pay attention to the impact that corrupted and absolutized myths have exerted on the poor and the dispossessed throughout the course of American history. I have tried to achieve this objective by listening closely to minority voices, especially the voices of African Americans in various periods of American history.

As I bring this book to a close, I pick up a theme that Robert Bellah introduced in his Foreword to this text—the theme of American empire. After speaking of "the role of world empire which has been thrust upon us," Bellah writes, "America's world power has no precedent; we could even say that everyone in the world today has two nationalities—the one they were born with and American." He returns to this theme at the end of his Foreword and asks, "To what extent can we help America become a responsible empire and to what extent must we stand against empire altogether?"

These observations raise the troubling question of the role America's myths will play in the globalized culture of the twenty-first century. If Americans absolutize their myths in the face of globalized culture, the fallout for the poor and the dispossessed throughout the world could be disastrous indeed.

An absolutized myth of America as the Chosen People might suggest that America has been chosen for privilege, wealth, and power and need have little or no regard for the plight of poor and suffering people throughout the world.

An absolutized myth of America as Nature's Nation might suggest that whatever foreign policies America might put in place are by definition just and right, regardless of their impact on marginalized people, and that the rectitude of those policies should be self-evident to all the people of the world.

An absolutized myth of America as a Christian Nation might suggest that whatever behavior America implements is at the very least righteous, if not Christian, since by definition America is a righteous nation.

An absolutized myth of America as the Millennial Nation might suggest that the United States has a divine obligation to export and impose its cultural and economic values throughout the world, regardless of the impact those policies might have on poor and marginalized people.

An absolutized myth of America as the Innocent Nation might suggest that America stands innocent, regardless of the suffering that American policies might inflict on poor and dispossessed people in other parts of the world.

While Americans often absolutize their myths during peacetime, they *must* absolutize them during wartime. Indeed, all wars are finally based on mythic views of the world that have been absolutized, and "wars that lose their mythic stature for the public, such as Korea or Vietnam, are doomed to failure," as Chris Hedges reminds us.[1] Hedges, who has witnessed war firsthand in a variety of cultural contexts, goes on to explain how human beings typically absolutize their myths during wartime.

> We demonize the enemy so that our opponent is no longer human. We view ourselves, our people, as the embodiment of absolute goodness. Our enemies invert our view of the world to justify their own cruelty. . . . Each side reduces the other to objects—eventually in the form of corpses. . . . In mythic war we fight absolutes. We must vanquish darkness. It is imperative and inevitable for civilization, for the free world, that good triumph, just as Islamic militants see us as infidels whose existence corrupts the pure Islamic society they hope to build. . . . By turning history into myth we transform random events into a chain of events directed by a will greater than our own, one that is determined and preordained. We are elevated above the multitude. We march toward nobility. And no society is immune.[2]

At the height of the Vietnam War, Martin Luther King Jr. implicitly critiqued the absolutized myths that sustained America in that conflict. In effect, he raised the question that so many have raised since September 11, 2001: "Why do they hate us?" King responded that, by absolutizing its myths, America had simply lined up on the wrong side of a world revolution.

"All over the globe," he said, "men are revolting against old systems of exploitation and oppression and out of the wombs of a frail world new systems of justice and equality are being born. The shirtless and barefoot people of the land are rising up as never before. 'The people who sat in darkness have seen a great light.'" King lamented that "the Western nations that initiated so much of the revolutionary spirit of the modern world have now become the arch anti-revolutionaries."

King never called for Americans to rethink their national myths, but he did call for a revolution of American values. "A true revolution of values," he wrote,

> will soon cause us to question the fairness and justice of many of our past and present policies. . . . A true revolution of values will soon look uneasily on the glaring contrast of poverty and wealth. With righteous indignation, it will look across the seas and see individual capitalists of the West investing huge sums of money in Asia, Africa and South America, only to take the profits out with no concern for the social betterment of the countries, and say: "This is not just." It will look at our alliance with the landed gentry of Latin America and say: "This is not just." The Western arrogance of feeling that it has everything to teach others and nothing to learn from them is not just. A true revolution of

values will lay hands on the world order and say of war: "This way of settling differences is not just.[3]

A true revolution of American values will not call on Americans to scuttle their national myths. Rather, a true revolution of values might well ask Americans to embrace the myths in their highest and noblest form. A true revolution of values will, however, ask Americans to embrace those myths with extraordinary humility. It will also encourage Americans to learn to see the world through someone else's eyes, perhaps even through the eyes of their enemies. In this way, their national myths might yet sustain the promise of the American Creed "that all men are created equal, that they are endowed by their Creator with certain unalienable rights, that among these are Life, Liberty, and the Pursuit of Happiness."

Notes

1. Chris Hedges, *War Is a Force That Gives Us Meaning* (New York: Public Affairs, 2002), 21.
2. Ibid., 21–24.
3. Martin Luther King Jr., "A Time to Break Silence," in *A Testament of Hope: The Essential Writings and Speeches of Martin Luther King Jr.*, ed. James Melvin Washington (San Francisco: HarperSanFrancisco, 1986), 240–41.

INDEX

RICHARD T. HUGHES is the author or editor of more than a dozen books, including *How Christian Faith Can Sustain the Life of the Mind* and *The Primitive Church in the Modern World.* He is a distinguished professor of religion at Pepperdine University.

ROBERT N. BELLAH is the author or coauthor of numerous books, including *The Broken Covenant: American Civil Religion in Time of Trial* and *Habits of the Heart: Individualism and Commitment in American Life.* He is Elliott Professor of Sociology Emeritus at the University of California at Berkeley.

The University of Illinois Press
is a founding member of the
Association of American University Presses.

Composed in 9.5/12.5 Trump Mediaeval
by Celia Shapland
for the University of Illinois Press
Manufactured by Thomson-Shore, Inc.

University of Illinois Press
1325 South Oak Street
Champaign, IL 61820-6903
www.press.uillinois.edu